An

UNBREAKABLE

Spirit

My Life with Brittle Bones

An UNBREAKABLE *Spirit*

My Life with Brittle Bones

GREGORY J. SMITH

IGUANA

Copyright © 2021 Gregory J. Smith
Published by Iguana Books
720 Bathurst Street, Suite 303
Toronto, ON M5S 2R4

Editor: Tamara Hart Heiner
Front cover design: Meghan Behse
Background photograph, front cover: Jordan Wozniak on Unsplash.com
Other photographs, front cover: courtesy of Gregory J. Smith.

ISBN 978-1-77180-501-8 (paperback)
ISBN 978-1-77180-502-5 (ebook)

This is an original print edition of *An Unbreakable Spirit: My Life with
Brittle Bones*.

For Mom and Dad

Foreword

This story is dedicated to anyone who has been labeled as "different." It is for the physically, mentally, and emotionally challenged, and for anyone looking for hope and inspiration. It is especially devoted to those few of us who have Osteogenesis Imperfecta (OI) and families and loved ones connected to someone with OI. My wish and prayer for you is that, in some small way, my story will offer encouragement to overcome any adversity and be the best you can be. Don't ever give up!

My story is for the able-bodied too. Perhaps in some small way, it will help to break down barriers, raise awareness, and allow everyone to see that we are not so different after all. Although I hope to take the reader inside my world to feel what it is like to break bones, this story is really about the heroes around me: my parents, my family, my friends, my co-workers, my doctors, nurses, and other special people in my life — both now and in my past. It is for those who prayed for me, took care of me, supported me, encouraged me, guided me, and loved me. I thank them with all my heart, as without them, I would not be here today.

———

Some special thanks are in order:

To the iconic Pro Football Hall of Fame writer Ray Didinger, for his invaluable guidance, kindness, and wisdom during the writing process. Not once did Ray stop believing in my story. His faith was incredible. His advice on the pacing and narrative arc of the manuscript were spot-on. I found out first hand why he is such a brilliant writer. He is an even better person. Thank you, Ray! Much appreciation to the tremendously talented director, actor, and musician Joe Canuso for his steadfast encouragement, gentle honesty, and title suggestion.

Words cannot express my gratitude to the amazing author Jodi Orgill Brown for her faith and wonderful ideas during the post-writing period. Jodi unlocked so many doors to make this dream come true. I am grateful beyond words.

To the remarkable Mindy Scheier, owner of a heart of gold, thank you for your kindness and encouragement.

It was pure joy and magic working with my sensational editor, Tamara Hart Heiner. You are brilliant! Thank you for your patience, encouragement, and significant suggestions.

To Greg Ioannou and all the wonderful people at Iguana Books. Thank you for everything! You are the best!

So many in my journey who I need to thank so much: my family, Bobby Rydell, Richard Marx, Barry Manilow, all the healthcare professionals who took care of me, and the many friends and acquaintances I have been blessed to have in my life. So many special people you will meet in the following pages. I love and appreciate all of them.

My loving parents, who I know are proud. This is for you, Mom and Dad!

Much love to Holly for her everlasting love, support, encouragement, and always-upbeat outlook when I needed it most of all. Her time and skills proofreading the manuscript, as well as her valuable creative suggestions, were so appreciated and welcome. Without her, this book never would have been born.

My love to Bud and Katie, to Louie, Tiny, Fluffy, Peewee, and all the other wonderful animal friends who made my world so joyful. Their unconditional love was always like a warm beam of sunshine in my life.

Tommy, rest in peace, my brother. Sue, my dear sister-in-law, rest in peace.

"A lesson for all of us is that for every loss, there is victory, for every sadness, there is joy, and when you think you've lost everything, there is hope."

— *Geraldine Solon*

"To heal, we must remember."

— *President Joe Biden*

Introduction

Think of all the things in the world that break every day: Vases. Glasses. Phone screens. Hearts. Windows. Contracts. Promises. Mirrors. World records. Dreams. Eggshells. The list goes on and on.

Breaks can be positive things. Wishing a performer to "break a leg" is good luck in show business. Dawn breaks. "Give me a break" can be a request for a favor or leniency. Coffee breaks and lunch breaks are always welcome. Prisoners break out of jail (a good thing for the prisoners).

Almost everyone breaks a bone at least once in their lifetime. There are 270 bones in the human body at birth; 206 when adulthood is reached. Breaking a bone is a feeling almost everyone can relate to, even if it's a tiny one like your pinkie finger or little toe.

I break bones. Lots of them. I may have broken more bones in my life than anyone else in the world. This is my story. The story of a broken body and an unbreakable spirit.

Chapter 1
Another Bad Break

We parked close to the medical building in a handicapped spot. Sliding out of the car while using my transfer board, I tumbled into my wheelchair. Damn it! Still no cut curb or ramp at the sidewalk.

Mom tilted my chair backward, like a thousand times before, to gain access to the curb. This time she lost her balance and fell. I went back with her, crashing into the parking lot. I was still in the chair, pointed upward to the heavens, like an astronaut ready to rocket into space.

Everything happened in slow motion. That eerie anticipation while falling; which bone would break this time? Where would it hurt? The awful feeling of devastation, the sharp pain knifing into my leg at warp-speed as reality cruelly set in. My right femur, the strongest bone in the human body, split in two upon impact. I heard it crack like a tree branch, as I often heard my bones break during a fracture.

"Ow!" I cried out. "What happened?"

I heard Mom somewhere behind me. "Oh my God! Greg, are you all right?"

The all-too-familiar feeling of warm blood rushed to the fracture site, a feeling I hadn't experienced in a long time. Those moments felt like forever, the exchange of screams and anguish. Oh, no . . . not again.

Two nurses ran over and peered down at me. They had watched the entire accident unfold as they returned from their afternoon walk.

"My leg! I broke my leg!"

They debated what to do: carry me to the nearby emergency room or wheel the chair?

"Let's take the chair!" one suggested. "Where does it hurt?"

"Here!" I yelled, rubbing the upper part of my right leg. "I have brittle bones."

I yelled with pain again as they turned the chair upright. As they lifted it onto the curb, I held on, slumped in my wheelchair, still screaming during the sprint down the sidewalk and through the automatic doors of the ER.

"Get out of the way!" one of the nurses yelled. Thank God the hospital was next to the medical building.

"What happened?" someone called out.

Chaos ensued inside. Faceless figures in green and blue scrubs gathered around me. The world was going crazy. I was in shock, mumbling repetitive, nonsensical words to anyone willing to listen.

"Okay, let's get him on the stretcher. We have to lift you on the stretcher . . ."

"No! It hurts."

"One, two, three — "

Several nurses scooped me up in one motion. I cried out in agonizing pain. "We need to take your jeans off." They unzipped my jeans and slowly slid them down my twisted legs.

Questions flew at me: What was my name? Did I want to be called Greg or Gregory? Where did I live? What was my age? They knew I had brittle bones from the sight of my stunted legs. I sat up on the stretcher, afraid to lay down, afraid to move, afraid of everything. I was cold and scared, wearing only my white underwear, a midnight-green Eagles sweatshirt, and gray socks. *This can't be real . . . it can't be happening*, I thought, my world changing in an instant. I looked at my right leg and the femur was throbbing, swollen to twice its size. Warm to the touch, the upper leg was turning blush-red from the gruesome trauma.

A nurse named Theresa saw me shivering and hastily threw a brown blanket over my legs. She asked if I wanted to lie down as she hooked up my left arm to a blood pressure machine. Exhausted, I didn't care what they did to me anymore. *Just make the pain stop.*

"Where's my mom? Is she okay? Mom, where are you?"

"Your mother is here. She's okay. She's right outside. Do you want to see her?"

"Yes, please. I need to know she's okay . . ."

Theresa gave me a shot of Toradol, and it didn't take long to work. I still experienced pain, but the intensity decreased. Maybe they would cast it and send me home? Maybe I could rest for a moment? *Please just let me rest. I'm so tired.*

Theresa pushed aside the curtain, and there was my mother. She looked so sad, so pale and withdrawn. Tear tracks ran down her face. "I'm so sorry, Greg!" she cried over and over. "I'm really sorry."

"Mom, it's not your fault. Are you okay?"

I tried to convince her it wasn't her fault. She was eighty-two years old and frail. I was forty-seven. She never should have been put in such a situation.

"Greg, we're taking you to X-ray. Ready? He'll be back in a few minutes, Mrs. Smith. You can wait here if you'd like."

The warm blanket was tossed aside in X-ray. I never did miss those hard, cold X-ray tables. My leg still hurt like hell during the transfer, despite the painkiller, and I screamed again. They took several X-rays and got me back on the stretcher. We returned to the tiny cubicle where Mom was waiting patiently.

The X-rays showed how my right femur had shattered. A vicious spiral fracture. It wasn't going to be something simple like casting my leg and sending me home this time. No, this time I needed surgery.

Chapter 2
China Baby

The day was just dawning, the weather seasonable for the middle of November, a brisk forty-four degrees at daybreak. An estimated 274,940 other babies would be born this day, an average of 191 babies per minute. Since Osteogenesis Imperfecta affects fewer than 20,000 births annually in the United States, there is a good chance I was the lone winner of that unlucky lottery on Friday, November 16. Eisenhower was President; "Love Me Tender" and "Blueberry Hill" were racing up the record charts; Don Larsen had just pitched the first (and only) perfect game in World Series history; and a bestselling book, *Profiles in Courage*, by a junior senator named John F. Kennedy, was capturing the hearts of Americans everywhere.

It was an uneventful birth. Everything seemed normal to the doctors and nurses. Yet they couldn't understand why I wouldn't stop crying until much later. Only when I was safely cradled in my mother's arm did I find peace.

The doctors didn't know I had OI. No one knew how brittle my bones were. My parents didn't know. Nowadays a genetic condition like OI would be detected in the womb. Back in 1956, there was no Internet to do research. My parents only knew what the doctors told them about my rare condition: it's a genetic disorder, often on the mother's side of the family. OI is caused by a defective gene that affects how the body produces collagen, a protein that helps strengthen bones. Type I is a tame version of

Me Standing

OI. Most children born with Type I OI live normal, healthy lives into adulthood. My case was a mix of Type III and Type IV, the more severe kinds of OI. Life expectancy averaged twenty-five years. Most OI-related deaths result from respiratory failure due to weak lungs. The most severe types result in death at birth or shortly after. There is no cure.

Mom claimed I was walking up until my first fall. I may have been born with fractures, as so many babies with OI are. I'd rather not think about the possibility of broken bones at birth. It's an uneasy thought, having fractures in the womb, being slapped by the doctor and crying. Was it a healthy cry or a cry of pain?

The condition didn't manifest itself until one night when I was twenty-one months old. It was bath night. I loved going into my room as the tub filled with bubbling water, grabbing a dry washcloth out of the drawer, then tossing it into the water with a splash and watching it sink to the bottom. Little things like that made me happy. On this night, the linoleum in my bedroom was wet. I slipped on my way to the drawer, tumbled, and snapped the femur bone in my left leg.

That single moment was the start of a new life. I was rushed to the local hospital where they put the fractured leg in traction. During my stay in the hospital, someone moved the traction. A nurse, cleaning lady, or family member by mistake? My left leg started to swell, my toes turning blue. Poor circulation, but why? They couldn't figure it out.

I was transferred to one of the big city hospitals, the old Children's Hospital (or CHOP) in nearby Philadelphia, Pennsylvania. That was my first encounter with the famous Dr. Jessie Nicholson. Dr. Nicholson was a world-renowned orthopedic surgeon and bone specialist. He was my savior. Seeing him meant I'd sustained a fresh fracture, yet he always had a calming effect on me. The doc would take the pain away. He would make things better. I trusted him.

Nicholson was short and thin, with sharp, blue eyes behind round wire-rimmed glasses, and snowy-white hair. He had a very distinguished air about him, almost British in nature, but he had grown up in Camden, New Jersey, walking in his father's footsteps as a physician. He had a friendly, Marcus Welby sense about him.

Once Dr. Nicholson saw my leg, his first reaction was anger. Why had they waited so long to transfer me to Philly? He whisked me into surgery without delay.

In surgery, Dr. Nicholson pondered the issue before him: the bone was not knitting properly. All the marrow and calcium were leaking underneath the tissue. That was why the leg was growing to several times its normal size. Over a cup of coffee in the hospital cafeteria, Dr. Nicholson reviewed the events with my parents: how he had to step away from the operating table, the smell from the leaking marrow so odorous; how he had to make a quick decision to amputate the leg or save it; and how he cleaned up the mess, deciding to get me a chance someday to walk. Life-changing decisions made in a matter of seconds.

My folks had to have been a wreck. One moment they were the happy parents of an almost two-year-old, rambunctious, seemingly healthy little boy, and the next moment they were parents to a kid with a life-threatening condition. It was the first time my parents heard the term "Osteogenesis Imperfecta." No matter how well Dr. Nicholson tried to prepare them, there was no way my folks could ever imagine what they were facing.

So began the vicious cycle of fracturing a bone, wearing a heavy plaster cast for six to eight weeks, and then fracturing it again. In and out of hospitals was my "normal" routine. Ambulance trips anytime, day or night, from anywhere — school, church, or home.

I broke all my limbs and my back in every way imaginable: sneezing or coughing too hard, turning over, awake or in my sleep. The doctors started calling me "China Baby" because my bones shattered like porcelain. I was always thinking of the next fracture, afraid to move or twist suddenly, always with a certain degree of anxiety and constant caution. I didn't know any better. To me, being in and out of a cast every few months was normal. Not being able to do things other kids could do was normal. Pretty soon the words "Osteogenesis Imperfecta" were burned into my brain. The term was marked everywhere, from X-rays to charts. I would tell interns or nurses what my condition was even before they asked. Such long words from such a little kid. "I have Osteogenesis Imperfecta," I would say matter-of-factly. No big deal.

Listening to records

I didn't know the condition was very rare, didn't know the doctors were telling my parents I probably wouldn't live very long. If I lived past the age of sixteen, when my bones would get stronger and my body matured, maybe, just maybe I would make it.

Although the fractures were countless over the years, several stand out in my mind. The following is my Hall of Fame Fractures.

The Backbreaker: One of my older brothers was casually pushing me in a stroller down Fourth Avenue, where I grew up. We were getting ready to walk over to the park and watch our town's annual rite of spring, the Dogwood Parade. It was a warm day in May, the sky a deep blue. A beautiful, perfect afternoon.

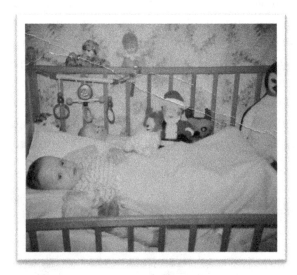

Early fracture

Then the world went crazy. We went over a crack in the sidewalk and two vertebrae in my back were crushed. I screamed in agonizing pain. Instead of going to the parade that day, I had an unexpected appointment with an ambulance and Dr. Nicholson. The worst part of this fracture was the need to wear a full body cast for several months. Only my arms and head were free to move. I couldn't do anything for myself, and I even had trouble eating since I was frozen in plaster. I lay flat on my back all that time except when they flipped me over like a turtle to prevent bedsores on my butt. After the body cast was removed, I wore a corset for a long time. A constant reminder of that beautiful spring day.

The Three-Limb Fracture: My father was carrying me home from church one Sunday morning. He used to carry me everywhere, like Tiny Tim in Dickens's *A Christmas Carol*. I was light and small, not into the wheelchair phase of my life yet. At the time we lived a block from our church, so he walked to and from church with me. On that winter morning, he slipped on a patch of black ice and fell backwards. Dad wasn't hurt, but I broke both my legs and shattered my right elbow.

How cold it was on that frozen ground! After getting his bearings, Dad slowly rose to his feet. He lifted me and carried me the rest of the way home as I cried in pain. I never saw Dad so upset, blaming himself for the accident. I tried not to cry on the sofa as we waited for an ambulance, not wanting him to feel bad. I could deal with the leg fractures. They were a dime a dozen. The elbow fracture was different, since the bone was literally broken into pieces.

The elbow was casted and put into traction until surgery. Spasms shot through my arm every few seconds. They tried to control the pain with medication, but pain management techniques were pretty archaic compared to today. I was never so glad to see Dr. Nicholson in my life. We had a true love/hate relationship: I loved him for his help to take the pain away and I trusted him immensely; but I also dreaded seeing him, as this usually symbolized pain.

Back in those days, there weren't different pain medicines or even pain specialists as there are now. I remember taking Tylenol with codeine later in life when the pain was bad; otherwise, I honestly can't recall taking many meds. I almost grew immune to the aches and pain after a fracture. If I had pain, two aspirin were supposed to do the trick. Toughing it out was normal.

The Birthday Break: It was my seventh birthday, and I was getting another cast removed that morning. We were having spaghetti for dinner, my favorite. Mom always asked us what we wanted for dinner on our birthdays, a family tradition. So much to celebrate!

Right before dinner, I slipped on a rug and went down hard. It wasn't just a bump or bruise like other kids might have from such a tumble. Another fracture, along with another ride to Children's Hospital in Philly. A fresh plaster cast awaited my arrival. So much for the spaghetti. When I got home, I still had enough energy to blow out the candles on my birthday cake.

The Bean-Bag Break: There was a game in the sixties called "Toss-a-Cross," a variation of tic-tac-toe where you throw a bean bag to turn over an X or an O and try to get three in a row to win. It was sort of like the cornhole game played during tailgate parties nowadays at sporting events.

Christmas Day, circa 1969. This was a hot game that holiday season, so I was anxious to play. I sat on the sofa in the living room while my brothers set up the board. A few bean bags in, I flung the deciding bean bag underhand, "putting a little extra mustard" on the winning toss, hoping to yell out in victory. Instead, that terrible, familiar feeling hit me as I snapped my right tibia merely from the force of the throw. Another trip to the hospital, even on Christmas, and another eight weeks in a plaster cast.

I remember that fracture and how bitterly cold it was outside as they loaded me on the stretcher into the back of the ambulance. The warm blankets covered my fragile, shivering body. Mom rode in the back of the ambulance with me while Dad followed by car. The hospital was nicely decorated as they unloaded me from the warm ambulance into the icy Philadelphia air, then inside to the noisy lobby. People rushed inside, all bundled up, carrying red and green wrapped presents with big bows. I wanted to stay in the warmth and security of the ambulance blankets, dreading what was to come. They rolled me down the hall to the Cast Room and transferred me to the hard, cold table with the thin paper sheet as I waited for a doctor to arrive to set and cast my broken leg. After the plaster dried, Dad carried me to the car, lifting me into the back of our station wagon. We made the thirty-mile journey home before the early winter dusk fell, home to celebrate what was left of Christmas.

When I wasn't fracturing, I had nightmares about fractures. Sometimes I woke up screaming, dreaming of falling. It was a terrible feeling, knowing I was falling, knowing I would break a bone, knowing it was going to hurt, knowing what would happen afterward: the chaos, the ambulance ride, the cast, the pain. No matter how many times I broke a bone, it always seemed surreal. Reality blended into my dreams. Was this another nightmare, or was this real?

Even later in life, the nightmares continued. The vivid dreams shattered my sleep. I'm sure I had PTSD — Post Traumatic Stress Disorder — something that was never treated. Back when I was a kid, PTSD wasn't taken as seriously as it is now.

That was my early life: fracture, cast, fracture, cast, fracture, cast. Over and over and over. Even at an early age, I tried to rationalize how breaking bones was better than the alternative: at least I was alive.

I grew very familiar with Children's Hospital. It was like my second home. The old, gray stone building looked like a cold English castle from the outside — or a gruesome mausoleum, depending on your outlook. The room I dreaded the most was the infamous Cast Room. It was a small room on the first floor, painted all white. The dusty scent of plaster hung in the air. This was the place where they applied and removed all the casts. The room of broken bones. Different sizes of electric saws hung on the wall. The sights and sounds filled me with terror.

I remember the whirring sound of those saws and the heat when they buzzed too close to my skin. Smokey white plaster dust flew everywhere in cloudy white puffs. After Dr. Nicholson split the cast in two, he pried apart the plaster with what looked like a giant pair of tongs. There was the frail leg, wrapped with cotton and gauze, as weak and fragile as a newborn chick just hatched from an egg. I glanced at the so-called leg like it was detached from my body. I wiggled my toes, the fresh air feeling cool on my skin. Were those really my toes on the other end of such a lifeless limb?

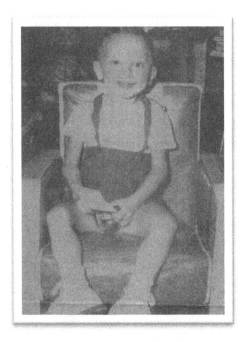

Always smiling

Casts were always uncomfortable, especially in the summer. I got pretty good at scratching an itch with a pencil or a ruler, even though Dr. Nicholson always frowned upon this tactic. The worst cast of all was the kind that went over my hips and around my chest. It was hard, if not impossible, to sit up for weeks or months at a time. When I broke both legs at one time, there would often be an annoying plaster bar between my knees. This was meant to keep my legs apart and was also a way people could lift me. Dr. Nicholson would often saw the cast in half and I would go home in the shell. In a few days I would feel strong enough to leave the smelly old cast behind and face the world without the plaster protection. Funny, I hated being in the cast for months and couldn't wait to be free, yet I hesitated when it was time to "leave the nest," so to speak. I recall how soft my leg felt against the cool bedsheets after months of rough, irritating plaster.

If it all sounds barbaric, well, it was.

Chapter 3
Heroes

More importantly than the building or a specific room, I grew familiar with the people within the hospital — the nurses, doctors, technicians, orderlies, and other patients. They knew me, too, since I was there so often. "Back again?" was the usual greeting.

There were so many people over the years, so many names and faces, like the nurse from the Philippines who cheered me up one painful night during a hospital stay by singing, "You Are My Sunshine." Each night-shift during my stay, she would come into my room, and we would do a duet of "You Are my Sunshine." I remember the cheerful orderly who cracked jokes and made me smile, taking my mind off the surgery happening in a few moments at six in the morning. He somehow made me laugh on the elevator, telling me stupid, corny knock-knock jokes. I never knew his name, but I always remembered his kindness.

One special friend was a young girl named Michelle. She seemed to be in the hospital as much as I was. She was a teenager, a few years older than me, with long brown hair and a nice smile. She loved Davy Jones and The Monkees. We became friends and consoled each other during those tough times, complaining about the food and the needles. I never fully understood why Michelle was in the hospital. What was "leukemia," anyway?

One day we unexpectedly bumped into Michelle's mom at the hospital elevator. She was there to pick up her daughter's personal belongings. Michelle had died earlier that morning. Her mother reached into her bag, wanting me to have something special. It was a picture of Michelle, a school photo. It simply said on the back, "With love, Michelle."

———————

Dad was quiet and unassuming. My hero. I knew him as a "Ralph Kramden" regular guy — without the roaring bluster of Ralph (my father loved "The Honeymooners"). The kind of guy you would want to have a Ballantine beer with, talking sports. He grew up in an orphanage after his mother tragically died when he was an infant. He was a World War II veteran, a survivor of the Battle of the Bulge in Europe. He was wounded and awarded the Purple Heart (like many veterans, he did not like to talk about the war). After the

Dad, Paris 1945

war he worked as a machinist at the B.F. Goodrich tire plant for over thirty years. It was normal for Dad to work overtime and weekends just to make ends meet. My parents lived paycheck to paycheck. Every Sunday evening, we went to the local bowling alley. Those were fun nights, watching Dad, who was the Captain of Sacred Heart White, his team in the Catholic League, do battle with the other squads from local churches in Phoenixville. At one time, the entire five-man team of Sacred Heart White was made up of family members, consisting of Dad, his youngest brother (Uncle Franny), and three of my older brothers. My father's team never won the championship. They were always underdogs.

Every fall into spring, we chased the dream of a championship season, just like our Phillies. Every year we came up short (just like our Phillies).

Cowboy Greg and Dad

After Dad was gone, I never went to the alley again. It just wasn't the same without him. Forty years later, we found three of his bowling balls and a box full of his old bowling trophies in the basement. Those relics of days gone by would gather dust over time, but the memories of my father and my uncle remained fresh and alive.

Dad loved baseball too, and we went to as many games as my health would allow. The Philadelphia Phillies were our passion, win or lose (we barely survived their monumental collapse in 1964), living and dying with each game. We always looked forward to baseball season and picking out games to attend when the schedule was finally released. It was a thrill getting the tickets in the mail or venturing down to venerable Connie Mack Stadium in late winter to buy tickets for the far-away summer.

The Phillies didn't win much while I was growing up. They were perennial underdogs, never giving up; a team I could identify with. I watched all the games on TV and listened to games on the radio. Like every kid, I had a transistor radio tucked under my pillow at night so I could listen to the late West Coast night games. Legendary broadcasters Harry Kalas, Richie Ashburn, and By Saam were like family every summer. Listening to the Phils' battle icons like Koufax and Mays kept me riveted. If I fell asleep before the game ended, Dad would always stick a note on the bedside rails in the morning before he went to work. "Phils won, 3-2."

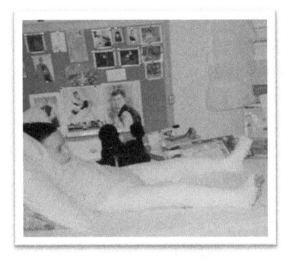

Recovering from another fracture

Like most kids in the early 1960s, I collected baseball cards. There was nothing like the smell of bubble gum upon opening a fresh pack of cards. It was always a hit-or-miss thrill to open a pack and find out what players you got to complete your checklist. Then, of course, you would either trade your doubles with other kids in the neighborhood or "flip" cards (a way of winning cards by tossing them on top of each other). I was a pretty good flipper in my time and won extra cards for my collection on our front porch every summer.

My favorite player was shortstop Bobby Wine. He couldn't hit a lick, but he was the best defensive shortstop of his time. He had a rocket arm, great range, and his glove gobbled up ground balls like a vacuum cleaner. I loved his style and ease while playing the field. "Scrappy" was a good term for Wine.

Dad knew someone from work who was a neighbor of Bobby Wine (Wine lived in the Philly suburbs too). As a surprise, Dad arranged for Bobby to call me on my birthday one year. Imagine getting a call from your favorite ballplayer on your birthday!

The following season was my first live game. I prayed that nothing would happen to mess it up. I had fractured the morning of an Eagles-Vikings football game we were planning to attend together. Instead of seeing our Birds take on the Purple People Eaters, I spent my Sunday afternoon at CHOP. That spring, my beloved Phillies were playing the dreaded Los Angeles Dodgers. It was a hot ticket as the Dodgers had a great team, led by the Hall of Fame pitching duo of Sandy Koufax and Don Drysdale. David vs. Goliath. I hoped the Phils would put up a good fight.

My heart raced as we approached Connie Mack Stadium (formerly known as Shibe Park). It was nice to be in the city for some fun instead of for broken bones. The huge light towers of Connie Mack drew closer as the stadium came into view. We had a brief panic when I thought I'd forgotten the tickets, but all was well when we found them under my seat. Dad gave a quarter to a scruffy-looking kid hanging around our station wagon. He promised to "watch" our car for us while we enjoyed the ballgame so "nobody stole the tires." That was nice of him, I said to Dad, who just shook his head.

Dad carried me as he walked up to the stadium gates. I peered inside and saw the parrot-green grass of the outfield. I had never seen anything so beautiful in my young life! The delicious smell of hot dogs, peanuts, and onions hung like a cloud over the fans. The buzz of the crowd, the chants of "Get your program here!" the excitement all around us as people streamed through the turnstiles in droves — so different from TV or the radio. After buying our programs (we always kept score with the little red Phillies pencils), we descended the steps and kept going until we reached the field level. Dad had somehow secured box seats, right next to the Phillies' dugout on the third-base side of the field.

I soaked in the entire atmosphere, everything in front of me: the players, the enormous grandstand, the field, everything in color. Back in those days, our televisions were still black and white. The vibrant colors amazed me, from the vivid red Phillies' caps to the blueness of the Dodgers' jackets. It was a perfect Sunday afternoon, the sky so blue, the sunshine so toasty, and the slight breeze so fresh and soft. I closely watched the players, both Koufax and Drysdale right there, literally yards away, almost close enough to touch. There was Jim Bunning, the Phillies' ace, warming up in front of us. A grilled hot dog (with yellow mustard) and a box of popcorn made my world complete. Who could ask for more?

Suddenly, out of the Phillies' dugout popped the familiar number seven, Bobby Wine himself. He walked over to our box, said hello, and shook my hand. He autographed a ball and a photo card as we chatted for several moments. I have no idea what we talked about, but it didn't matter. I got a chance to touch his glove, that same glove where countless baseballs went to die. It was like touching Babe Ruth's bat.

Bobby said he would try to get a hit for me. He got two hits — and the Phillies beat the mighty Dodgers that day. I watched the light towers slowly vanish from view as I peered out the back window of our wagon, wishing the day had only just begun, already looking forward to the next game later that summer. Baseball, so pure and innocent in the sixties, allowed us to share a common bond and spend special times together, father and son.

Baseball came into my life again the following June. My Uncle Joey lived in Atlanta, Georgia, at the time and knew some people in the Braves' organization. They found out about my illness and sent me a bunch of stuff in the mail: signed baseballs, yearbooks, stickers, plus a nice get-well letter from their manager. Soon I was receiving packages almost daily from different teams. The excitement built each day as Mom went for the mail, holding another envelope or box with the return address and logo of the Pirates, Cardinals, or Yankees on the front. I was stunned when the iconic Yankees sent me their 1966 yearbook. I wasn't a Yanks fan, but I was an awe of their majesty in baseball. It seemed like New York was always in the World Series. From their traditional pinstripe uniforms to venerable old Yankee Stadium, the Yankees oozed old-school baseball.

The St. Louis Cardinals overwhelmed me with everything they sent: signed photo, an autographed baseball, stickers, you name it. Their legendary manager, Red Schoendienst, also wrote a personal letter on Cardinals stationary, saying the whole team was praying for me.

I hated the Cardinals up until then. They always beat my Phillies, stealing the pennant from Philadelphia in 1964 after the Phils choked, losing ten games in a row to end the season. Our neighbor, Mr. Leininger, was a huge St. Louis fan. Every time I saw him in the neighborhood he was wearing his stupid red Cardinal cap or Cardinal jacket. He would gently tease me about the Cards "going all the way" that season while my Phillies languished in the cellar.

My loyalty to the Phillies and my scorn for the Redbirds temporarily flew out the window when I opened that box full of Cardinal memorabilia. Maybe Mr. Leininger was right after all?

I always cringed when I heard that an athlete refused to sign an autograph, especially for a kid. They had no clue how good signing your name could make someone feel.

As much as we wanted our Phillies and Eagles to finally win a championship, there was always next season. A new baseball or football season gave me a reason to keep fighting as the fractures piled up and my body grew weaker. The frustrating defeats faded into renewed hope each year, hope that kept my dreams alive and made me fight to live even more. It would've been so easy for my parents to put me in a home for handicapped children and let someone else deal with the situation. But they were fighters too and refused to send me away when Dr. Nicholson advised my admission into the Seashore House in Atlantic City, New Jersey.

Mom often remarked how "God never gives you more than you can handle" in life. Mom was my champion. She suffered just as much as I did. She felt every broken bone in her broken heart. Yet she was never bitter or angry with God because of my fate. Instead, she remained a fountain of hope, love, and faith.

Mom was the rock of the family. A former nurse practitioner, she quit her job to take care of me when my OI developed. She would often spend the night in the hospital with me or sit by my bedside all night at home. Alone while Dad worked, she drove the Schuylkill Expressway each day to visit me in the hospital. Mom always brought me a toy when I was in the hospital, often a stuffed animal. She would walk around the corner from the hospital to a little store. One time a cop stopped her and warned her about the dangerous neighborhood. He walked her back to the hospital that evening.

Cowboy Greg and Mom

She bathed me, fed me, and helped with my bathroom duties. Daily sponge baths were the norm when I was in a cast. She held my hand when I was in pain, read to me, or prayed with me. I know she had always endured a sense of guilt about my bone condition, like she was the cause of my brittle bones. She wasn't, of course. But I always knew that deep down inside, she endured a personal sorrow in her heart that lasted a lifetime.

Like most wives and girlfriends around 1944, Mom watched Dad go off to war, leaving behind my brother Jimmy (who was only a toddler). She would get an occasional letter and postcard from Dad, who was embedded on the Western Front of Europe. For security reasons, the soldiers were not allowed to tell anyone where they were located, so often the mail would simply say "Greetings from Somewhere in Holland."

My parents' wedding

Christmas Eve, 1944. Mom received a telegram (which was usually bad news). The telegram read that Dad was wounded. No explanation if he was dead or alive, no clue where he was or in what condition he was in. Dad was wounded during the famous Battle of the Bulge (which was the largest battle ever fought by the United States Army). He sustained shrapnel wounds in his right leg and was flown to England to recuperate. The Gold Star banner hanging in our window at home turned silver to indicate that a wounded soldier resided there. We kept our Christmas tree up until Dad came home the following March.

Mom was a big believer in getting me outside as much as possible. She didn't want me to become a "shut-in." Often we took leisurely walks to Reeves Park, where we would have ice cream cones and bask in the fresh air. Ann & Harry's was a tiny drugstore around the corner from where we lived. It was where I got most of my baseball cards. We often stopped in for an ice-cold Coca-Cola (poured from the old-time Coke bottles into an old-time Coke glass) and a bag of candy (consisting of all my favorites back then: tiny Tootsie Rolls, green leaves and orange leaves, Bazooka bubblegum, and penny gummies). Charles Music Shop was where I bought all my 45s and LPs back in the day. Charlie knew the kind of music I liked and kept me alert to new releases. He kept the Bobby Rydell records well stocked.

Many of these quaint stores were not accessible to someone in a wheelchair; almost all had a step or two to negotiate. It didn't matter. Mom was always determined to make the best out of any situation. If we were out for the day, she made sure I would have fun. My folks never gave up on me and wouldn't allow me to give up on myself. "Things could always be worse" was their motto. When I think of all the hardships and heartaches they endured, I know they shared an unbreakable spirit, too.

My siblings had to deal with the chaos an unexpected fracture would bring at any moment. They often had to fend for themselves, like making dinner or cleaning the house. Many times, they kept me company at home, playing a game or reading to me, even though they could've been out playing with friends. My siblings tried to involve me in their lives, even if it was something as simple as a backyard wiffle ball game. When there is a special-needs child in a family, so much is focused on that child and his or her caretakers, especially the parents, that often other family members are overlooked. My siblings sacrificed so much. They were heroes as well.

Friends were a big part of my early childhood. Visitors brightened my spirits. Get well cards hung on my bulletin board near my bed. Many people prayed for me, but Monica stands out in my mind as someone who touched me so much during this time. She lived around the block. She went to the same church as my family (Sacred Heart), so her family knew mine well. She was sixteen. Moni would stop by after school and bring me a bag of candy to share from Ann & Harry's. She made me cards for every occasion, and we often colored on my bedroom floor or read books together. She babysat for me too. She was my first "crush." She was pretty and would eventually be the springtime May Queen at our church.

I would look out the front window for Moni on the days she didn't stop by. Once, during a snowstorm, I watched her have a snowball fight with a group of kids across the street, wishing I could join in. "Monica needs time with her other friends too," Mom would say. I wished I could be one of her "normal" friends, but I knew she thought of me as special. She cared, and for a teenager, that was unusual. The things she brought me — the toys, the candy, the small gifts — she bought out of her own allowance. She was a big inspiration to me, a shining example I would never forget. Moni got married and had kids, and I saw less of her as the years went by. She moved away and became a nurse.

———

Bobby Rydell was a popular singer from South Philadelphia. He was a teen idol in the late 50s and early 60s. I remember at four years old watching Bobby on American Bandstand, my coal-black hair slicked back in a pompadour like his. I collected all his records, singing all his songs and spending hours listening to old 45s on my portable record player as I rehabbed from another fracture.

I always wanted to be a singer. I had my first gig at the age of four. Mom used to haul the record player and a stack of 45s to the local convent so that I could perform all my Bobby Rydell hits before the Sacred Heart nuns on Sunday afternoons. I even had the body gestures down pat, dressed in my butterscotch jacket and bow tie. The good sisters got a kick out of it. They had to be hard up for entertainment. There I was, pointing at the circle of sisters and singing, "Wild One, I'm gonna tame you down," as the nuns smiled or looked stunned.

Meeting Bobby Rydell, 1961

It was my father who arranged for me to meet Bobby Rydell at the old Steel Pier in Atlantic City. He was performing there in the summer of 1961. I remember sitting on Bobby's lap, singing "Volare" with him in his dressing room before the show. I kept the many autographed photos and his personalized scrapbook he gave me that day. Whenever I needed to smile, I would page through the homemade scrapbook (which Bobby's mother had made for him). I kept it updated with loving care.

Bobby was very kind. During the show he dedicated "our" song, "Volare," to me as we watched from the audience. We said goodbye in the dressing room after the show.

Several months after we met, Bobby wrote me a personal letter, commenting on how "sharp" I looked that day in my sporty blazer (I must've worn that jacket everywhere) and signature bow tie. Near the end of the letter, Bobby wrote, "If I ever had a little brother, I wish he would be just like you."

————

One of my fondest early memories is taking a family summer vacation to visit my Uncle Steve in California. He was a used car salesman out there. Born with a gift of the gab, Uncle Steve could talk anyone into buying anything. If you've ever seen a used car commercial on television where the salesman is yelling, "Have I got a deal for you!" well, that was my Uncle Steve in a nutshell.

Disneyland was on the agenda, a destination every little kid would be excited about. I couldn't go on all the rides because of my condition, but I did visit the "It's A Small World" and "Pirates of the Caribbean" attractions. The three-week cross-country trip was right out of the Griswold's "Family Vacation" movie. I left my favorite little pillow in a motel in Zanesville, Ohio; I was in awe of the giant oil wells in Oklahoma; and we watched Neil Armstrong step on the moon in a New Mexico hotel. It was also on this trip I first learned I had an accent.

We stopped in a diner in El Paso, Texas, for breakfast. As we gave the waitress our order, she commented, "You're all from Philadelphia!" How did she know? Did she see our license plate in the parking lot? No, it was our Philly accents, full of funny pronunciations of words like "water" and "door."

One of my favorite relatives when I was growing up was my Uncle John, the barber of the family. He had learned how to cut hair in the Navy, where he'd also played trumpet in the Navy band. He would cut our hair in our basement every six weeks. He carried a barber kit with all the accessories: scissors, comb, and a razor. Uncle John enjoyed his beer, so every time he cut our hair Mom would treat him to a shot and a beer. By the time the second or third brother was on the stool, the booze would start to affect his barber skills. Each one of us bartered over who would get to go first, knowing his haircuts got worse with each bottle of beer.

It was the sixties and every guy wanted to look like The Beatles. "You don't want to look like a girl, do you?" Uncle John would tease. No, we wanted to look like The Beatles! But in the end we would end up with the usual crew cut, even in winter.

My favorite part of an Uncle John haircut was the end, when he would whisk my neck and ears with a soft brush and scented talcum powder ("fufu powder," he called it). "Next!" he would call out as he downed another shot in one gulp.

We would cry for about a week after our haircuts, complaining they were too short. But I loved Uncle John because he was a really good guy, despite his dreaded razor.

The absolute best memories were made at home, times like spaghetti dinners every Sunday, when Mom made five pounds of pasta and homemade meatballs and everybody actually ate at the dinner table together at the same time. Penny poker games at the kitchen room table with my family; watching old black and white reruns of "The Honeymooners" with my father after dinner; quiet, rainy afternoons listening to records with my pet dog beside me; those were the times I cherished the most. The routine days were special because they were so few and far between. A day without a broken bone was always a good day in my world.

Chapter 4
Timmy

I spent the first eight years of my education in a special school for handicapped children in nearby Norristown, Pennsylvania. Back in the sixties, they didn't integrate the physically challenged with so-called "normal" students. I attended a school which was accessible — all ramps, with everything on one floor. Most buildings back then were far from accessible, with stairs a major obstacle to overcome.

I rode to school each day by taxi with four other disabled kids in my area. There was Denny, Timmy, Donny, and Sy, all with various challenges, all of different ages and limitations. They were my best friends. A jovial older guy with white hair named Joe drove the cab every day and kept us laughing. I hardly knew my grandparents, so Joe was like my surrogate grandfather. He helped me in and out of the cab every morning and afternoon. It was a big deal that I trusted him to lift me. Only Dad or Mom ever lifted me until Joe came along. And when I made my confirmation, I picked the middle name Joseph in his honor.

Our daily cab ride consisted of noisy trips full of stories and laughter, a time to bond with friends who could relate to what it was like to have a disability in the early sixties. We had the same classes and tried to do the same recreational things as other kids. We had arguments but never teased each other about our differences. We could spar about "your Mom is this or that," but we never mentioned disability. We were in the same boat and knew it. We didn't want others to judge us on our handicaps, so why should we judge each other? I had a crush on my pretty, red-haired second-grade teacher until I found out (to my horror) that she was expecting a baby. I took part in a few school plays, including a Christmas Pageant where I was asked to sing (I stunned the crowd with my own version of "Here Comes Santa Claus"). Luckily, I had experience with Bobby Rydell and the nuns. Kids played a form of kickball at recess. Only we didn't kick the ball. Some used their canes or other devices. We played the same games other kids played, only with the appropriate modifications and adjustments required. We ate lunch together, which was a big deal. I had a Flintstones lunch box and thermos or whatever superhero was popular at the time. Peanut butter and jelly or baloney sandwiches was the preferred menu, with a Tastykake for dessert (butterscotch krimpets or chocolate cupcakes).

I used a rolling walker, a clever device that allowed me to "walk" safely without fear of falling or tipping over. I did well in school but hated math, an old annoyance that would haunt me forever. There was little difference in curriculum. The teachers were real teachers who specialized in working with special-needs children. I loved my teachers and loved my school. Being at school was the one time in my early life I felt normal.

It was a sign that someone had died when we wheeled into class and found flowers on a classmate's desk. We were used to our friends dying young. Saying so long to my school friends overnight or over the weekend wasn't like saying "See you tomorrow" or "See you Monday," because it was entirely possible we wouldn't see each other ever again.

Timmy was my closest friend. Tim was a little older than the rest of us. Tall and thin, he had an loud, infectious laugh, which he used often. Tim was always happy. I mean always! Remarkable for a kid with a double-whammy of cerebral palsy and a seizure disorder. Tim walked but it was a challenge, shuffling along, braces on his legs, walking in a slow but steady sideways gait. He suffered from unpredictable, violent seizures that could occur at any moment. Tim nearly died several times (which was the norm for all of us kids).

He had a joke every day. He never complained or moaned "why me?" at least not in front of his friends. Every morning Tim greeted us with his bright smile, often sympathizing if one of us wasn't feeling well.

That was the usual banter in the cab. Poor Donny, always down, trying to cope with his illness, annoyed by Tim's perpetual joy. Donny was hard to understand because of his speech impediment from his muscular dystrophy. Sy didn't say much. The term "autism" didn't exist back then. People referred to Sy as "slow." Terrible how we were labeled. To us, we weren't different — the rest of the world was.

Tim was also the policeman of the cab. Since he was bigger than all of us, he broke up any arguments or fights in the backseat. I always sat in the front with Joe. Tim manned the middle of the backseat. He was like my big brother in the cab and tended to look after me, maybe because of my brittle bones or because I was the smallest guy in there.

When angry (which was practically every day), Donny would pick a fight with someone in the cab, usually Sy. Timmy was there to break it up. They would argue about the most stupid things, like who was the better ballplayer, Mickey Mantle or Willie Mays?

"I'll slap you down!" threatened Donny.

"Go ahead and try!" Sy retorted from the other side of the backseat. He knew Donny couldn't reach him, let alone have the strength to do anything physical.

"I'll slap you both down! How do you like that?" Tim said, settling the matter.

The truth was, no one could slap anyone down. It was all talk. You had a kid with a disability flailing away at another guy with multiple challenges, as Timmy took the brunt of the shots, and Joe, the ultimate boss, telling everyone to "calm down or else you'll have to walk to school!" (that wasn't going to happen, either). Most of the time everyone would be back to normal by the time we reached school. And there was no ratting on each other once we got home. What happened in the cab, stayed in the cab. It was a place where the guys could be tough, yet in the end, forgive until the next ride. All things we couldn't do at home. At home we were merely thought of as "handicapped kids." In the cab, we were like everyone else — at least for a while.

Diana Ross and the Supremes were Tim's favorite music group. Often, in his eternally good mood, he would sing at the top of his lungs the latest hit record of the group. "Baby Love" was his favorite, as Sy and Donny groaned. For no reason at all, Tim would suddenly burst into song, especially if Joe had the radio on.

As annoying as his singing could be, his cheerfulness was like a welcome breath of fresh air. That was Tim: fun, protective, encouraging, and my best friend in grade school.

Chapter 5
Pins

I went from "China Baby" to "China Boy" in no time at all. It was around this time in my life that we moved from my childhood home on Fourth Avenue to a smaller rowhome on Hall Street, still in beloved Phoenixville (a picturesque, lunch-pail town west of Philadelphia). Hall Street was where Mom grew up. My parents wanted to return to their roots. My oldest brother, Jim, and my sister, Phyllis, had moved out and were on their own, so there was no need for the bigger house.

Dad carried me up and down the stairs until we could afford to buy a stair lift. I still wasn't independent, and the new house wasn't accessible. But we made do. I crawled around the downstairs like an infant. I had a wheelchair, but I wasn't encouraged to use it much indoors, maybe because space was so limited. I slid on my rear end at lightning speed as I competed with the pet dog for floor space. It was an odd way of getting around until I used a wheelchair full-time.

I loved sitting outside in my wheelchair in the summer. Playing wiffle ball or Nerf Ball with my brothers or kids around the neighborhood was a common nice-weather activity. It made me feel "normal." Pushing my chair around the block, getting to know the neighbors, and enjoying the fresh air and warm sunshine was good for my bones. I had a sense of freedom when I was in my wheelchair. I didn't feel as isolated or confined, even if my ventures were just up and down Hall Street.

I had another crush on a neighborhood girl who spent some of her time with me playing cards and doing homework. I didn't have many friends around my age. Because I spent so much of my early life as a shut-in, I didn't develop close friendships with peers. There was no "hanging out with buddies." I mingled with whoever was around.

One of my friends was named Joe Pickett. Joe was slightly younger. He was short, African American, solid as a rock with muscles and had the brightest smile. Joe lived at the bottom of Hall Street with his mother and two older brothers. I saw Joe every day I was outside. He would walk up the street to the Civic Center, which was located around the block. He was a boxer and went to the Civic Center to train. Every single time he went by, he held out his hand, and we did a high-five as he passed. Every single time. Even if he just went home for a minute and then briskly passed by again, we always slapped five, no matter what.

"Yo! How's it going, little brother!" Joe would bellow out. Occasionally we would play chess together. Joe was a thinker, not just a boxer, and we had many a challenging chess match together. Joe went on to become a champion local fighter in the lightweight division. His boxing name, as well as his nickname on the street, was "Wicked Pickett."

Joe always put a smile on my face, even when I was down in the dumps. "If I can ever do anything for you, little brother, you let me know!" he would say.

———

Despite the continuing fractures, I was alive, which amazed the doctors. When I turned thirteen, they decided to try surgery. I had five operations on my legs. Dr. Nicholson did the honors, inserting stainless steel pins and rods into the bones of my lower legs, hoping my legs would be strong enough to stand and walk. My legs were slowly beginning to bow (or curve), a grotesque event, common in OI, so the pins would hopefully keep my legs straight as well.

However, a few months after each surgery, a scab would form on my leg. Soon, the shiny sharp point of the pin emerged through the skin. My body would reject the pins. Dr. Nicholson then pulled them out with a pair of pliers, and the process started over again. With each surgery, the pins were heavier and larger, yet my body continued to say no.

It was several years of frustration. All that work — a six-hour surgery, rehabilitation, and months in a cast — only to see the gruesome sight of the pin protruding from my leg with each try. Those were emotionally painful days where we were unsure when I would get home, unsure of the unknown aspects of the entire lengthy process. Days seemed like weeks, and weeks seemed like months.

With each operation, my legs became smaller and smaller. The doctors took bone out every time to make the pins fit, and thus my legs became stunted. The good news was that the pins kept my legs from bowing, at least until the pins were rejected; the bad news: my legs became dwarf-like, not in proportion with the rest of my body. The first time they took off the cast after the first surgery, I was horrified. I never expected my legs to be so disfigured. They didn't look great before with all the fractures, but now I looked like a monster. I cried looking down at my own legs. It was a terror I never really got used to, one I could never get away from.

It was during one of those rejections that Dr. Nicholson and I had our first disagreement. He would pull the pins out when they came through the skin far enough to grab. This time the rods were huge. My legs felt even weaker; the pain and past rejections were still fresh in my mind. I lost it when we reached the hospital. Maybe it was all that pent-up anxiety and sadness. It was like someone else was in control of my emotions. I wouldn't allow Dr. Nicholson, or anyone else, to touch me. I sat on the table in the cast room where I had suffered so many times before. This time I was determined I'd had enough.

Why not numb my leg when they pulled out the rod? Why did it have to hurt so much? People got a shot of Novocain at the dentist before a tooth was pulled, right? This was a stainless steel rod sticking out of my leg, for God's sake. Here I was, ready to have a dagger pulled out of the bone in my leg, and Dr. Nicholson wouldn't give me anything for the pain. It will only take a second, reasoned my parents. Be brave. I cried and screamed, "No!"

For the first time since I'd met Dr. Nicholson, close to ten years earlier, I felt he was out of touch with my feelings. He acted like he didn't have time for this foolishness. I had been courageous for so long. Maybe he took my tolerance for pain for granted. I felt helpless on that cold table. *Please, somebody help me* kept flashing through my mind in bold red letters. My parents couldn't say anything. Their hearts had to be breaking, yet they deferred to the medical staff. It had to kill them when assistants held me down and Nicholson yanked on the rod, successfully pulling it out. Screaming with pain, it was worse than a fracture.

I left the hospital in tears, my confidence shaken in my hero. I hated him. I hated him for making my legs so twisted and ugly. I hated him for failing. He was the symbol of the entire process. He personified OI, and I hated it. I never wanted to see him again. I feared surgery more than ever. Yet I knew I was trapped. I would see Dr. Nicholson again. I would frequent Children's Hospital in the years to come. Like it or not, there was no way around it.

I encountered many people in the hospital during those surgical years: children, nurses, doctors. Often, interns and doctors from foreign countries stopped by my room to gaze at my legs. Most of the time, I didn't mind; however, as I was growing older, I was becoming more self-conscious about my appearance, as any teenager would. I wished I only had pimples to worry about.

Sometimes I felt like an animal in a zoo. I was a rare species (as I was constantly reminded). My parents advised me to cooperate; anything to help the doctors understand OI better was worth the awkwardness of the moment. One time they wheeled me into this huge auditorium where I was greeted by a sea of white-uniformed doctors and nurses. I gazed at their curious faces as they stared back at me. Dr. Nicholson was there, front and center, with various diagrams, charts, X-rays, and a blackboard at his disposal. He lectured for a while, highlighted by the unveiling of my legs. Much to my relief, I was out the door pretty quickly.

Even though the surgeries didn't help me walk, as was the ultimate goal, the doctors were right about one thing: after age sixteen, I stopped fracturing so frequently. Instead of breaking a bone every day, every week, or every month, I was now fracturing every other month or once every six months or so. That was a miracle in itself. Less pain, less trips to the hospital, fewer casts. I could live a semi-normal life.

I was now officially wheelchair-bound. I learned the fine art of doing wheelies and speedy traveling. I had an electric chair at the time, but my medical team thought a manual chair would be more beneficial for exercise, the lighter the better. Mom reminded me to slow down, that, after all, I did have brittle bones. Like any teenager with their first car, I just wanted to go.

I got used to life in a wheelchair, and every few years I traded it in for a newer, improved model. As my physical needs increased, so did the variations on my chair. Getting a new wheelchair was always a big deal, like purchasing a new car. My chairs (I kept a spare in case I had a flat) were (and still are) my lifeline. Without a chair, I was immobile. My wheelchair went everywhere I went. When it was time to get a new set of wheels, it was important to get it right. A new wheelchair every five years was exciting to break in. From the new bearings and tires to that "new chair smell," I looked forward to test-driving and finally selecting my transportation. Pushing my chair was like an able-bodied person walking — I didn't think about it, I just did it. Soon, being in a chair or pushing a chair was second-nature to me. Like it or not, my wheelchair was a part of me — till death do us part.

Chapter 6
Praying for a Miracle

Mom was very religious. She attended Christmas Eve Midnight Mass *and* Christmas Day Mass, just in case Christmas Eve didn't count. Mom had prayed for a miracle since I was two years old. She had more faith than anyone I knew. She prayed the rosary every night and went to church without fail. Jesus was in my life for as long as I can remember. I drew my belief and my strength from her because, no matter the number of fractures or pain, she was convinced that someday I would walk.

I made my First Communion the day before my eighth birthday, November 15, 1964. There was a special eleven a.m. mass that Sunday morning. I was dressed in a white suit and a light-blue tie (foregoing my traditional bow tie). The family threw a huge party. Our relatives from Jersey were there, the ones we hardly ever saw (everyone has relatives in Jersey). When our relatives from Jersey made the trek to Pennsylvania, it had to be a big deal. To mark the occasion, a local photographer took my picture after church. My folks eventually had the photo made into a portrait by a local artist (it still hangs on my bedroom wall). It was kind of strange, having your own portrait hovering over you, like I was already dead, but I realized the picture was more for my family. It always reminded me how much I was loved and how afraid they were that my life would be a short one.

Around that same time, a real cardinal visited me at home (no, he wasn't from St. Louis). Cardinal Krol from Philadelphia was at our parish to do Confirmation. We had just moved to Hall

Street, and our little house was located behind the Sacred Heart Church. Our Monsignor Sengler told Cardinal Krol about my life. When the monsignor told him I lived at the other end of the churchyard, a surprise visit was planned after the ceremony.

I was watching TV in my bedroom, in a double-cast (two legs for the price of one), recuperating from a pair of fractures. My head was snapping back on the pillow as I dozed and snored. It was close to nine p.m. when Mom came bursting in the front door, climbing the stairs in record time.

"Greg!" she called out. "Greg! Are you awake? The cardinal is coming to see you!"

Turns out the cardinal, red robes flowing in the cool spring night, was walking through the churchyard at that moment, along with our Monsignor Sengler, heading for our place.

Mom gave me a quick once-over: clean pajamas, hair combed, face clean. Where are my rosaries? Not that I was praying at that exact time. Let's give Cardinal Krol the illusion that I was deep in reflective prayer when he just happened to drop by. I knew this was big for Mom, to have a real cardinal — someone who conceivably could be Pope someday — give us the great honor of visiting our humble home.

I knew of Cardinal Krol and I did pray the rosary. But I was just a kid. His visit didn't faze me that much. I would've rather have met a famous sports star. (Note: This same monsignor was friends with Philadelphia Eagles great Chuck Bednarik — old "Concrete Charlie" himself — and had asked the legendary

First communion, age 8

player to visit our parish for Communion Breakfast one year. Bednarik was a former altar boy, so he was only more than happy to oblige his friend. Meeting Mr. Bednarik was unforgettable: shaking his gnarly hands, my tiny hand disappearing inside his meat-hooks, his fingers twisted in all different directions from years of playing smash-mouth football. Needless to say, I was thrilled.)

Mom gave me a crash course in cardinal manners, advising me to call him "Your Eminence." I hoped I wouldn't forget and screw it up by saying something stupid. Pleasing Mom meant the world to me and would save me a lecture later. Before any more lessons were reviewed, we heard a firm knock on the front door. Mom clicked off my little TV and rushed downstairs, opening the door for the cardinal and the monsignor. She noticed that a nice-size crowd of churchgoers had escorted the two clergymen. I'm sure they had to be wondering where he was going and why.

I heard footsteps thundering upstairs. In a second there he was, Cardinal Krol himself, dazzling in red, standing in my doorway. Mom led the way, and I remember how red her face was, almost as red as his robes, blushing proudly with spiritual joy.

"Gregory?" Cardinal Krol asked.

"Cardinal . . . Krol," I replied, staring at the imposing figure walking toward my bedside. "Your Eminence." (I almost forgot that part.)

"I have a brother named Gregory," he said. "So I'll never forget your name."

I didn't know what to say about that, so I mumbled something safe like, "That's nice . . . Your Eminence." I saw Mom out of the corner of my eye nod approvingly and smile.

The rest of the visit was small talk, praying together, a short pep talk (I needed to offer my suffering up to Jesus), and an official blessing. I do remember two things like it was yesterday: first, the cardinal gave me a photo, a personal 8 X 10 shot that was taken when he was elevated to cardinal in Rome not long before. It wasn't signed, so I asked for his "autograph." I thought that was appropriate. Mom gave me a frowning glance at the request. I scrambled to find a pen, which wasn't a problem since I was into art back then and had about a hundred pens at my disposal. The cardinal quickly signed and handed me the photo, which would later be tacked on my bulletin board, along with other celebrities. Then came the real surprise.

Cardinal Krol reached into his pocket and produced a shiny gold coin. Only it wasn't a coin — it was a special medal, one blessed by Pope Paul VI. Cardinal Krol only had a few of these, and he gave one to me. I was awestruck.

A final blessing later, he was gone.

God was good, and I began to believe, even as a kid, there was a reason and a purpose for all of the pain.

———

It was my mother's dream to take me to Lourdes. We visited Lourdes when I was fifteen, the famous Catholic shrine in Southern France. The place of miracles. It was where Our Lady appeared eighteen times to a poor young peasant girl named Bernadette in 1858. My parents scraped together enough money to make the trip, borrowing, saving, and scrimping. Along with my youngest brother Mark, we embarked on our own little pilgrimage in August 1972.

Our Lady of Lourdes called for "penance" during the apparitions. Our own personal penance began as soon as we arrived from our long transatlantic flight. From Paris, we transferred on to Lourdes. The airport was small, and I recall my father carrying me down the stairs of the plane to a waiting wheelchair. Lourdes knew all about wheelchairs and accommodations for people with challenges. We weren't on an organized pilgrimage. We were on our own for three weeks. We couldn't speak French. So, looking back on it, we were either pretty brave or pretty stupid. Naïve was probably a better word for our introduction to Europe.

The first time we entered the shrine grounds was like "entering Heaven itself," said Mom. So quiet and peaceful, a world of difference considering the commercialism just outside the sanctuary gates, where souvenirs of all kinds were sold, everything from T-shirts to water bottles to rosaries to trinkets. Here was Lourdes in front of us: the majestic basilicas, the miraculous fountain, the Grotto itself where the Blessed Mother stood, where the hundreds of crutches and canes hung, testaments of miracles through faith and prayer for decades. A beautiful statue of Mary stood in the niche of the rock which she had graced with her presence.

On a French street, 1972

We prayed a great deal at the Grotto and in the numerous churches where masses were said 24/7. People of all nationalities knelt in constant prayer. Some sat on benches at the Grotto, saying the Rosary out loud, others on their knees, silently praying, their lips moving along with their beads between their fingers. No matter the hour, no matter the weather, people were there, praying for miracles. We stopped at the Lourdes Medical Building on the grounds of the shrine. The bureau was the place where the miraculous cures were reported, documented, and verified. Impressive evidence of physical cures with photos and old documents were detailed during the lectures. Royalty from all over the world secretly volunteered their time at the shrine, working in the hospital or as stretcher-bearers, their form of penance to Our Lady.

It was at one of these lectures where we met Brother Collins. This elderly Irish priest came to Lourdes each summer with a group of blind boys from a school in Dublin. Meeting these boys touched me a great deal. I began to wonder, why would God allow innocent kids to be so afflicted? I shook each hand, and they smiled in return. No pity. No sorrow. They returned each year to reaffirm their faith. If a physical miracle should happen, so be it. Spiritual healing was a miracle which never failed each summer.

Praying for a miracle

I didn't feel so helpless anymore. Why should I complain?

Each day at four-thirty p.m. was a daily Blessing of the Sick in Rosary Square. I was fortunate to be in the rows of sick people to receive these blessings from countless priests, bishops, and cardinals. Miracles often happened during the procession of the Blessed Sacrament. I still couldn't comprehend it, instantly being able to walk or see or hear. My life would be so different without OI. Here I was, worried about not breaking a bone while at Lourdes, yet what if the opposite occurred and there was a miracle?

We shared a common bond as I gazed over rows and rows of the sick, handicapped, and dying worshipers. Different ages, different ailments, different cultures, different languages, different stories, different needs, different expectations. All had sacrificed something to be at this place and time, at that moment, in this holy place. Maybe there would be physical cures that day, maybe not. All would leave touched by the message of Lourdes. No one left Lourdes empty-handed.

At the end of each day, we checked out French television in our hotel room while writing postcards to home. The French newspapers were only interesting for one reason: baseball scores. No details, no box scores, only numbers buried in a small section of the paper. Even so, it was like a breath of fresh air discovering if my Phillies had won or lost the day before.

The French cuisine wasn't bad. We tried to stick to our basic diet of American food and found that French fries were about the same as the fries at McDonald's back home. We were courageous to try rabbit one night (I kept thinking of Bugs Bunny) but passed on more exotic food like escargot (snails) and frog legs, delicacies in France. The gross plate of snails at a nearby table (nestled on a bed of parsley) looked too much like our front garden and drew a predictable disgusted reaction. We did enjoy the occasional glass of red wine offered at every meal. It made the odd sights and aromas of the French restaurants easier to swallow. My favorite was the soft, warm bread and the endless variety of pastries, almost as good as our local Tastykakes.

"Go drink at the spring and bathe in its water," Our Lady had said to Bernadette. My parents secured a pass to the Baths, so I was lucky to bathe in those very same miraculous waters, a rare privilege. After saying prayers and kissing a statue of Our Lady of Lourdes, a pair of capable attendants lowered me into one of the stone reservoirs under the mountain. It was a cold, damp place, a place that was hidden from the outside world, yet another place where miracles often occurred.

Wearing nothing but underwear, I was immersed in the ice-cold water. I experienced a feeling never felt before or since. Maybe it was the shock of the extremely frigid water, but a surge went through my body like a wave of electricity. A terrific pain knifed through my back, but not my legs. My legs weren't completely submerged. Mom noticed this and quickly splashed a handful of water over them before I was dunked once and out. It happened so fast.

Afterward I sat shivering outside the baths in the hot summer sun. Was I expecting an instantaneous miracle like those I heard about during the lectures? Honestly, no. Mom prayed fervently for a miracle. I was more realistic. Did my inability to truly believe I would be healed prevent me from being cured?

We filled bottles and jugs to carry the precious Lourdes water home for family and friends. Our own personal supply of miraculous water was available whenever we needed it. We knew the water did not contain special elements that caused miracles to happen. When cancer vanished or decaying bone was made whole again, it wasn't the water — it was divine intervention through prayer that made miracles real. Lourdes water was merely a brilliant instrument of faith and prayer from Mary herself.

Our last day in Lourdes was full of mixed emotions. We were all homesick. Yet it was sad to leave this special place. Who knew if any of us would ever make that long trip again?

Every Christmas for years, we received a postcard and letter from Brother Collins with best wishes from the boys. I often thought of them, impressed by their faith, still striving to believe more firmly.

Even on the return trip to America, the power of Lourdes continued to shine. Back in New York at customs, a tough-looking guard began inspecting our luggage. Tired after another grueling flight, we weren't looking forward to the anticipated wait. The guard noticed our jug of Lourdes water. I know Mom was fearful it might be confiscated. Instead, the guard mentioned that he wasn't Catholic, but he had often heard of Lourdes. He asked about our trip. Mom went into action and offered him a small bottle of water. He accepted it like gold and allowed us to pass through without inspecting our bags.

In the years to follow, much of the remaining water served as a source of hope and healing, helping many at home who were sick or dying. We were only too happy to share it. In that small way, we passed along the message of Lourdes.

With Pat Croce

Years later I met Pat Croce, the President of the Philadelphia 76ers. I loved his positive outlook on life. I sent him a get-well card after his near fatal motorcycle accident. He replied with a personal thank you note and asked to meet me at a future Sixers basketball game in Philly. Pat kept his promise and stopped by to say hello later that season. In appreciation, I surprised him with a gift: a small bottle of Lourdes water to help his recovery.

"You've been to Lourdes?" he asked. "Are you sure you want to give me this?"

As time went by, France seemed like a fading watercolor dream. Though I wasn't physically cured at Lourdes, I learned to accept whatever God had in store for me in life.

Chapter 7
The Box

Citizens Band Radio helped bring me out of my shell. Thanks to movies like *Smokey and the Bandit*, the CB radio was the craze back in the seventies. On the radio I could be "normal," make friends and explore the world without ever leaving home. Even in the middle of the night there was always someone to talk to. There were radio-related parties and picnics to attend. A whole new world was opening for me. A group of truck drivers found out about my situation, took up a collection, and bought my first radio. They hooked it up and installed the antenna on the roof. It was the truckers' way of spreading good cheer.

My first handle was "China Boy." CB'ers generally picked a handle (or nickname) that made light of themselves, so China Boy was mine. My second handle was "Smitty." Every male in my family was called "Smitty." The handle was a mini tribute to my father, who was the one and only "Smitty." My home channel was Channel 10. I hung out with people of all ages. Names like Catman, Wanderer, and Skateman became my buddies. For the first time in my life, I was pals with a group of "normal" guys. It didn't matter if I couldn't walk on the radio. Everyone was the same. Race, religion, and disability didn't matter.

There were occasional disagreements with neighboring channels, and we broke a few FCC rules (like playing music on the air or talking into the wee hours of the night without a break). Generally, our group kept it light-hearted and fun, and I became popular. I didn't like my high voice, so often I just listened to others or had the radio on while falling asleep on Channel 19, listening to the truckers converse.

My new friends liked my sense of humor. I could be myself on the air. My confidence soared. I even had a few girls talk to me on a regular basis. I fondly remember three: Marnie, a local cheerleader; Irene, a tall, blond Polish beauty in high school; and Kathy, a bubbly and funny chick who was a paramedic. Kathy was special to me because she was one of the few people on the radio who knew about my disability yet didn't care. She always made me smile with her cheerfulness and sense of humor. "Micro-Medic" and I talked every night on her way home from work. I had a crush on her but knew she was dating a guy in medical school. They eventually got married, and I attended their wedding.

That's how it was on the radio. People appeared on the air. Some stayed and some faded away after trying out the latest fad. I also used the radio as a tool for doing some good. I got involved in Phoenixville's Town Watch program. Every other Saturday night, I spent a few hours as a base unit, keeping in touch with mobile units as they patrolled the streets, alerting police if they found anything suspicious. Doing this volunteer work made me feel a greater part of my community. I was happy to finally be the one giving back to others.

It was always an interesting experience meeting someone from the airwaves, putting a face to a voice. Some were noticeably shocked when they met me — "Wow, dude, you really are in a wheelchair!" Girls seemed disappointed, knowing that smooth-talking guy on the radio was a little, brittle guy. I did feel better whenever I met someone from the radio. Even my CB friends came in all shapes and sizes. No one was perfect.

Cruising was a popular, pointless endeavor on weekends, driving up and down the main street of town, showing off your car and radio. Every Friday night I listened to the cruisers. It was on a typical Friday night when I experienced my first taste of discrimination on the radio. My story had made the local papers about the truckers helping this disabled kid, so I could no longer hide. I only hoped my real radio-friends didn't care. If they said the wrong thing, so what? If it wasn't said maliciously, I was okay with it.

There were a few on the air who were just plain cruel. They called me names like "crippled" or suggested I change my handle to "Daddy Longlegs." One guy threatened to find me (which wouldn't be hard to do) and dump me out of my chair, just for kicks. His idea of fun was to park at the head of my street and key up his powerful mic, covering my conversations. It was trash talk and no physical action. Who was bluffing and who was a serious, card-carrying nut? At times I allowed the rude comments to get to me. I would stay off the air for a few days, retreating into my shell. Other times I snapped and let them have it on the air. There is only so much a guy can take.

I didn't know how to deal with the ignorance. I knew the comments came from losers who had nothing better to do. But knowing the source didn't stop it from hurting.

I felt trapped in my body during my teenage years — a normal person inside a very abnormal body. I got used to being stared at. Kids stared a lot. I didn't mind because kids were honest about it. Often a kid would come up to me at a mall and ask, "What happened to your legs?" All it took was a simple answer like, "Oh, I broke my leg. It's getting better, thanks!" with a smile. That usually satisfied their curiosity. Kids were naturally curious. Ignoring their questions would only deepen the mystery. Answering with anger would only make them afraid of me and the next person with a disability they'd encounter.

Adults were worse. Adults stared too, quickly looking away. Anything "different" was best ignored. At times parents hauled the kid away, scolding, "Don't ask him things like that!" I always felt that was the wrong approach. Just because adults had disability hang-ups didn't mean the next generation needed to feel that way.

Maybe it was just my imagination, but it seemed I got more stares than other people in wheelchairs. I looked different because of my short stature. People who are paralyzed might appear "normal" to the casual eye; I stuck out like a sore thumb. I was way too embarrassed to ever wear shorts during the summer. My legs got plenty of stares, even with jeans on. "Why do you have tiny legs?" or "Why don't you have feet?" were two popular questions. Adults often thought I was an accident amputee. I was too young to have served in the Vietnam War. When I told the truth and explained about brittle bones, no one had ever heard of OI before.

I could relate to the movie *The Elephant Man*, the scars of fate one could never hide from. My legs were useless. I even contemplated asking Dr. Nicholson to amputate them. Why were they there? It was a question I often pondered, from childhood to old age. Not "Why can't I walk?" or "Why me?" Instead it was always, "Why are my useless legs here?" Like a modern-day Scarlet Letter for all to see.

Adults also tended to talk "over" me rather than to me. Someone would ask Mom, "How is he doing?" even though I was right there. Conversations happened behind my wheelchair, as if I couldn't hear or understand.

I was always impressed when people made eye contact, or even got down to my level when we were talking. No one wants to be looked down on. As I got out in the world more and more, I learned more about prejudice and being considerate of feelings other than my own. Those times when I was treated as a human being rather than a curious object were a precious gift. I wasn't this repulsive creature after all — I was a human being. And the CB radio helped me see I wasn't so different after all.

During my junior high days, teachers came to our house after regular school hours. I was still fracturing in my teens, too fragile to attend school. Plus, the school was not accessible (as so many buildings were not back then). It was nice having class one hour a day, but I missed the interaction with friends, people to share lunch with or do homework with or just talk to. I became socially isolated. I missed being in school.

I also noticed a misconception in life. Society's labels continued to become more pronounced. A wheelchair user was automatically either paralyzed or mentally challenged. Able-bodied folks would raise their voices to me, as if being in a wheelchair meant I was hard of hearing too. I felt patronized and started complaining about it. Often the complaints fell on deaf ears. Doing well in school meant showing society that even though my body wasn't perfect, my mind was good. I tried not to buy into the labeling.

My high school days were also home-bound. An intercom system was hooked up from my bedroom to school. I affectionately became known as "The Box" for three years. Students unplugged me and carried me from class to class. Depending on the class, I spent the hour on the windowsill or on my own desk. One day I didn't have class at all because a student forgot me in a bathroom.

The box was great because I could interact with teachers and students by merely pressing a button. I still missed being there, missing things like proms and football games and partying. My weekends were spent with family, not with high school friends. All during my high school years, I missed school activities that I knew were happening. If fate had been kinder, I would have been doing them too. A few classmates would stop over at the house after school to tutor me (in math) or do homework together. It was great putting a face to a voice. They were just as curious about me. Who was this kid in the box? Some Fridays I wished school never ended. I missed my friends until Monday. I kept busy on weekends with family activities, but no matter how tough school was, sometimes I couldn't wait to switch on the box at eight a.m. on Monday morning, just to hear those familiar voices again.

Subjects like geometry were tough since I couldn't see the blackboard. Most of the teachers were understanding; a few felt awkward with me and didn't interact much. Some classes I passed without doing much work at all. Some teachers cut me some slack when it came to grades and tests. Sometimes I had school in my pajamas. One afternoon I fell asleep during class, only to be startled to attention by a loud voice on the other end asking, "Greg, are you all right?" Temporary malfunction of the intercom was my excuse.

Exams were generally held after school hours. It was as close to being in class as they could make it. I cheated one time during a test, checking my textbook for an answer. Later my Catholic guilt kicked in and I never cheated again. Plus Mom gave me the "God is always watching" lecture, and that erased any cheating ideas I may have hatched. Letting Mom down — let alone God — was forbidden.

My high school English teacher was Mary Como, Perry Como's sister-in-law. She said Perry was a nice guy, as laid-back as he was on stage and on his records. My Spanish teacher, Miss Bregatta, assigned Spanish names to all her students. Somehow, she couldn't quite translate Gregory into Spanish, so everyone started referring to me as "Jorge" for the year. ("Jorge" meant George, but I was used to people forgetting my name.) When I complained to Mom, she reminded me how, if I had been a baby girl, I would've been named Gertrude. My parents didn't know what to name me before I was born. Mom had this thing about naming kids after whatever saint's feast day fell on the day we were born. Since November 16 was St. Gertrude's Day, naming me Gertie wasn't going to work. She looked at November 17 — St. Gregory the Great's feast day — and the rest is history.

I knew a few members of the football and basketball teams from my daily interactions on the box. I did attend a few high school football games on Saturday afternoons in the fall. I remember sitting outside of one of the end zones, in the shadow of a goal post, intensely watching the Phantom players. I felt a part of the school when I sang our school song ("The Purple and the White") before the football game. It was a Homecoming game, so it was cool to feel a part of those activities.

My parents never "fought." They had "discussions" from time to time, but they never screamed at each other. I do recall one argument over the high school football games. My father worked on Saturdays because he had to. It was time-and-a-half on Saturdays, good money. Mom suggested to my father that he should take me to the home Phoenixville games, especially since it was my senior year. She knew how fleeting this precious time was before my high school days were over, and she wanted me

High school graduation

to be as involved with school life as possible. It's not that Dad didn't feel the same way. He felt just as bad that I was missing out on many of the normal school activities. He was right when he said he needed to work on Saturdays. But so was Mom. I wished I could've climbed into my wheelchair and pushed all the way to Washington Field myself. I didn't want to be in the middle.

Dad worked the following Saturday, and that started sparks flying. Mom said fine, she would take me to the game. Mom didn't understand a lick of football. She sacrificed her Saturday afternoon to make me happy — and to prove a point to my father. Dad needed the car to go back and forth to the tire plant, so determined little Mom pushed my chair to Washington Field, a good mile away.

It was a bright, cool afternoon in the middle of October. The leaves were brilliant with vibrant reds, oranges, and golds as we strolled the tree-lined streets, bravely dealing with the frequent cracks in the sidewalks and obstacles like high curbs at every corner. It was hay fever season. Along with being left-handed and having dimples, I also inherited my father's hay fever. Around August 20, from about the Little League World Series until the first frost, I would sneeze my head off. It was no different on this breezy afternoon. I loaded up on tissues before we left the house, yet by the time we reached the high school grounds, my tissues were raggedy. Sneezing a good ten times in a row (I counted) without even breaking a sweat was the norm, even while taking my allergy meds. With every sneeze, I'm sure my mother gritted her teeth and thought of Dad.

And so there we were, sitting outside the end zone, Mom in a lawn chair next to my wheelchair. She pretended she was interested in the action, even asking me questions about the play, but I knew she would rather be home baking or attending a bingo matinee somewhere. Instead she was beside me, smiling. She did love the marching band and the cheerleaders.

Long afternoon autumn shadows followed us home. Dad was already there, hanging out in the kitchen. I'm sure he felt guilty because he proudly proclaimed that he had come up with a compromise: if he couldn't take the entire day off on home-game Saturdays, he would only work half of a day (or go in even earlier than seven a.m.) and still make it home to take me to future games. Peace reigned from then on.

––––––––

The one time I did attend school was for my graduation on the football field. I finally met so many voices I had become familiar with over the years. I got a standing ovation from the graduation crowd when a fellow student received my diploma and walked it over to me. The feelings of achievement and accomplishment were a welcome difference in my life.

I did well in high school, averaging a B. It bugged me that society still tended to see the wheelchair first, associating the chair with "stupid." I needed to believe in myself before anyone else would believe in me.

Chapter 8
An Unexpected Twist

What next after high school graduation? Sitting around, wasting away doing nothing was not me. The summer of 1975 was mostly spent sleeping until noon and having fun. No job, no college prospects, no future plans. I became quite familiar with morning game shows and afternoon talk shows. I could get used to those lazy days of a carefree life. I almost fell into the trap of getting too comfortable with my life. Mom and my Aunt Sue, although they meant well, were advocates for "let Greg take it easy" far beyond summer. They felt I should just accept my disability, stay home, and stay away from the outside world. Enjoy sleeping late and watching Phil Donahue every day.

Disability checks were great for those who really needed them, but I felt I was more "normal" than people gave me credit for. I didn't want to play into society's conception that a person with a disability should stay home and not work. Stay in your corner, like a potted plant, don't bother anyone, and don't make waves. That was the attitude I got in the late 1970s and early 1980s. The Americans with Disabilities Act wasn't even on the horizon yet, so it was still pretty much the Dark Ages for folks with a disability. I was never one to listen to society. So, I began to make waves.

It was fine to want to break the mold but I needed to have a plan. I had no training in anything productive. I was good at drawing, often doodling in bed as I recovered from fractures. I considered commercial art, even applying for a "Draw Bambi" mail-order course. I saw the ad in a TV Guide and thought, "Hey, not a bad idea!" My parents went along with whatever I wanted to try. Dad seemed to be a little more realistic than Mom in his attitude toward my abilities. Soon I found the competition in art to be very tough, and I wasn't talented enough to make a living out of my doodling.

The lost Easter eggs

My enthusiasm for art wasn't wasted. I became the "family artist." Every year I was counted on to design and color our annual Easter eggs. I painstakingly etched personal hard-boiled eggs for all family members, complete with names, logos, and crafty decorations. I was proud of myself, and if I failed to color Easter eggs one year, they would be missed. Hardly anyone ever ate the eggs or took them home. They were just there on the Easter dinner table, a colorful holiday decoration. It became a modest family tradition, encouraged by Mom, that "Greg paints the Easter eggs." Forty years later, we were cleaning out the basement and found two cardboard boxes full of musty, dusty Easter eggs. My mother, God bless her, had secretly kept my finest artwork all those years. Somehow the eggs had survived. Those memories, once as faded as the colors on those time-worn eggs, became vivid and vibrant again, proof once more how much Mom loved me.

I always loved sports. I thought of studying journalism, with a goal of being a sportswriter. I contacted a journalist who wrote for the local newspaper. "Well, you really have to be able to get around," was his answer. I appreciated his honesty.

It was just another trickle-down effect of my OI. Like anyone at a crossroads of life, my decision about what to do with my life was confusing and a bit more of a challenge than most young adults my age. My profession needed to meet my abilities and limitations. I was willing to try anything I set my mind to do. Reality, in the form of physical barriers and discrimination, often got in the way.

———

Around this time, Vocational Rehabilitation became involved with my case. They hooked me up with a special training program they were sponsoring with the University of Pennsylvania. The course was Computer Programming, and it was funded by Vocational Rehab and the Wharton School of Business. Not too bad to have on a resume.

Back in the mid-1970s, computers were scarce compared to today. Home computers were non-existent, and they were even foreign to many businesses. But it was a growing field, and they promised a good-paying job at the end of the nine-month course. I was more of a people person, never liked math, and still wasn't completely sure about my direction in life. But what did I have to lose? I couldn't say no and didn't want to be branded a loser or a person with a disability who could work but didn't want to. Despite my reluctance, I signed up.

Every morning Mom drove me to a parking lot in nearby King of Prussia to meet a van with other physically challenged people from around the area. It was like being back in grade school again. These ten guys were older. We were stuck in the same familiar rut of life. This was our chance to get a good job, make decent money, and get off disability. I'm sure we all shared the common bond of wanting a certain amount of respect and dignity in our lives, no matter the different circumstances.

Most of the time I stayed quiet in the van. I felt like an outcast with these guys, who were clearly more streetwise and independent. They often talked about what they would do after the course was over, yearning for the chance to prove themselves. Some wanted pretty big things, like a handicapped-accessible van or their own apartment, while others wished for the basics such as having a few bucks in their pocket for a movie. They talked a lot about girls, a subject still foreign to me even into my early twenties. I listened intently, envious of their aspirations, fearful of the real world I was facing. The more these guys bitched, the more I felt they were losers. Then what the hell was I doing there? I had to be a loser too. Who was I to judge anybody? Maybe they had good reasons to complain about their disabilities and their lives. At least they were on that van every cold morning like I was, chasing some sort of dream.

This older fellow named George kept the van lively, telling stories and singing songs from the fifties. He seemed stuck in time, commenting how he was on the van to "give this damn program another shot." Apparently, his case had been open with Vocational Rehabilitation for many years. He was still looking for a job. He would start a course or a job, then quit, then start again. George knew he was in a rut but seemed incapable of pulling himself out. I didn't want to be another George in thirty years.

Our professor was a middle-aged gentleman named Alvin. He was brilliant at what he did, despite the fact his thin, twisted body was racked with cerebral palsy. He sat in a wheelchair, wearing a crumpled suit and tie, and lectured every day. I admired his courage and intelligence, even if I hated the course. I *did* want to be another Alvin in thirty years.

I hated catching the van so early in the morning and getting home so late at night, studying in the evening, then having to do the same thing all over again the next day. King of Prussia was often the last stop at night, so we would be riding around the area in icy, winter weather for a while before we reached the parking lot where Mom waited. I dreaded leaving Mom in the morning, watching her car pull away as the driver buckled my chair into the floor of the van. It was like starting kindergarten all over again.

That was reality. I was trying to learn a skill I had no interest in, so the entire process was even more difficult to deal with. Plus, this was my first time in the real world. Things shifted from my health to my future. A different mindset.

The course itself was dry. We hardly ever saw or used a computer. That would come in the second half of the course, after the new year. We did get to see the very first computer, which was built at Penn, a mammoth machine made of tubes and wires that filled a gigantic room. That was cool. Maybe if we'd used real computers from the start, everything would've made sense to me. Instead we talked about computers, what they did, how to access them and run them, and listened to droning lectures and read boring textbooks. It didn't connect with me.

After several weeks we took our first exam, and, not surprisingly, I flunked it. I had never failed a test before in my life. I continued to fail as the course slowly inched toward Thanksgiving. My family thought I was doing great and having fun, happy that my future was becoming clearer. Little did they know the truth. I didn't want anyone to know of my failures. No way would I survive the entire course.

I needed the Christmas holidays of 1976 to get my act together. I needed to grow up too. It was time to stop being a baby. I said that I craved independence, to be like everyone else, yet here was my chance and I couldn't cope. I dreaded returning to school after the break. The weather had turned even nastier — bitterly cold, snowy days — which didn't make things any better.

Just when I thought things couldn't get any worse, they did, in an unexpected way.

It was just another New Year's Eve. Company came over to celebrate. Mom set out cold cuts, and we played cards while watching Dick Clark from Times Square in New York City. We laughed and reflected on 1976. The Bicentennial was unforgettable, especially the wagon train caravan rolling through town on the Fourth of July.

Dad always went to his family doctor to get his blood sugar checked, every month without fail. Back in those days, you couldn't check your blood sugar on your own. Our family doctor was vacationing in Florida for the holidays. Instead of seeing the doctor who was filling in, Dad decided to skip the check-up.

On New Year's Day, Dad became violently ill — vomiting, fever, and chills. He stayed in bed over the holiday, thinking it had to be the flu. He became so sick that Mom grew frightened and called an ambulance. Dad couldn't get out of bed on his own, so the paramedics carried him down the stairs on a stretcher. I was downstairs in Dad's favorite brown lounge chair, shaking with fear as I watched him go out the door and into the freezing January air. He looked at me, so pale and sick, mumbling, "I'll be all right, Butch. Take care of your Mom."

Later that day they transferred him to Philadelphia. After a week, we thought he was turning a corner with the blood infection. It all started with a sore on his right foot, a complication from his diabetes. The Philly hospitals were the best. He was in the right place. He was getting better, and we prayed he would be home soon.

Two weeks later, he died after a sudden turn for the worse. I never had a chance to say goodbye.

I heard the phone ring that morning, heard Mom say, "He died?" She had just come from the hospital hours before. I heard her sobbing, then saw her at my bedroom door, checking to see if I was awake. I was and asked what was going on.

"Daddy died," she said softly.

The words left me numb. He was going to get better, wasn't he? I couldn't cry. I just lay awake the rest of the night. Before I thought of what his death would mean to the future, I fell asleep thinking of all the memories. It was less painful to dream than to face reality.

I remembered how we went to ballgames together. The Sunday night bowling matches. How he had worked so hard for all those years. What a great guy he was. Hard to believe everything would just stop. We needed him. Mom was taking care of me and now had to look after everyone on her own. It didn't seem fair. Dad was only fifty-five.

On January 27, the day before his funeral, the snow piled up to nearly a foot from a blizzard a few days earlier. Someone had shoveled a path for my wheelchair to reach the car. The cemetery was windy and cold, the sky steel-gray, the trees bare and lifeless. They struggled to push my wheelchair through the enormous drifts of snow, at times needing to carry the chair just to reach the gravesite. A taste of the harsh reality to come.

Well-wishers stopped by our quiet house after the funeral. Mom was so brave. Late at night we were alone again. Dad wasn't coming back. His favorite brown recliner in the living room sat empty. He was all around us but wasn't there. And in my room — alone — I finally cried.

I would always feel his presence in my life. Like on the day I graduated from college. And the night the Phillies finally won the World Series. Or the day I was hired for my first real job. He was always there.

————

The holidays were over. So was the funeral. Now it was time to return to school. I was determined to give it another shot — for Dad. He always wanted to see me make good. I went back for him.

I was still failing in February. In a bout of depression, without even consulting Mom, I decided to quit. I hated that word. I was not a quitter. Yet here I was, throwing away this opportunity. Would anyone understand?

Down at Penn, I told Alvin and the people from Vocational Rehabilitation that I couldn't go on. I got a stern lecture from a staff guidance counselor, who laid it out — how I was throwing away a great job, independence, the chance to be somebody. Did I want to go back to being labeled as "disabled"? She was right. I wished I had a plan to fall back on, but I didn't. I would return to a do-nothing life and an empty future. She asked me to stick it out another month. I said no. Vocational Rehab was disgusted with me. An all-expenses-paid education, leading to a good job, down the drain. Did I realize how many other guys in my situation would die for this chance?

At least Mom understood. She knew how hard things were at home. She worried about me, out there in the wicked weather and the wicked world by myself for the very first time. In my heart, I felt like I did give up. I felt like a failure and a loser, like I had let down so many people who had faith in me. I was sure I had let my father down. All this time, trying to please others and do the right things, yet torn up inside.

And yet, a little voice inside reassured me that somehow, someway, everything would be fine. The failures in 1977 would only serve to make me stronger and more determined down the road. I couldn't see it then, but everything happens for a reason. Like one big jigsaw puzzle, every piece fit into place.

Chapter 9
Aftermath

After Dad died, my Uncle Henry became like my second father. He had a big influence on my life and never treated me differently or dwelled on my disability. My uncle was tall and thin, with dark-framed glasses and a perpetual tan. He worked for many years at a local tire plant, just like Dad. Many of our family either worked at tire plants or the local steel mill. We were descended from immigrants who came to Pennsylvania looking for work in the coal mines and steel factories.

Uncle Henry and Aunt Sue argued often over petty things, but that was how they lived and loved for nearly sixty years. It wasn't uncommon for him to half-jokingly threaten to "throw her in the trunk" during one of our many day trips together. Salty and colorful with a heart of gold, I'm convinced my uncle loved my dear aunt. As she would say, "He's like an antique. I can't get rid of him now." He didn't mince words, and although my aunt was his leash and advised him to "mind your own business," it didn't stop Uncle Henry from putting in his two cents everywhere he went.

Uncle Henry's passion was gambling. He was happiest behind a card table or at the racetrack. Of course, he taught me the ins and outs of cards and the ponies. He liked to play blackjack in Atlantic City. He was good at the game but better at poker. He held his own at the tables, told off the pit bosses when he lost, and led a fantasy, Frank Sinatra-type of life (his idol). He told stories in the car about Sinatra, along with his usual hunting and fishing yarns. I was a captive audience during our excursions to Atlantic City, but I found his stories interesting: amazed how he knew all the good fishing holes around the area, amazed how he once stayed up in a tree for twenty hours waiting for a deer to pass by. To say that he embellished his yarns a bit would be an understatement. If nothing else, he was always entertaining.

Sometimes he told the same story twice. "Did I ever tell you this one?" Yes, but I didn't mind hearing it again (although Aunt Sue would groan in the backseat). He had hundreds of stories. Nearing eighty years old, my uncle was eager to share his wisdom with anyone willing (or not so willing) to listen. Uncle Henry enjoyed time with me almost as much as I looked forward to seeing him. He focused on my abilities (like my new-found ability to play blackjack), which was novel to me. He made me feel good about myself. The only time he mentioned my disability was in passing, almost as an afterthought, commenting to others, "Shame, isn't it? He doesn't have any legs."

I did have legs. They were just short and stunted underneath my trousers. Why Uncle Henry always thought I didn't have legs was something I never understood but didn't bother to ask.

The racetrack was also a favorite hang-out of ours. Nothing like sitting outside on a warm summer evening in Brandywine, Delaware, intently studying a program, trying to pick a winner. We followed a local harness driver named Wade, and when Uncle Henry saw in the morning paper that Wade was going to ride in a race that night, he always called me up and asked if I wanted to go. We didn't have much money. My uncle had his pension and social security, so we were strictly two-dollar bettors. But we had fun at the races. They served as a diversion from life. We didn't win much (although Uncle Henry did hit a long-shot exacta once for over $2,000). "We will get them next time" was our usual lament on the ride home.

We met the baseball player Pete Rose at Brandywine one night (way before he was publicly labeled a gambler). My uncle spotted him in the clubhouse while placing a bet and wasn't afraid to go up to him and ask him to say hi to me. Sure enough, after the races ended that night, Uncle Henry positioned my wheelchair near the escalator, and there was the familiar face of Pete Rose riding down the escalator with a group of people. Uncle Henry followed behind him, smiling broadly, and I could read his lips. "He doesn't have legs . . ."

Aunt Sue and Uncle Henry

Pete stopped for a moment, shook my hand, and gave me a pre-signed autographed photo. "How are you doing, buddy?" He grinned before his bodyguard whisked him out the door into the summer air.

Uncle Henry kept life fun. He went out of his way to make me smile. Behind a poker table, he was in his glory. Crafty and shrewd, he was notorious around town as a bluffer. He feasted on the younger, inexperienced players. He played at all the local fire houses and church events, especially ruling at his weekly late-night game at the Moose Lodge hall. He could go hours without winning a hand, but when the dust cleared, he usually was a winner (or at least broke even). He could be rude, not caring who was across the table from him, but he was admired and respected in town, especially by the older guys who he hung out with. He loved the famous song by the great Kenny Rogers "The Gambler," often telling me, "Know when to hold them and fold them." We used that song as our guide when we gambled together. "You never count your money at the table," he whispered to me when I started stacking my chips or quarters. It was like Kenny himself was playing next to me.

After playing poker for over sixty years, several times a week, my uncle claimed to never have gotten a royal flush, the highest hand in the game. The odds of getting a royal flush are very low (649,738 to 1 to be exact), yet to never have beaten the odds once was remarkable. He always chased that elusive royal flush, both on and off the card table. It kept him going in life.

One memorable Uncle Henry incident was the time he forgot about Aunt Sue's lottery tickets. She played the same numbers every day for many years. It was their 50th wedding anniversary, and she played 5017, which stood for 50 years and the date they were married, November 17th. For some reason Uncle Henry forgot to get tickets that day of all days, and guess what the Big 4 number was that night? Unbelievably, 5017 came up straight — $5,000 down the drain. It wasn't the end of the world, but close to it. My uncle was at a loss for words when he got home that night from fishing and Aunt Sue asked if he had the winning tickets. That little memory slip would haunt him for years, and whenever a disagreement came up, the infamous lottery incident story was rolled out again.

An idiosyncrasy he had was never buying candy before a holiday. The day after Christmas, Valentine's Day, or Easter, Uncle Henry could be found prowling the local stores for half-priced boxes of chocolates. "What the hell," he reasoned, "the candy is still good."

Our fondest memories were coming home from Atlantic City and stopping at Pat's Steaks in South Philly for a tasty cheese steak at four in the morning. My uncle was in his glory, chomping down a steak on the streets where *Rocky* was filmed. He grew up in the city, so he was familiar with this atmosphere and soaked it up.

Uncle Henry helped us out after Dad died. He was our handyman, and since he had a lot of free time after retirement (when he wasn't fishing), he would stop by and fix a leaky faucet or whatever needed to be done around the house. He often dropped off a basket of fresh corn on the cob at our front door, asking nothing in return. He took me under his wing, got me out of my doldrums and out of the house. My uncle knew what he was doing. Maybe he lacked formal education, only going as far as sixth grade, but he had more common sense than anyone I ever knew. He smoked like a chimney (the aroma of his trademark cigars lingered on his clothing, just another thing to irritate Aunt Sue). He ate bacon and eggs each morning, didn't care about cholesterol, and drank beer in moderation. He lived each day like it was his last. His feeling about life was like the smoke at the end of one of his cigars: witness it, experience it, and then let it flow.

———

After my father died, we moved into a new rancher across town. Mom used the money she received when Dad had taken early retirement prior to his death. It wasn't the full benefits he would've gotten had he survived, but half was better than nothing. It allowed Mom to purchase the one-story home. Most of my siblings were on their own by then, and without steps to contend with, life would be easier for both of us. Some people thought she was crazy, selling the house. But Mom knew what she was doing. It was a move which would change our lives forever.

Things always happen for a reason. If Dad had not died, we never would've moved. And if we hadn't moved, my life would've turned out entirely different. Dad was looking down on us, and after the Penn fiasco, I firmly believed he was guiding me every step of the way.

Back in the late seventies, houses weren't required to fit the needs of a person with a disability. We were still seen as outsiders in society, accessibility not being a high priority.

Without stairs, I began to assert my independence. I had learned how to toilet myself, shower myself (with the help of a shower chair and shower spray), and now had the freedom to push my wheelchair all around the house, or even outside if I wanted. No more crawling around the floor like a little creature. It may seem like a small thing, but I finally felt free, like I was released from a prison. I was not fracturing as often, and now I had new-found independence. I felt almost "normal." Pushing my chair whenever and wherever I wanted to go — from my bedroom to the kitchen, or sitting outside on a summer night — felt so liberating. My self-esteem and confidence grew, and I wondered where all this freedom would lead me. I finally could savor the feeling of a simple act like getting a drink of water by myself.

The doorways were still too narrow, the kitchen cabinets too high to reach, and even though there was a ramp in the front, the ramp going to the backyard was built too steep, and I couldn't use it without assistance. Mom advised me not to worry. She was there to help.

———

The late seventies were a confusing time in my life. Painful fractures, hideous leisure suits, and bad disco music dominated. I met iconic actor John Ritter (at the old Mike Douglas Show in Philly), flew to California to visit my Uncle Steve (with Mom and Aunt Sue), and eased into a meaningless lifestyle again, watching Johnny Carson every night until late and not waking up until The Price Is Right. That was how my life was for several years: timed by television programs. Often I stayed up until the playing of the national anthem, a beeping test pattern signaling the end of my programming day. Holidays and weekends were just any other day. Summer vacation wasn't special; every day was vacation. Did I even care anymore to make changes in my world?

Easily the dumbest thing I did during this era (and possibly ever) was get a perm. I looked up to my brother Pat, who was two years older than me. Pat was a good athlete and a good-looking guy. He had all the best rock albums and dressed cool. When he got braces on his teeth, I wanted braces on my teeth. When he got a perm, I wanted a perm. Guys getting perms was the weird style at the time. Mom tried to talk me out of it. I did have nice hair, but it was straight and boring. I wanted to be like everyone else.

Once again, I should've listened to Mom. I looked ridiculous the moment I saw myself in the mirror — a combination of Shirley Temple, Richard Simmons, and a chia pet. It was dear old Uncle Henry who told me the truth. "You look awful," he said bluntly. It took a few haircuts to cut the curls out, and I was back to myself again. Lesson learned. It's not always good to try and be someone else. Thank goodness no photo exists of my stupidity. Only the awful memories of my curls.

I needed something to happen in my life to rescue me from myself.

Chapter 10
Cards & Cigars

There was a nursing home called Phoenixville Manor just a block away from our new house. I noticed an article in the local paper looking for summer volunteers. I had never been in a nursing home before. I didn't know what to expect. But that little voice inside, which guided me so many times in my life, told me to apply.

I was growing tired of doing nothing all day. My self-esteem was shot; I hated myself for failing at Penn. I was tired of using my disability as an excuse for not challenging myself. Sitting around only made me dwell on my challenges even more. I had to get out of the rut I was trapped in. The nursing home was the first step in that process.

I began working in their gift shop. It was a fun place to work because I got to meet many of the residents who drifted in during the day to browse or buy small items like candy bars or nail polish.

One couple who came in all the time was Bill and Dolly. Both were always dressed to the gills, like two figurines on top of a wedding cake. Bill was normally decked out in a dark suit, tie, and fedora hat, while Dolly always wore a dress, heels, and a pearl necklace. They were both very tiny, in their eighties, and cute. All dressed up with no place to go, other than up and down the halls. Bill sat on the sofa in the middle of the shop and chatted about our days working together for the Pennsylvania Railroad. Dolly patiently waited for him to finish his conversation, then off they went again, holding each other under the arm, slowly pacing down the hallway. Dolly occasionally whacked Bill over the head with her handbag for no apparent reason, which didn't seem to faze him.

I learned that I could easily talk to older people and enjoyed it, and they seemed to like me too. I was willing to listen. They looked at my disability differently than most of the world. They seemed to trust me, like I had a clue what they might be going through. I soon became a fixture at the nursing home, not only volunteering in the gift shop, but doing part-time odd jobs, such as making posters for the Activities Department, putting my past art skills to good use. I must have made thousands of posters and signs over the years. I had a purpose in life now. I couldn't wait to get up in the morning and wheel the block to the nursing home. I was making friends there and people needed me, which made me feel good.

Staff drifted into the gift shop daily. I got to know the day-shift nurses and aides. Normally they ran in, made their purchases or browsed a bit, then left. Then there was Fred.

Fred wasn't his real name. To be honest, I forgot his real name. I called him Fred because he had a squirrely face and a brown pompadour hairstyle similar to Liberace, and the tank-like body of Fred Flintstone. He was a friendly guy, and when I started working in the gift shop, he was nice enough to drop by and introduce himself. Fred happened to be the Director of Nursing.

We had a sofa in the middle of the gift shop. It was there for residents like Bill and Dolly to sit and rest before going on their way. Fred stopped in every day to chat, often plopping himself down on the sofa. He asked me a bunch of questions, like how I liked my job or what I did for fun. I enjoyed the company during dead times in the store. Fred wanted to be friends and I looked forward to his visits and our chats. Fred was in his fifties and had a wife and adult children. We talked about his family, but he mainly wanted to know everything about me. It was nice to have someone so interested in my life, and as a nurse, I thought he may have been fascinated with OI.

He started hanging around the gift shop more and more, for longer and longer periods, until even I had to wonder, "Doesn't this guy have a job?" I noticed he hung out with me in the gift shop much longer on Saturdays, when the usual staff wasn't around and a skeleton crew manned the day shift. Fred asked me to visit his office sometime, as he had all kinds of plants that he took care of (I was into plants back then as well). But I didn't have the time. I was more interested in spending my required time in the store, locking up, and then visiting residents for the remainder of the day.

Fred noticed how I would blush when a pretty female nurse or aide would come into the store. He started asking me if I had a girlfriend or if I ever had sex, topics which made me feel uncomfortable. He noticed I would get flustered by the subject and backed off. But he increasingly started asking me more intimate questions every time he visited. I began to sense this guy was a real weirdo, but I kept quiet.

One time he asked if I noticed the new private duty female nurse working down the hall. I said yes, I did meet her, and she seemed very nice. He asked if I thought she was attractive and I admitted that yes, she was very attractive. He then proceeded to tell me everything about her, including her age and that she was single with no boyfriend. "I have her phone number," he informed. "I could get you a date with her."

I didn't like the direction this was going. Wasn't all that information supposed to be confidential? Still, I said I would think about it. How could I call a girl I barely knew? Wouldn't she know how I got her number? Fred said not to worry. He could arrange things. "Stop thinking and worrying . . . just enjoy life," was his advice. My self-confidence soared.

The next weekend Fred stopped by, excitedly sat down, and asked if he could shut the gift shop door for a few minutes, as he wanted to tell me about the "date" he had set up between me and the private duty nurse. The arrangements were set, and he had her phone number with him. But first I had to do something in return. He wanted to touch my private parts.

An icy chill came over me, but instead of being scared, I immediately shouted, "What's wrong with you, man?"

I've never seen someone turn so white so fast in my life. His face looked like a beached whale. He probably thought I was this passive little guy who would do anything he wanted. Fred was surprised I wasn't a half-wit after all. He started apologizing profusely, saying he was sorry, that he "didn't mean it that way," pleading that I not tell anyone. He never threatened me or made me feel guilty, like I was the pervert. He just kept apologizing, suggesting we forget the whole thing.

Maybe he thought I would reconsider when I had time to ponder the missed chance of having a date with the pretty nurse down the hall. Truth is, after he opened the door and scurried out, I was shocked at my own spunk. I was scared to death but wouldn't let Fred the Predator know that.

Now I wondered what to do. I could either forget the whole thing and go on with life or report Fred. But who would ever believe me? I was just this new volunteer, a young guy in a wheelchair, looking for a way to spend my time in a nursing home. He was an adult male, married and with a family, probably a well-respected person in his community, with a real job, and an important one at that. The more I pondered it, the angrier I became. The fact I was a volunteer and had a disability shouldn't matter. What did I have to lose? I wasn't the pervert. Damn Fred for putting me in that situation! And if he hit on a guy like me, who knew what he was doing to other staff members, or worse, to the helpless, innocent residents?

There was an older nurse who also worked weekends, generally every other week when Fred was off. Her name was Mrs. Hoover, but everyone called her Mrs. H. She was cool with the staff. She was an assistant to the director and was also a fixture at the nursing home for many years. Mrs. H. liked to joke and always had a smile on her face. But she always let everyone know who was boss. Staff respected her and felt at ease going to her with problems. She was a "nurse's nurse" — gentle and kind, a professional in every way, someone who took the nurses and aides under her wing to teach and counsel, not humiliate. Yet when she had to be tough behind closed doors, she was. I wondered why Mrs. H. wasn't the Director of Nursing, but she shrugged off that suggestion as "facility politics" and claimed she was "happy doing what I'm doing." If anyone would understand, it would be Mrs. H. I made an appointment to see her in the Nursing Office after I closed shop one Saturday.

I told her everything. She listened intently, occasionally taking a drag from her cigarette (back in the early eighties it was okay to smoke, even in the Nursing Office. Funny how so many nurses and doctors I worked with over the years smoked, even though they would tell their patients never to smoke). Apparently there had been some other complaints about Fred and his aggressive behavior toward staff. I sighed, relieved that I wasn't the only one who thought Fred was a problem. There wasn't enough proof to get him fired, but the evidence was building. I was glad Mrs. H. believed me. In fact, her face grew redder and redder as I told my story. I could tell she was angry that her Director of Nursing was trying to hit on someone at work, let alone someone in my situation.

"Don't worry," she assured me through clenched teeth as I departed, "I'll take care of it."

From then on, I saw Fred passing by the gift shop, but he didn't stop in anymore. He barely waved hello, and he seemed to always be in a hurry whenever he bumped into me in the halls. Then I heard through the grapevine that he had resigned. Who knows if it was voluntary or forced? The important thing was that Fred was gone forever.

————

During the summer, I was assigned to spend time with John Dickert. He was a friendly elderly gentleman in his eighties, always dressed in western garb — a string tie and vest, always in rusty brown. For some reason he often neighed like a horse between sentences, out of pain or habit. He reminded me of Grandpa Joad from the classic movie *The Grapes of Wrath*.

The Activities Director thought it would be a good idea for me to visit John for an hour or so after I closed the gift shop. John had a family, but they rarely visited him. He was lonely and needed a friend. He felt forgotten. Staff became like surrogate families for residents who never saw a familiar face other than on Christmas. That was John.

John and I became quick pals. I always called the residents "Mr." or "Mrs.", unless they asked me to call them by their first name. Nursing home resident or not, they deserved the respect due to them. I met him for the first time sitting in his wheelchair at the second-floor nursing station. Head in hands, he was dozing off as he waited for a cigar. I hated to wake him up, but after a few taps on the shoulder, he lifted his head, befuddled, mumbling, "Who the hell?" before spotting me, his thin, wispy white hair messed up. I shook his hand, introduced myself, and he eyed me suspiciously with his sharp blue eyes, wondering what a "young fella" like me wanted with a "forgotten old guy" like him.

We started talking about anything and everything: the weather, sports, anything to break the ice. John enjoyed reminiscing, so I allowed him to do most of the talking. Listening turned out to be a valuable tool. I learned that most residents, like John, really wanted someone just to listen to them.

John was proud to show me his grainy yellow photos that he kept in his pocket or under his leg, photos of himself as a young man, his wife, his children, old cars, and old clothes. Nothing current: everything was from the past. He laughed at himself, musing, "Didn't I look good back then? I grew up in Philadelphia when Broad Street was a prairie." He stared at those memories, wishing he could transport his aging body through the photos and return to his youthful days. It was fascinating to gaze at the styles of clothing, the different kinds of automobiles and old houses. John's stories were interesting to listen to, even though he tended to repeat himself quite a bit, and he insisted on staring at the same pictures each time I visited. Maybe it was closure, a way of validating his life. Imagine everything this guy had seen in life, all the history he saw and lived through. He reminded me of my Uncle Henry. I was a captive audience again, but I really did enjoy his reflections and our chats.

"My daughter!" he would exclaim. "What a great girl . . ." His words faded away like the fading photos. It had to be so painful to know she didn't visit anymore.

Cards and cigars — John loved both. With each visit, after closing the gift shop, I met him at the nurse's station, where he first had a smoke, crying like a baby when the nurse was late with a match. I tried to find some common ground between us, something that would get him out of his doldrums. He didn't care to talk about sports or old movies. I noticed he had a beat-up pack of playing cards tucked into the side of his wheelchair, and I asked him what he played. "Pinochle," he replied, perking up. "Do you play?"

"Do I play? What luck to finally find someone who likes pinochle!" I crowed. I didn't know a thing about pinochle. Not a damn thing. But I hit on something that the old man liked, so I went with it.

"Want to turn over a few?" he asked around his cigar, raising his bushy white eyebrows while holding up the pack of cards. We headed for the dining room. John ordered a few residents to "Beat it" as we took over the nearest round table.

Cards were a bright spot for the old man. Finally having someone to play with was big for him. He taught me how to play pinochle. After our first game he eyed me suspiciously, especially after he corrected me on more than a few moves.

"Sorry, I haven't played in a long time." ("Never" was a long time.) I caught on after a while, basically following his moves until I had a grasp on the game — or at least I thought I did.

One afternoon a nurse was watching our game as she took the old man's blood pressure. "What are you guys playing?" she asked.

"Pinochle," John replied. "What's it to you, sweetie?"

"That's not pinochle," she said. "I have no clue what you're playing." As it turned out, neither did we. John got confused and taught me versions of pinochle, rummy, and whist all rolled into one. The blind leading the blind. Ah, what the hell . . . it didn't matter. We were having fun, which was the main objective of our games. So I went from not knowing how to play pinochle, to thinking I knew how to play pinochle, to not really knowing how to play pinochle.

Every afternoon that I was working for close to a year we "turned over a few." We soon became known as the "afternoon card players" by the nurses and staff. Lord help any residents at our favorite round table in the dining room (the one near the entrance, in case the old guy had to quickly rush out to pee).

When John caught pneumonia the following winter, I visited him in the hospital. I brought him a brand-new deck of cards. "We will save these for when you get back," I encouraged him as he lay in bed, hardly able to talk.

"My buddy," was all he said, recognizing me through cloudy eyes.

The nurses at the hospital told me how much John looked forward to our visits and how he lamented whenever I couldn't make it in. I thought about that a lot, how much my visits meant to one lonely old man.

John never did make it back to the nursing home. John was the first resident I spent time with, the first who touched my heart. He gave me a purpose and showed me I could make a difference in someone's life by a friendly hello, a simple visit, and a deck of cards.

————

Wheelchair Willie was one of my best friends on the CB radio. He was in a car accident several years earlier which left him paralyzed from the waist down. He was a young, husky guy, a St. Bernard in human form, burly and friendly, cut down in his prime when he totaled his car on a rain-slicked highway. "Me and a tree had an argument," he surmised. "The tree won."

He went through the usual stages of denial and anger before finding acceptance. Once he did, there was no stopping Willie. Hell on wheels, literally. I always thought it would be tougher to adjust to a new disability. Willie had had a taste of able-bodied life, which I never had. I was used to my life, whereas he needed to adjust. He finally found a purpose in life and moved on. Willie was a guy who didn't sulk. It had to be like a nightmare you can't awake from, but he never complained about it.

Willie was everything I wanted to be. He drove a specially equipped revved-up dark-green van with a hydraulic lift and hand controls to drive. With his other car, a beat-up Chevy, he just climbed into the driver's seat, threw his folded-up chair in the back seat, and took off. He wasn't above getting under his van to fix it or plopping out of his chair to the dirty ground to garden. He reminded me of everything I was missing in life — shooting pool, wheelchair basketball, picking up girls. He showed me that I was limiting myself by thinking I was handicapped. He didn't preach, he simply showed me by living. Disability or not, my life could be so much better than it was.

In many ways, I wanted to be like Willie, yet in other ways, I was afraid. Like when Willie strapped himself in his chair and used himself as a human bobsled to plow down a snowy hill. After all, I did have brittle bones. I admired his fierce determination and will to enjoy life. He had come so close to death when he had his accident. It took that brush with death to make him live life to its fullest. Instead of retreating into depression and isolation after his accident, Willie threw himself into life even more. "If I never grow up, I'll never grow old" was his philosophy.

Willie knew how much I loved working at the nursing home. He put the idea in my head that I could get paid doing what I loved to do. I had no clue what social work was or what a social worker did. I did some research about the field — the academic qualifications, the salary. I needed to earn my college degree, at least a bachelor's degree. That was four years of school. Becoming a social worker sounded like a great idea. Helping others in need. Giving back what was given to me all my life. Couldn't find a nobler profession.

It just so happened the current social worker at the nursing home was a guy (a rare thing). Jack was the spitting image of singer/songwriter James Taylor. I asked him for his advice the first time I expressed this crazy idea to anyone. "You'll never make a lot of money in social work," he said honestly. "But some things are just more important than money."

Great advice. Plus, to my surprise, he didn't laugh at my dream.

Chapter 11
The Road to Independence

After the Penn debacle, an intense desire and determination was burning inside me to prove to everyone, myself included, that I wasn't a quitter. I wanted to show Vocational Rehabilitation I could do it. I had thrown away a great career and a promising future. Would I do it again? Why should they invest their faith and money in me again? I did need help with grants and loans. I was making peanuts at the nursing home. I needed my disability benefits and was limited to what I could earn. How could I afford school without help? I couldn't. What about the cost of textbooks and gas to travel back and forth to school?

I took that hard first step on the road to independence. I applied for every grant and student loan I could find. Huge amounts of red tape and paperwork. Vocational Rehab saw I was serious this time and agreed to help me. One of the toughest steps was just saying I was going to do it. I needed to try, after settling into a comfort zone of doing nothing with my life for so long. When I brought up the idea of college to Mom and my family, it surprised them. There were doubts as well as encouragement from family and friends. Mostly doubts.

Mom, always supportive and protective, didn't want me to get hurt again. But she agreed. Maybe she knew, deep down inside, this was the first step to independence.

There was one main difference between college in 1984 and Penn. This time I wanted it so bad. The idea of becoming a social worker was perfect. I already knew what a difference I was making in someone's life, as I had with John and the rest of the residents I helped at the Manor. Earning a degree and getting a good job would give me the respect and dignity I craved. A degree would change my life and make others look at me in a different light. It would give me the self-confidence I needed to excel in all aspects of life down the road. Making more money wasn't a bad idea either.

I took the entrance exam and thought I did okay, although I struggled with the math section (no surprise there). I waited anxiously until the results came in. Doubts crept into my mind. Was I looking for a way to back out? A total waste of time? Maybe it was better just to stay at home after all.

To my surprise, I passed the exam. I registered at the community college and was accepted.

The plan was to carpool with Wheelchair Willie. He was a semester ahead of me, but his schedule on campus was practically the same as mine (he was a social work major), so it would work. I appreciated Willie because he cared, and he was willing to help a guy like me catch a break. He understood my life as few people could. Mom wasn't too thrilled with the idea of carpooling with wild Willie every day. She half-heartedly believed him when he swore not to be reckless with me in the van.

Early September 1984. A new chapter of my life was just beginning. I climbed into Willie's van; he folded up my chair and tossed it in the back. Gunning the souped-up engine with "You Might Think" by The Cars blasting over the speakers, off we went. I waved so-long to a skeptical Mom on the porch. I was worried too, but I was also ready for the incredible journey ahead.

My first day at the community college was also my very first day in a "regular" school with able-bodied students. As I waited for the elevator to take me upstairs to my very first college class, I watched the rush of students file into the wide student plaza, the early morning September sun shining through the glistening windows. Kids sporting mohawks and parachute pants, listening to their Walkmans, lugging backpacks, many wearing blank stares, wondering what to expect next. We were all in the same adjustment boat, though mine was particularly stressful. I had to get used to a desk, lockers, a blackboard, and a teacher in front of me. I was changing classes on the fly instead of a student unplugging my intercom box in school. It was tough enough getting used to college life, let alone getting adjusted to things students usually took for granted.

I still worked part-time at the nursing home, trying to supplement my disability benefits to purchase textbooks. Mom, Vocational Rehab, and a combination of grants and student loans helped with books as well. New experiences were happening at blinding speed. A few weeks into the semester, I smoked my first joint. Willie chain-smoked cigarettes like a chimney, but on this crisp fall morning he showed up at my house smoking a joint. Mom was standing on the porch and couldn't see.

"What's that funny smell?" I asked. I took a few sniffs of the repulsive air before he explained.

"Smitty, it's weed. Take one puff and see if you like it. It's good for you."

Willie was into herbal medicine back then. A fore-runner to present-day medical marijuana, so to speak.

Weed? I remembered the term from my brothers (not that they ever used it). I also knew the weeds in the backyard were annoying.

"C'mon, man!" Willie insisted. "Just one puff. Who knows? You may like it! If you don't, no big deal. At least you tried, right?"

He had a point there. I was out and about in the world now. I was sure all the younger college kids smoked pot. Why not be cool?

"Okay, I'll try it," I reluctantly agreed.

"That's it . . . go slow, man," Willie advised as he passed the joint over to me.

I had no clue what I was doing. I put the joint between my quivering lips and inhaled. Right away, I started coughing and wheezing. It tasted awful, and I felt a burning sensation on my tongue and down my throat. The van seemed to spin. Suddenly the song "White Rabbit" played on Willie's radio.

Willie laughed until I began spitting up green fluid all over his van. "Hey, watch that, Smitty! I just had the inside cleaned yesterday!" He held up his half empty can of beer. "Do you want a drink?"

I coughed all the way to West Chester. Willie just shook his head. I guess he thought I was a real nerd. One puff, and I never smoked pot again.

It was important to do well in my first semester. I needed to maintain a certain average to keep my student grants. I took six classes in the fall of 1984. Eighteen credits. Was I crazy? I had to cram all those courses into a few days to fit my schedule (and Willie's). I loved my courses, especially my social work and psychology classes. All I did was study and attend classes. A typical day was classes starting at eight a.m. and not ending until ten at night. I came home, studied, caught some sleep, worked the next day, studied some more, then prepped for classes the next day. That was my life for four years, and I poured my heart and soul into it. This was my shot, and I wasn't going to waste it.

I aced all my classes that first semester. I put a lot of hard work and determination into it. When Vocational Rehab saw the six As, they were more willing to help financially, and I was grateful to accept.

Most of all, the great first semester made me believe in myself. My confidence soared. I wanted more. I couldn't wait for the second semester to begin after the holidays. I started to believe. What worked in the first semester should work again in the second, right? I tried not to stop and think too much. I just did it. From class to class, test to test, term paper to term paper. I didn't slow down, even during the holidays and summer breaks. I just kept pushing ahead, as if I was pushing my chair through a pile of snow. Tough sledding, but in time my goals were conquered.

I survived obstacles like bad weather, pushing hilly sidewalks across campus, my history book being stolen out of my locker, and the embarrassment of dropping everything — papers, books, pens — right in the middle of campus as I rushed to another class. But I did it.

My faith in the world grew too. Students on campus held open doors and offered to carry my heavy textbooks or even to push my chair. I learned to graciously accept assistance. I wanted to be as independent as possible but learned that it was okay to accept help. When I refused, students often seemed disappointed. So I just sat back and enjoyed the ride.

It was an advantage to be an older returning student. I was twenty-eight when I started college. Making friends was cool and got easier with time, but I was there for a reason, not just to party. That doesn't mean I passed on fun when it came my way. I just had my priorities straight.

———

Around the holidays, another unexpected twist hit me hard: Willie quit school. He said he was having "problems," but he didn't elaborate on the phone. Instead of taking a semester off, he dropped out completely. My role model, the guy who had encouraged me to enter school, just quit.

Willie had his bad points, but he was a good guy. I learned a lot from him, like believing in myself. I'll never forget the time we needed to use the lone small elevator at school to get upstairs for our next class. It took forever to arrive on the first floor. When the door opened, we found out why: the elevator was loaded with able-bodied students.

"What the hell?" Willie bellowed. "Ain't the stairs good enough for you all? How did you get an elevator key anyway? Maybe me and my little buddy here should just use the steps while you jackasses ride the elevator all day?"

On and on it went as the elevator emptied. Silent, red-faced students quickly filed out and dispersed. I wanted to crawl under the nearest rock, but Willie was right. And as we rode up together, he glanced at me, sort of agitated at my silence, and remarked, "Sometimes you got to speak up, Smitty. Especially when people just don't care."

I lost a friend but also my ride to school. I put an ad on the bulletin board at school. Mom started driving me, forty-five minutes each way. She sacrificed a lot, getting up early, driving in bad weather, picking me up late at night. I prayed for an answer.

It was then I met an angel named Lori. She was also majoring in social work. An older returning student, a single mother of two kids, she had her own unique story. Divorced, on welfare at one time, now working two jobs and going to school. An independent free spirit raised in California, she was fun and refreshing with her open attitude.

I admired her a great deal. Lori was a survivor too. Since we were taking the same classes, she saw my flyer seeking a ride and asked if I wanted to carpool with her. She offered to go out of her way to pick me up at home and claimed she didn't mind. She needed the company and the friendship.

Mom met Lori and trusted her instantly, maybe because Lori was in her forties and a mother too. She knew what she wanted in life and what she didn't want. She smoked in the car, we laughed a lot, and we quizzed each other on the way to school before a big test. We would carpool together for the next four years.

The eighties were my coming-out era. I was in school, making new friends, and my bones stopped breaking so easily. Life was getting better.

Dating opened a whole new world to me. I was always so self-conscious about my legs. I was meeting girls at college. Even though I was afraid to ask them to study together, to my surprise, girls were asking me! I felt bad that I couldn't drive. It seemed awkward asking a girl to pick me up, fold the wheelchair, then toss it into the car. I could get in by myself thanks to my transfer board, but handling the chair and driving were something I couldn't do. My friends at school encouraged me not to worry about it, especially Lori. "If a girl likes you enough, she won't mind," she advised.

I was limiting myself by not giving myself a chance to have fun. A guy with a disability with a girlfriend was becoming more common. Back in the day, God forbid a person with a disability had sex. And if you did, it had better be with another person who had a disability. Here I was, allowing society to dictate what I should and shouldn't do, buying into the stereotype. So, when I had the time, I started going out and having fun. I was meeting girls face-to-face, girls who made me believe that my chair was no big deal.

My first real girlfriend was a chick I met through the CB radio. Her handle was Silver Fox. I found her like magic one night as I was cruising by Channel 20. She was talking and I stopped to listen. She sounded cute. I said hello, she ignored the guy she was talking to, and we ended up talking the rest of the evening.

Fox lived nearby with her folks on the other side of Valley Forge National Park. She was twenty, and I was pushing twenty-eight. It didn't matter to either one of us. She sounded sweet and she flirted a lot that night (I did too). Fox claimed she was an interior decorator and teased me about driving over to check out my house, especially the colors in my bedroom.

I stammered and tried to act cool. I wanted to meet this girl, yet I was scared it might lead to something more than meeting — or maybe rejection. I had been hurt before by girls from the radio who wanted to meet, then mysteriously disappeared once they saw my wheelchair. One girl came over to meet me, said she had to get something from her car in the driveway, and left without saying goodbye.

In the midst of our conversation, while she was laughing at my stupid puns and corny jokes, I told Fox about my disability. She didn't seem to care. When she kept asking to meet, I thought, why not? If she satisfies her curiosity and drifts away like the others, so be it. I agreed to meet her.

"Over the weekend?" I offered.

"How about tomorrow night?" she suggested.

"What did I just do?" I whispered to myself, wondering what I had gotten myself into.

We agreed on the following night, which gave me overnight and the entire next day to stress about it. I wanted to call it off but, the smooth operator that I was, I forgot to ask for her phone number and couldn't find her on the radio. Fox was going to be at my door, like it or not. With Mom at bingo, I prepared for my first ever "date."

When Fox came to the door, I was stunned. She was gorgeous, tall and shapely with long, curly brown hair and green eyes. She smelled great and smiled when she saw me. All the stress suddenly flew out the screen door when she opened it.

She came back the next night. And the next. And the next.

I had a girlfriend. Not a crush this time. Not a feeling of love either. I had never experienced such a feeling before and couldn't explain it. But it was nice, and I liked it.

I was a little confused by this sudden attention. All my life people stared at me in a bad way, and here was a girl who looked at me lovingly, and that was a welcome change. Fox and I got along like old friends. We didn't have all that much in common. She was younger and liked to dance, drink, and hang around a younger crowd. I was more sedate, shy, and didn't drink. Fox was still exploring, unsure where her future was going. I was exploring, too, but knew what I wanted in life and in a relationship. I liked Elton John's music and she hated him. She loved Fabio and I couldn't stand him. We compromised on Bruce Springsteen and Top Gun. Still, we got along great.

She was much more experienced — in life and especially in sex — than I was. She was fun and had a good sense of humor. After years of social isolation, I needed someone like Fox in my life. She was like a fantasy to me, something I always wished for but never imagined would come true.

Fox didn't mind tossing my chair in the back seat of her little car. Safe to say she certainly broadened my horizons. She loved Billy Idol and Huey Lewis, so it wasn't unusual to hear songs like "White Wedding" or "Heart of Rock n' Roll" blasting from her car radio as we cruised on a Friday night. It was nice to have someone to care about and someone who cared. Nice to have someone to call first thing in the morning and after school at night. Nice to have someone call me too. Sometimes Fox dropped by school during breaks and we had lunch together. We would drive to Valley Forge Park since it was spring, to have lunch or talk (usually).

My brittle bones didn't break during the relationship. We were both very conscious of that. Regarding sex, as much as Mom wanted me to be a priest, I had feelings like any other guy. A whole new world was opening. To be honest, I liked cuddling and hugs most of all. Feelings of being wanted and needed were big to me. It still amazed me that a woman (an attractive woman at that) would find me attractive. All I had to do was look at my battered legs to get discouraged. But I was soon learning that many women were interested in much more than what my legs looked like (much more!).

I admired the great Christopher Reeve and his openness about disability and sex. He showed the world that just because he had a physical challenge, didn't mean he was forced to extinguish any natural feelings or desires. With me, because my experience with women was so limited, it made me more sensitive, passionate, and romantic when I did find a girlfriend. Love made the intimacy so much better. I was no longer ashamed of having a disability. Despite the challenges, I could still enjoy life, feel good about myself, and say, "Maybe I'm not such a monster after all."

Fox was unpredictable. Like Wheelchair Willie, she was bringing me out of my shell. I wasn't spending my Friday and Saturday nights at home anymore, at least not alone. I was getting out and doing things, meeting people, and feeling like a "normal" person. I really didn't know how to act when it came to going out to dinner or to the movies on a date. I was learning fast in this whirlwind relationship. For instance, I hadn't seen a movie with a girl (other than Mom) in twenty years since we saw *Old Yeller* as a kid. The first movie Fox and I saw together was the big hit that summer, *Back to the Future* with Michael J. Fox. It was an appropriate title for my life now. To Fox, it was just another Saturday night date. For me, it was wonderful and special — the sights, the sounds, the smell of popcorn, being with a crowd of people. So, this was how the rest of the world lived!

Fox's parents were nice but guarded. Meeting them wasn't the easiest thing in the world. They didn't openly discourage the relationship, but they weren't doing cartwheels either. They treated it as though it wouldn't last long, so why get upset? I could sense their patronizing tone. Maybe they had been down this road before, or maybe they simply knew their daughter very well. I'm sure they had to be saying to her privately, "What are you doing? You are young and pretty. Why are you seeing this guy?"

It was true. I couldn't be the buddy most fathers wanted, working on cars together with their daughter's boyfriend or watching sports together. Her dad didn't warm up to me, especially when he had to help me up a few steps into their expensive condo. Her mom was nicer, but I could see the disapproval and sympathy in her eyes. Fox told them over dinner about my college plans and the fact I was going to be a social worker and would be making big money (wrong). That didn't seem to impress them much. What kind of future did their daughter have with a guy like me? It was a natural concern. I got it.

Fox didn't listen to their advice. Her parents had tons of influence on her life, especially since she still lived at home. She listened more to her friends, as peer pressure was always greater. They viewed me as sort of a joke. Once the novelty wore off, I would be a goner.

Mom, on the other hand, didn't mind that I now had a girlfriend. She was surprised, but she was getting used to sudden changes in my life. She was aware of college girls coming to the house to study. All she kept repeating was, "Be careful. I don't want to see you get hurt." And she didn't mean physically hurt.

But end it did, roughly two months after it began. There were other guys on and off the radio. It really hurt when I heard her flirting with another guy on the radio late at night. Her parents knew how frequently they met their daughter's new boyfriend of the month. I was just one in a string of guys. But that was Fox. She was young and didn't want to be tied down. I guess I couldn't blame her. I was just the opposite. I wanted something I'd never had before, an old-fashioned type of relationship, one girl, one guy. Just like in those old black-and-white movies.

I didn't regret being a hopeless romantic. I sent flowers because I really liked her. I also sent flowers to try and keep her. As Madonna sang, "We are living in a material world." Without her I would return to lonely nights. I loved going to the movies or out to dinner. I didn't want to go back to the way it was before. I was stuck between my heart and my head.

To my family and friends, everything was fine. I didn't want to hear warnings, so I pretended like everything was cool, even when Fox no longer stopped by every day. She was just "busy," that was all.

In the end, I was the one who said enough. That was tough, even though I was relieved to end the arguments and heartache. I was a wreck. My schoolwork was suffering, something I vowed would never happen. I would miss the laughs and the intimacy. But things were no longer fun.

Fox had courage to share the stares when we went out. She was willing to do things for me, such as driving, handling the wheelchair, things she didn't need to do. I refused to view my first girlfriend as a "user." I had finally found someone. First love can be painful, even at twenty-eight. You can have a broken heart, even in a wheelchair.

I was depressed for weeks after the break-up. I didn't want to go back to the old me. I wanted it all — school, friends, independence, and a girlfriend. It was time to refocus and move on. My relationship with Silver Fox was a lesson learned. It wasn't wasted time, and I couldn't crawl back into a hole.

Meanwhile Fox was moving to Connecticut. She found a new job there that her older brother set up for her. I suppose she needed a fresh start too. New relationships, marriage, and children awaited her in New England. On Channel 20, the same channel where I first found her, I listened to her fade away up the turnpike on her way to a new life. When she ended by saying she loved me, my heart felt a twinge. But onto better things in life, with so much more to do, and more to look forward to in the months and years ahead.

I faded away from CB radio. My "Leaning Tower of Pisa" antenna, famous for the way it leaned to one side on our roof, came crashing down in our backyard during a violent summer thunderstorm. That was the end of my radio days. But the radio had served its purpose. They were times I would never forget, important times which helped me grow in many ways, times that molded me into the person I became later in life.

Chapter 12

I Made It Through the Rain

Barry Manilow played a big part in my life in the eighties. Bobby Rydell would always be special to me, someone who had helped me through the dark times as a kid. Now Manilow's music was doing the same thing. He came along in the seventies, the same time my life was a confusing mess. Dad died, I was still fracturing at an alarming rate, I failed at Penn, and I had a rainbow of leisure suits in my closet. I felt like such a loser. Barry's music inspired me when I needed a lift most of all. He was singing about not giving up in emotional ballads like "All the Time" and "I Made It Through the Rain." I could relate to the music and the lyrics because I was living many of those same emotions.

His fan club started a pen-pal program during the summer of 1984. I applied, not knowing what to expect. The goal was to match fans from all over the world and share in the music. Even strangers from different lands had Manilow's music in common. Going to concerts (my first was at Resorts in Atlantic City, seated in Row Z, the very back of the theater), I met many fellow fans, some local and others from across the country. The pen-pal program was a different experience.

The fan club matched me with a young woman from Oslo, Norway. She was single, twenty-five-years old, a second-year law student. Her name was Mari.

Mari had been a Manilow fan since the early eighties when she heard the early hits like "Mandy" on Armed Forces radio. She loved his music and scoured the stores in Oslo for any Manilow albums she could find. Imported albums were not easy to find back then. But what solidified her devotion was seeing Manilow in concert when he came to Oslo in 1983. She had middle row seats near the stage, the first person in line for tickets. Of course, there were only two people in line, and the other one was an American. After that, she joined the fan club, and the rest was history. She wrote for a pen pal on a whim, and the fan club matched us. They did a pretty good job — both around the same age, both in school, both originally from small towns, and both die-hard fans. We were fans who not only listened to the music and went to concerts but taped every Manilow performance we could find on TV, saved newspaper columns and reviews, and appreciated the album cuts, not just the hits.

For two years we wrote about music, listing our favorite songs and albums, sharing our feelings of why we liked each song and what made each album special. Her letters were warm and friendly. A letter every two weeks was like touching base with someone I had known forever. Her personality glowed out of the many pages.

Mari wrote of her hometown, her life, and her dreams. She was a law student, struggling with her tuition but not her studies. Her financial worries sounded familiar. As I learned more about Norwegian culture, I admired Mari even more. Women in Norway were usually advised to be nurses, secretaries, or housewives. Very stereotypical views, especially for the eighties. Mari had the courage and determination to break the mold and become a lawyer. For now, just paying her apartment rent at the university was a main concern. That, as well as passing the rigorous exams. Two more years until she would finally earn her law degree.

Mari's father had also died when she was young. On weekends and holidays, she took the train home, a journey of several hours. She lived there with her mother, who worked as a gardener. Soon I read about her family: an assortment of aunts and uncles, nieces and nephews, and a sixteen-year old canary named Olav. They became real to me, as my family did to her.

We had so much in common. We loved old black-and-white movies, trivia games, and Italian food. It was safe to say we drifted away from the topic of Manilow music in our letters. She did relate how, at the Oslo concert, Barry almost picked her to sing "Can't Smile Without You" with him. She was in the front row and he pointed at her and asked, "Do you want to come up here?" While she stammered in disbelief, he picked someone else, and her chance at stardom went down the drain.

Her letters, which now arrived every few weeks (aside from cards and special items sent in between), were like a breath of fresh air. There was someone special out there, an ocean away, a friend I could relate to. Along with studying, now my evenings were spent writing back to Mari. We were growing closer and until a new letter arrived, I read her old ones again and again. I was surprised she felt the same way, claiming she couldn't wait for my letters.

It was a very innocent, simple way of getting to know each other. Sort of old-fashioned, like an old black-and-white 1940s movie. I listened to Manilow music, and my thoughts would drift to Mari. We started to add little surprises to our letters, which soon turned into packages; Manilow posters, articles, and tapes. I began searching for books on Norway, reading all I could about her culture. The country and the names of the cities and small towns were no longer foreign.

The pen-pal thing was turning into much more. Every time I tried to reign in my heart and remind myself that this wasn't *The Love Connection* but a friendly way to correspond with a fellow fan, our letters said otherwise. Since I had never felt this strange way before (and it was a good feeling), my heart won over my head. Overseas, Mari was taking an equal interest in the United States. She didn't need a drastic crash course in lifestyle and culture as I did. America had always been special to her. It was her dream to visit the States someday, especially New York City.

It was during this time that Manilow released his jazzy *2:00 AM Paradise Cafe* album, his masterpiece. There was a smoky atmosphere to the record, like one is sitting alone in a quiet jazz cafe late at night, listening to beautiful ballads while the autumn rain gently falls outside. It was an album for lovers, an album to share with someone special. We both rushed out and bought it during that winter, the warm music melting those long, cold nights. It was our favorite Manilow album of all time.

We thought about meeting someday. Would meeting spoil the magic? I was afraid to tell her about my OI. I had this crazy fear that she would stop writing if she knew I had a disability. I just wanted this fairy tale friendship to continue forever.

"So, you see," she wrote, "there will be no jealous boyfriend when we go on our tour of New York City together." Tour of New York? I had trouble getting off my own block!

Her dream date was a walk through Central Park, a tour of Manhattan, a Manilow concert, a quiet candlelit dinner for two at a cozy Italian restaurant with good food, a glass of wine, and then dessert. "Want to join me?" she asked. No wonder my heart was racing like Secretariat.

We exchanged romantic cards and gifts over Valentine's Day. She wasn't kidding about meeting. With hard work over the next year, she might be able to save enough money for a vacation in the summer of 1986. Until then, she invited me to Norway. Oslo was such a beautiful city: the famous Sculpture Park, the Viking Museum, the many quaint sidewalk cafes and shop, the mountains and fjords, those hills overlooking the city.

I had lost all common sense. I wasn't sure how to handle the situation. I knew it was time to be honest. I wanted the truth to be more personal than a handwritten letter so I sent Mari a tape, recorded on a late spring evening. I explained everything, about the fractures and hospital stays, the surgeries and long rehabilitation. I told her about the loneliness, the prejudice, the pain. How I used a wheelchair to get around. Everything else in my life — from college to my family life — was all true. I mailed the tape and braced myself for an answer.

Mari was surprised but also admired my courage for telling her the truth. She had normal questions about my life (which I encouraged): Did I have special care needs? Was there a chance I would ever walk? Those questions were easier to answer now. New York or not, she still wanted to visit if I wanted to meet her. There was no one like her in my life. Mari was special, and I agreed to meet her in a year.

————

I saw Dr. Nicholson for the last time on a sentimental examination when he wanted to update his records and called me for an appointment. It was closure for him, since he was officially retiring. He examined my legs, the wheels turning in his mind as he carefully made verbal notes, mumbling under his breath, something about the surgeries, gazing at my bowed, stunted legs with a sense of regret in his hushed tone. His wife took notes on a yellow legal pad. She was his secretary now; it was the first time I had ever met the pleasant Mrs. Nicholson. He was more than just my doctor. He had a life too, with a wife, grown children, and grandkids.

I felt bad for him. He tried hard to help me all those years, and he did help me. He eased my pain and tried to make my life better. The goal of walking wasn't achieved, and I'm sure that frustrated him. I thanked him for everything. I was doing well now. I was alive, thanks to him.

Maybe it was a last gasp of hope when Dr. Nicholson threw out the idea of me going to the world-famous DuPont Hospital in Delaware for "total reconstruction" surgeries — repairing my legs, back, all of my deformities. It would mean months and years of surgeries, pain, and rehabilitation, all with the goal of walking. This time the answer was no. I was old enough to make my own decisions. There were no guarantees that the process would work. It might even leave me bed-bound and unable to sit, let alone stand. I decided enough was enough. I was going to school. My fractures were fewer and fewer. I had a semi-normal life. I was happy. By now I was used to my lifestyle.

"I don't blame you," he said.

Dr. Nicholson died in 1987. But his legacy would live on. I grew to remember him not as a source of pain and suffering, but as a healer, someone who ultimately saved my life.

Physically, I was feeling better. Psychologically, I was feeling better about myself, my self-esteem at an all-time high. Now I decided to tackle my smile. I sure had more reasons to smile, and I wanted my teeth to look nice. OI often affects dental health, making the teeth brittle and discolored. My courage increasing, I decided to do something about it, especially since my brother Pat had braces and the results were great.

I floated the idea to Mom, and she was all for it. She was getting used to my new-found independence. After a lengthy process of having my teeth filled, cleaned, and bleached, I was ready for braces. I wanted to visit the same orthodontist my brother saw. Steps leading into his office were an obstacle. This was well before the Americans with Disabilities Act was passed, making it a law that all buildings and businesses, especially new ones, be accessible. So, I tried another orthodontist in town. His office was accessible, so I scheduled an appointment.

I met the doctor, an older guy with receding white hair. He wasn't the friendliest guy in the world as he eyed me suspiciously. When I told him that my disability was due to brittle bones, he mumbled something like, "You don't see that very often."

After the exam, the dentist looked at me, wearing a frown, muttering, "Braces cost a lot of money. You're in a wheelchair. Do you really need braces?" The fact he said "need" instead of "want" surprised me. I suppose he was trying to be honest in an awkward way, but I couldn't believe he was saying, "You're crippled. Why do you want straight teeth?" If he had honestly explained that he was afraid to do braces for fear of breaking my jaw, that would've been acceptable. But he didn't. He let the stupid comment hang there.

I had experienced discrimination in the past, to the point of once being patted on top of my head in an elevator like a puppy dog. But I had never faced this kind of ignorance. I felt like running over his toes. I went home from that orthodontist discouraged but not beaten. I wasn't going to let one jerk stop me.

It was Mom who encouraged me to make an appointment with my brother's orthodontist. My Uncle Henry said he would help us with the steps if the doctor agreed to treat me. It wouldn't hurt to seek a second opinion.

"Sure, we can do it," Dr. Gerald reassured after examining my teeth. I knew my condition had to be a concern. He did explain the risks involved and said he would do everything he could to straighten my teeth, keeping in mind my fragile condition. There were limitations and there would be pain. I was happy he was in tune with OI, grateful he was willing to face the challenges with me. With that in mind, I signed the consent papers, hoping I was doing the right thing.

I was thrilled. I had to be the happiest patient he ever had. And so I wore braces for two-and-a-half years. The pain was worth it (what was a little more pain in my life?) — the rubber bands, the loss of eating certain foods for a while (chewing gum and corn on the cob were the biggest losses), the monthly visits to tighten the metal, the rough wires scraping my gums, the struggles up and down the steps each time — all worth it. Sometimes Dr. Gerald saved us a trip up his steps, especially when it rained or snowed, for simple repairs or tightening, treating my braces in the front seat of Mom's car.

When the braces were finally removed, my smile was so much better. So was my self-confidence. I was proud to open my mouth and flash those dimples. It was a well-earned victory over prejudice and a triumph of dignity. I planned on hanging around life a while now, and my smile would always be with me. I never forgot to use it.

In the eighties, I was honored to be a godfather for the first time. My brother Pat and his wife Linda had a baby son named Adam, and they asked me to be godfather. I left all jokes about Marlon Brando outside the church as I attended the baptism with Mom. Adam would go on to be a star athlete in high school and college, later becoming a very successful sports broadcasting celebrity in New York City. I had nothing at all to do with his success, but I was extremely proud to be his uncle/godfather.

I remember how joyous my own godfather was, and how much I looked forward to his visits. Uncle Frank lived in North Jersey where many of Mom's relatives of Slovak descent resided. Uncle Frank made the trip from Jersey to visit a few times a year. He had a big smile and was always tan, with slicked-back salt-n'-pepper hair and a hearty laugh. His personality was infectious. He usually ended a sentence with the word "right."

"I just so happened to be passing a donut shop, right? So, I brought a box of donuts with me, right?" "Buy something nice for yourself, and think of your Uncle Frank, right?"

Every time he was ready to leave for his return journey up the Jersey turnpike, he gave me a big hug and we shook hands. Inside his palm would be a folded twenty-dollar bill, which he slipped into my hand, smiling, like he was Houdini. For a kid, twenty bucks was a big deal, and although I loved my godfather for non-monetary reasons, I also looked forward to the cash.

Mom would make a big spaghetti dinner when she knew Uncle Frank was visiting for the day. Or perhaps it would be a meal of real ethnic food such as pierogi. Uncle Frank was happy with a pot of freshly brewed coffee nearby while the family sat around the kitchen table and talked.

One Easter I was in a body cast and confined to bed. Uncle Frank sent the largest chocolate Easter egg I ever saw. It had to be at least ten pounds, filled with jellybeans, marshmallow chicks, and chocolate goodies. Uncle Frank never failed to remember birthdays, send get-well wishes, or call me when he couldn't travel. Christmas was special when he dropped by over the holidays, stocked with presents for everyone.

When he died from a sudden heart attack, we attended his funeral in Passaic. Hard to believe it was Uncle Frank laying there so peacefully. And when his casket passed by in church, I reached out and touched the smooth cherry wood, whispering, "Thank you, Uncle Frank," for always making me smile.

———————

Mari sent me a Norwegian language book that Christmas, which promised to teach me to speak Norwegian in only ten minutes a day. I rifled through the flashcards from the book and pasted the tiny word stickers around the house. Everywhere I looked, there was a Norwegian word for this and that, from "bathroom" to "stove." If I could've stuck one on the dogs, I would have. I was determined to learn a respectable amount of Norwegian to surprise Mari the following summer.

I graduated from community college with a grade point average of 3.95. I received a standing ovation at graduation and won the Alumni Award, an honor which goes to the student who has achieved academic success and has overcome adversity in life. They gave me a plaque to take home and a similar plaque was hung in the school's gym for posterity, along with previous winners. Guy Buford, the first African-American astronaut, was our keynote speaker at graduation. "Reaching for the Stars" was the message. Overcoming adversities and discrimination were topics I could relate to. But so far, we had only reached the moon. The stars were the next goal.

I had my associate's degree in Human Services, a far cry from where I had started two years earlier. I converted doubters into believers along the way (most of all myself) and made some good friends, especially Lori. I was so happy when she received her diploma.

I wasn't ready to stop. An associate degree was a start, but it wasn't good enough to get a decent job in the social work field. I needed a bachelor's degree at the very least, which meant two more years of school. Lori felt the same way, so we went through the process again, even before graduation. We started looking into local universities, something affordable and accessible. Lori and I were a team. I was glad she was willing to go wherever I was going, not only because of my transportation but also because we were friends and loved carpooling together. We gave each other support and encouragement. If we both needed a kick in the ass to stay motivated, we offered that too.

When it came to choosing a school, we didn't want to travel into Philadelphia unless we really had to. We applied to numerous colleges and universities, going through the red tape again, applying for more grants and loans, taking the necessary entrance exams, meeting the required people who did the interviews and made the decisions. We finally decided on West Chester University, a small school in the suburbs. It was a state school, so more affordable. Twenty minutes each way from home, locally respected for its social work program. It was intimate and accessible (for the most part), small yet still a university. And the staff seemed friendly when we visited.

The converted farmhouse on the south side of the sprawling campus was where most of my core classes would be held. To my dismay, there were several small steps to contend with. I mentioned the inaccessibility to Mrs. Joyner, who was the head of the social work program. Nothing a ramp can't fix. She laughed when I naively asked if my 3.95 GPA was good enough to consider admission. She never let me forget that.

In the end both Lori and I were accepted at West Chester. We couldn't wait to get started, excited about the upcoming two years. More hard work awaited us, even harder than anything before. But "no pain, no gain," as I knew so well in my life.

I watched the sea of people in the overseas terminal at JFK airport in New York. Reality was setting in. Travelers happily and tearfully greeted each other all around us with kisses and hugs. So many different languages. Luggage was everywhere. People held up homemade signs to attract their traveling friends.

I admired Mari's courage, visiting a strange country. She had been to Italy only a few years earlier, but never America. Summer had arrived so fast. After all the planning, here it was! We planned on taking in New York and Philadelphia, along with the obligatory summer trip to the Jersey shore. Summer activities like a Phillies baseball game and family cookouts were also on the agenda.

"Is that her?" Mom asked as a pretty blond with a bright smile approached us. She was carrying one large suitcase and a shoulder bag. She looked the same as in her photo — tan, short, and blue-eyed, dressed in a crisp white sleeveless top and slacks.

"Hi," Mari said sweetly, politely shaking hands, very business-like. I was awe-struck.

Uncle Henry kept things lively with his stories on the way home. I glanced into the backseat a few times just to make sure Mari was there. We got home around midnight. Mari invited me into the guestroom as she unpacked. Our first time alone. She sat on the edge of the bed with clothes, film, and other travel items scattered about. The smell of spring flowers filled the night. She hugged me without a word.

"It's so good to see you," she whispered.

"It's good to have you here," I softly replied. And then I asked her a question that had been on my mind for a long time. "Are you disappointed?"

"No way," she answered, hugging me tighter. I believed her. She was soft and smelled great. "Anything else you want to know?"

"Yeah," I said, picking up the hot-pink swimsuit on the bed. "When are you going to wear this?"

Warm hugs after so long sure beat writing letters.

———

Watching television together was a nice relaxing time on our first day together. Mari couldn't get enough of our commercials ("Where's the beef?"), television shows (*Wheel of Fortune* and *The People's Court*) and movies (anything Richard Gere). We played a lot of Trivial Pursuit (which was the latest craze). One afternoon we sat in the cool shade of Reeves Park, watching children in the playground, thinking of the future and talking.

Our first evening alone, I gave Mari a little gift I had been saving for so long. It was an emerald necklace, her birthstone. "You're crazy," she teased, kissing me.

It was a perfect romantic evening. We listened to our hearts. It felt as right as the rest of the summer.

Mari tolerated baseball, loved a real Philly cheese steak and soft pretzel, got drenched in a muggy thunderstorm as we waited to see the Liberty Bell at Independence Hall in Philadelphia, and had a fun day at the Philly Zoo, taking tons of pictures (she was a real photography buff) of me and the other animals. We also spent plenty of time listening to Manilow music, the reason we were together.

Life was perfect. After a life full of pain and rejection, I had found someone who didn't look at my legs but into my heart. It was so different than Silver Fox. This was real. From tanning in the backyard (the pink swimsuit was worth the wait); meeting other local Manilow fan club members (including Vicki, who soon became one of my best friends); buying eight Manilow albums at one time at the mall (the ones Mari couldn't find in Norway) and getting a strange look from the heavy metal, tattooed music cashier; discovering popcorn at the movies (no popcorn in Norwegian theaters); learning Norwegian daily in lessons from a pro . . . all wonderful times.

A sun-splashed late-summer day greeted us in New York City. The highlight was strolling around the Statue of Liberty together, the towering Manhattan skyline across the glistening, sparkling bay, watching the small boats dotting the windy harbor. It wasn't the private time we dreamed about, alone on a romantic carriage ride through Central Park, a candlelit dinner for two, and a show, but it was pretty cool.

Mom made her famous spaghetti and meatballs dinner the day before Mari went home, as family dropped by, bearing gifts, bidding their farewells. Mari had become like family that summer and we were all sorry to see her go. She kept saying "I'll be back." I tried to keep it together inside. When my eyes misted, I wheeled into the bathroom. Mari knew I had been crying.

"Be happy for me! I'm going home but I'll be back," she reassured.

————————

"...And that was for Mari, love always, from Greg. Thanks for a great summer."

We hugged in the dark after the disc jockey played my request: "Somewhere Down the Road," by Barry Manilow. The summer was over.

There we were, sitting in the JFK Airport again, this time waiting for Mari to board her return flight home. An airline employee offered to take me aboard first, thinking I had a ticket. Wishful thinking.

Mari hugged Mom, saving one final warm hug for me, whispering, "I'll write back first. Thanks for everything. I love you."

In an instant, she was gone. We watched her jet soar overhead, its red tail a blur in the distance. Away went my heart, disappearing into the clouds.

With my hard-earned associate's degree proudly displayed on my wall, I took a deep breath and continued. The new school year would bring exciting challenges: new faces, new classes, and new experiences. Another year of student loans, crazy hours of classes, and long hours of studying. Nothing could stop me now. That bachelor's degree was mine for the taking. I was more determined than ever to reach my goals.

Chapter 13
Don't Ever Lose Your Sense of Humor

My two years at West Chester U were just beginning. I joined a disability activist group on campus, and we helped make the university more accessible. I had two internships to keep me busy too.

I did my junior practicum at the Manor. My internship consisted of three days a week on the job, with full days of classes the other two weekdays. It was great working there, this time in a shirt and tie, helping the residents I had grown to love. I worked with a fine social worker named Ellen, who was Director of Social Services. She taught me the ins and outs of nursing home social work. She was extremely patient, even when I made the inevitable mistakes. Ellen was always smiling and in a good mood. That impressed me a great deal. How she could remain so upbeat and positive with so much sickness and sadness around her every day? She was a special person, and I soon found out it took special people to do her job.

Although I couldn't sign any of the documents, I did smaller things around the office: copying, filing, stuffing envelopes, more or less the grunt work we all go through when we're learning the ropes. Ellen did show me how to complete the forms. I was quickly learning what it took to be a social worker in a nursing home setting. I attended meetings, such as care plan reviews and the morning stand-up meetings with fellow staff. I learned about teamwork and what it takes to work with others and how to be professional; how to be on time for work, dress nicely, and be neat with my work, things I never forgot.

Counseling residents and families would always prove interesting. Different cases came up daily. I saw how hard the staff worked: the doctors, nurses and aides, the unsung heroes in nursing homes. I saw how the administrator and business office worked behind the scenes to keep the place running. I heard about nursing homes being "dives" — places filled with horrible sights and dreadful odors. But I could honestly say this wasn't one of them. Most importantly, they treated the residents with great care and dignity. It was far different from being a volunteer, which is important work, but now I was seeing so much more. I had a different perspective and a better appreciation of nursing homes. The residents already knew me from my volunteer days. They trusted me, knowing I could relate to many of the same feelings they were experiencing — feelings of despair and loneliness, feelings of sadness and pain. My OI was an advantage, for once.

I'll never forget Ellen's final piece of advice on my last day of the internship. I thought she was going to lay some long, deep theory on me, something serious and profound. Instead, her advice was very simple. "Don't ever lose your sense of humor," she said. Life goes on, the sun rises the next day, and all those clichés. The shelf-life of a social worker in the field was only four years. Four years! The work is so emotionally draining. I was determined not to be one of the casualties.

———

My senior practicum was spent at the local hospital — the place where I was born, the place where my OI first surfaced. Now I was a "pretend" social worker. Much different than nursing home social work. My supervisor this time was Jean, an older lady with beautifully coiffed gray hair. She had twenty years of experience in the field. She did not have a degree; she was hired back when that wasn't needed. Her knowledge and networking skills were tremendous. She knew all the resources in the area, phone numbers, and information by heart. Jean oozed common sense too. What I was learning in the classroom was important, the different theories and such, but it was in the field that I got out and did it, applied those theories and used basic common sense and sensitivity, which was real social work at its finest.

Jean was retiring later that year. I was her very last intern. I would get the best training from a seasoned pro. Social work in a hospital was different and unique from what I experienced in my first internship. Different population, different age groups, different cases. It was a great experience to grow out of my comfort zone, not only as a social worker, but as a person too. Some days I worked on the hospital units. Much of it was discharge planning or setting up home care and equipment (like a visiting nurse or a wheelchair). It was fast-paced, and it felt good helping people go home. I always loved going home when I was in the hospital.

Some days I worked in the Emergency Room. That may have been the toughest part of the job, comforting families after an accident or during a crisis. Not everyone could do that particularly emotional part of the job. But comfort I could do; computers, not so much.

One of my first cases was talking to a young teenage girl named Lisa who had tried to commit suicide. Only fourteen, she had swallowed ninety-two aspirin. Luckily, someone found her on her bedroom floor and rushed her to the ER, where they pumped her stomach and saved her life. It was my task to find out why she had done it.

Entering the room, I was probably more scared than Lisa was. The pretty girl with the long red hair looked at me suspiciously. She asked who I was, and I replied, "A social worker here to talk."

She groaned. "Oh, you're only a social worker? I was expecting a psychiatrist."

"Only" a social worker? That hurt.

I admitted to Lisa that I was scared too. We had some common ground there. After that she opened up to me a bit. Turned out she overdosed because of a forbidden romance. Her next-door neighbor was twice her age. She visited him to "do homework and watch television," but when her parents forbade her to see him, she took the pills. How does anyone survive taking that many pills? Lisa did. There had to be a reason she was alive. I had no magical answers. She didn't want my advice anyway. No lectures or speeches. Highlighting points of common sense and offering reminders was all that was needed. Her parents wouldn't listen, and her peers didn't understand. I listened intently during my twenty minutes with Lisa. Nothing heroic or special on my part. I listened and I cared.

She thanked me for stopping by. I felt better as I left the room. My first case completed! In the end, I wrote up my findings, discussed them with Jean, and referred the girl and her parents for post-discharge counseling. I never forgot her name, and several years later, while paging through our local newspaper, I smiled when I saw her name listed as one who had graduated with honors from high school.

With each success, I gained more confidence. I worked with alcoholics, drug addicts, patients with hospital insurance issues, you name it. Great experience! I still loved the nursing home atmosphere because I saw the residents every day, whereas a patient in the hospital might be a onetime deal. But the knowledge I was gaining at the hospital proved to be invaluable down the road.

———

I was breezing through most of my classes at West Chester. There was a pair of required courses I still needed to take: a language and my old nemesis, math. I didn't dread the language as much as I did the math. I really wanted to take American Sign Language as my requirement. I thought that sign would come in handy in my profession. I encountered quite a few clients and residents who were hard of hearing or who could only read lips. Sadly, the classes were only offered in downtown Philadelphia. Lori didn't want to drive into the city twice a week, and I couldn't blame her. We both decided to settle for Spanish instead.

I studied Spanish in high school, although I forgot a lot over the years. If you don't use it, you lose it. Spanish 1.0 was a stroll in the park. Simple words and phrases. Spanish 2.0 would be harder, learning different tenses. Spanish 2.0 was offered during the summer. Fifteen weeks' worth of Spanish crammed into five weeks. I wanted to graduate on time, so Lori and I signed up for the summer course.

It was a sizzling July. There we were, five days a week, every morning for four hours. Professor Diaz was friendly, a short, chubby guy with a full beard. He often strolled into class wearing Bermuda shorts, sandals, red socks, and a brightly colored flowered shirt. On our first day he said, "Look, I don't want to be here as much as you don't want to be here. We all would rather be on the beach. But we are here, so let's make the best of it."

It was hard work, the hardest so far at West Chester. A test every Friday, sink or swim. Learn it fast or don't. No in-between. While the rest of the world was on vacation, we became a tight-knit group of survivors in that class. That was my life for five weeks that summer; go to class, come home, work at the nursing home, study at night, then back at it the next day. I only took one course that summer, so I ate, drank, and slept Spanish. If I had stopped to think about the frantic pace of the course, I never would have gotten through it. I didn't stop and think. I just did it. Students dropped out of the class each week. We hung in there as the weeks melted away. When the dust cleared, I ended up with an A for the summer course. Spanish 3.0 loomed ahead in the fall semester, the one course that was needed to meet the language requirement. I heard horror stories about the course but I wasn't too worried. With a little hard work, I hoped to breeze through.

Instead, Spanish 3.0 turned out to be a nightmare. Much more difficult lessons and assignments. We were to only speak in Spanish after the first day of class, unless it was an emergency. We were only writing in Spanish. Different tenses, elaborate phrases. Spanish Lab, which we attended once a week, was the toughest part of the course. I didn't have trouble reading or writing the language, but I couldn't seem to catch it when I tried to listen to the words. The language was spoken rather quickly, so listening to Spanish and trying to decipher words, answer questions, and make sense of it all was a major challenge for me. I wanted to say, "Slow down." I wasn't cocky any longer about my language abilities.

To make matters worse, the professor was the strictest wacko guy I ever encountered in college. Tall and rail-thin with badly spiked hair and an equally bad goatee, he was a real tyrant in class. Let's call him Professor Moriarty (Sherlock Holmes's arch-enemy).

Screaming, ranting, and raving, he laid down the law the first day of class. He demanded perfection and wouldn't tolerate anything less. He wasn't above ridicule, and often brought the female students to tears by calling them stupid or making fun of their answers. Even the guys in class quaked and stuttered, on the verge of breaking down. Odd to see big, macho footballers ready to cry. Nowadays if a teacher did that, he would be reported and suspended for abuse. But this was the mid-eighties, so we didn't know any better. He put up with no nonsense and no excuses. Earning this grade would be tough. The professor made it clear from the start that he didn't give many As or Bs in his world. And he didn't give a damn if we cried or quit.

One day he walked into class with a huge yardstick, cracking it against his desk and threatening to use it if we didn't study hard. He treated us like children. Motivation was one thing, but this was ridiculous. We stayed because the class fit our schedule. There didn't seem to be a way out. Lori and I had heard rumors about Professor Moriarty before the semester. Everyone dreaded the guy, so his reputation was known on campus. It sure turned out to be a challenge, and after a while it was survival of the fittest. The faint-hearted dropped out like flies, from thirty-five students to twelve in the first few weeks of the fall semester.

Fear made the survivors study harder. His pacing in class was not needed and annoying as hell. Everyone was constantly on edge. Never knew where he would stop, hovering over a shoulder and suddenly challenging us with a question. He called me "Smith" and didn't treat me any differently. At least he didn't ridicule me.

"Smith!" he challenged in broken English. "I want to hear you roll your Rs. Do it, Smith! Roll the Rs! I hit you with stick!"

Damn! I tried, but my tongue wouldn't cooperate. No one actually thought he would use the stick, but one never knew. I started to answer in English and was abruptly cut off. *"En Español, por favor,"* he reminded as I stammered.

"Smith, Smith, Smith . . . what am I to do with you?" he muttered, walking away. I had dodged another bullet. Saved from the dreaded stick.

I was trying hard to get into it, even watching Spanish cable TV channels at home. It was refreshing to understand what they were saying. I constantly reviewed my notes and flashcards. Lori and I endlessly quizzed each other in the car during our commutes. It was as though our other classes didn't exist. It got so bad I forgot myself and wrote out a birthday card in Spanish by mistake. I was brainwashed. We were still hanging in there as Christmas neared. The final exam loomed, the last hurdle to freedom from Professor Moriarty. The final test covered the entire four-month course. A truly make-or-break test. I had earned a solid B so far, so unless I totally bombed the final, I was hoping to at least pass.

"Faith," the latest song by George Michael, blasted from someone's Walkman as we waited, studied, and worried in the hall outside of class. There was dead silence when we entered the classroom, like we were all doing the last mile to the electric chair. Deep down inside, I was scared to death. Confident that I knew my stuff, yet hoping I wouldn't freeze (as I was prone to do when stressed-out).

After we got settled in and Professor Moriarty marched into the room, dressed in black as usual and pushing a small cart, a strange miracle occurred. He broke out into a wide grin, and before the exam started, he offered everyone doughnuts and coffee, encouraging us to come up front and help ourselves. Take a damn crawler back to your desk to munch on while you take the most important exam of your pitiful life!

He was a different guy that morning. The tension eased. What was up? It didn't hurt that the students had taken him out to lunch a few days before the big exam. We went to a local Mexican restaurant, got a few drinks into the professor, and he loosened up quite a bit, even calling us by our first names.

The final exam wasn't so bad after all, the answers flowing easily. I hated to admit that his tactics had ultimately worked. He made us work hard, and it paid off. He made sure we would never forget Spanish — or him — again. As we exited, there was the professor, standing outside the door, waiting for each student to come out. He shook my hand, smiling, and told me what a pleasure it was having me in his class. I thanked him for not playing favorites, for treating me as rotten as he had everyone else.

He turned out to be a pussycat after all. I earned that B. I took the challenge, accepted it, didn't quit, and victory never tasted so sweet. Lori let out a yell as we left the building. Like we had conquered Mount Everest. We watched the other students filter out, exhausted and relieved, wishing them a nice holiday break. Lori had a smoke in the car, as if she'd just had sex. I took a nap.

———————

I'll never forget my thirty-first birthday in 1987. Mom asked me how I wanted to celebrate. The usual spaghetti dinner at home, featuring her homemade sauce? Or a special dinner out with Uncle Henry and Aunt Sue? The choice was easy. It had been quite a while since I had been to my home away from home, the Atlantic City casinos. Some much-needed fun down AC would help to ease my stress.

I must have won a few bucks that night, because I wanted to treat everyone to a soft pretzel before heading home. We stopped at a little pretzel cart right outside the door of the Sands Casino. It was close to midnight. No one noticed the guy who followed us out the door. I was digging into my wallet for four one-dollar bills when this guy suddenly reached over my shoulder and grabbed my pouch (I carried a pouch to keep all my stuff together — hair brush, gum, stamps, tissues, an old Phillies pocket schedule, pens, and oh yes, my wallet).

It happened so fast. I yelled, "Hey!" as this guy tugged on my black pouch. I hung on for dear life as Mom yelled, "What are you doing?" My aunt and uncle looked stunned and didn't say a word.

It was a tug of war between me and the mugger until I felt the wheelchair sliding toward the curb. I let go of the pouch when I started to slide out of the chair, grabbing the wheels. The mugger gave the pouch one final tug before running into the misty, damp November night. A crowd of people saw what was happening and started chasing the guy down the fog-shrouded street. Just that fast, we heard a police siren and saw a cop car whiz by us, racing along the front of the casino, lights flashing red and blue. Shocked, I realized how close I had come to being pulled over the curb and into the street — within inches.

After a few moments, we heard a distant cry: "They got him!" The cops came back to tell us they had captured the fleeing mugger. We needed to follow them to the police station to press charges. Apparently, he tried to throw the pouch away as the police and a handful of citizens cornered him. Everything was saved.

None of us wanted to take a trip to the Atlantic City police station, but we did. We had gotten over the initial shock and were now running on anger and adrenaline. At the station we gave statements and were asked to fill out a few forms and sign to press charges. As I was ready to sign on the dotted line, I looked up and got my first look at my mugger. They were holding him in an adjacent room. I could see him through the glass window. The mugger was standing, his hands behind his back in cuffs, head lowered. Then we made eye contact for the first time. It shocked me how young he was. He appeared haggard, with shaggy brown hair and a scruffy, stubbly face. When our eyes met, he began shaking his head. I wasn't sure what that meant — either "No, don't press charges," or "I'm sorry for what I did." The cops were asking him questions. One rolled up a paper ball and lightly tossed it at the guy, the paper hitting his chest and bouncing harmlessly away. When the cops found out it was my birthday, they were even more disgusted.

This scene seemed to last forever, the mugger shaking his head and me responding with an affirmative yes.

Even though he ruined my birthday, I couldn't help but feel bad. I signed the papers with the handcuffed mugger staring at me, his helpless eyes haunting me on the ride home. While everyone else talked about the incident (What if he had a gun?), I kept quiet. I didn't want to talk about it.

We were afraid we might have to return to AC for a hearing, but they didn't need me any longer. The cops thought it was pretty low, trying to rob someone in a wheelchair. Turns out he was known and had a long record for possession and selling drugs. He pleaded guilty and was sentenced to jail for three years. Justice was served. My birthday was over, but I would always remember my birthday mugging.

————

There was one final challenge looming ahead in school. The big, ugly monster which stood in front of me and my diploma — math. Such a small word, such a daunting task ahead.

I hated math. It went all the way back to my days at Penn. Any kind of math was horrifying, even simple stuff like fractions. It was a requirement, so I picked the most basic math course I could find, skipping physics, geometry, algebra, and all those other fun courses. In other courses I was determined to get an A. With math, all I wanted to do was survive.

Battle-tested from Spanish 3.0, I bought a new pocket calculator, sharpened my pencils, and went to work. Of course, this was way before smartphones and personal computers. Basic handheld calculators were new. You had to figure out the answers on your own.

Our professor was an older guy with frizzy white hair, like an Einstein lookalike. Upfront, he informed the rather large contingent of students in his class that most people did fail his course and needed to take it over, so not to worry. He listed a detailed chart on the blackboard, showing the grades from his classes over the last five years. There was a heavy slant toward the "F" column. Extremely encouraging!

Whereas Professor Moriarty from Spanish 3.0 was dramatically emotional, this guy was like a robot, spewing out facts and figures. Everything was charted and logical, with no emotions or feelings. It was odd how he was so smart when it came to numbers and logic, yet he couldn't remember my name, always calling me "George" or "Gary," never Greg. When events weren't pre-planned and coordinated, he was like a fish out of water, a mere mortal like his students.

Everything was so challenging now, with graduation just around the corner. I would not recommend saving the toughest courses to the end, but that's exactly what I did, which added to the pressure. As it turned out, the basic math course was kind of fun. Einstein brought a pair of dice to class to help illustrate some of his points. Odds and probabilities. The next time down Atlantic City there would be hell to pay at the dice tables. Cool! I could relate to dice. What's next . . . a deck of cards?

I did well in the first exam until we started studying statistics. Then things went downhill fast. I studied hard, then went totally blank in class. I knew the formulas, but I froze. That was a helpless feeling, and it didn't help that I was psyching myself out so bad. Like always, I was putting pressure on myself. Why couldn't I get this? I wanted to be a social worker. Why did I need to know what the odds are of rolling a seven as opposed to a two?

Meanwhile, across the Atlantic, Mari was having her own problems with school. She vowed never to be a tax lawyer. Taxes were her Achilles' heel. She had mountains of reading to do. Her average final exam lasted nearly four hours. She had five of them to take. Our second planned vacation together was put on hold again.

Mari was also having trouble with her student loans. With no student loan, getting through law school would be impossible. She started working a part-time job at a department store in Oslo, in their women's clothes department.

Between her law exams and my math, our plates were full that spring. Her letters encouraged me. "You can do it, love! Don't give up! Give it all you've got!" she wrote. Problem was, I was giving it all I had and it still wasn't enough. I was holding a low C in math, far below my standards in school. Maintaining that C until the final exam would be crucial.

I prayed a lot. Thought of Mom and Dad. Thought of Mari. Thought about how far I had come. Thought about the future. I had worked too hard to let it all slip away now. *They are only numbers*, I kept telling myself.

Lori was having similar difficulties. We were both people-people, not logical robots. She was in danger of failing too, and I knew she was thinking of her kids and her long fight out of poverty. We did our usual cramming in the car, followed by a pep talk, and we were ready to go. This last exam started at eight a.m. I tried to stay calm as Einstein passed out the test. I glanced over at Lori as she diligently scribbled side notes, her lips moving. I swallowed hard and kept going.

Like the Spanish 3.0 final exam, I wasn't sure if I had more right answers than wrong, but I gave it my best shot and waited for the results to come in. Win, lose, or draw, I felt like a great weight had been lifted off my shoulders. I felt even better when the results were posted the following week and I did hold on to the C. Lori was delirious with her D-minus. We never pretended to be rocket scientists. We were destined to be social workers — and we were on our way! Another mountain climbed.

We celebrated by going out for pizza. Damn our budgets! After all, you only live once.

Chapter 14

I'm Not Superman

With all the craziness of school around me that final year, I was due a little fun. So, I did something I had never done before and may never do again.

Barry Manilow had written a book called *Sweet Life: Adventures on The Way to Paradise*. I bought the first two copies of the autobiography from our local bookstore. I read it that night, cover to cover, in six hours. The other copy I sent to Mari. The book was great, tracing Manilow's life as a kid growing up in Brooklyn, New York, straight through to his superstardom in music. A promotional book tour was being planned for key cities across the country, with autograph signings at various bookstores. The very first stop, as I learned from the fan club, would be in Cherry Hill, New Jersey, just across the river from Philadelphia. I found a tiny notice in the Sunday paper that week, announcing his appearance at the bookstore at twelve-thirty p.m. the following day.

Vicki and Chris were an engaged couple from Philly I had met through the fan club. Vicki had her own local club. They soon became my friends. We always had fun together, going to dinner or the movies whenever they needed a break from city life. They weren't fazed by my wheelchair and were fun to hang around with. I loved their zany sense of humor and Vicki's passion for everything Manilow (she even named her firstborn son Barry).

They planned on camping out overnight in the parking lot of the mall where the bookstore was located. They asked me to join them. They wanted to save a spot to meet Barry the next day, and Vicki wanted to be first in line. A few years earlier, I would've automatically said no, finding an excuse not to go. It was a crazy idea. My common sense said, "Don't do it, something will happen. That's for kids." Then I remembered Wheelchair Willie's advice so long ago about only living once and taking a chance. I may never have this opportunity again — why not go for it? When Lori agreed to take notes for me in class the next day, that sealed the deal.

The biggest seal of approval I needed was from Mom. Of course she worried, but she was slowly letting go of the apron strings. She acted like I was going away to boot camp. I told her I would call later that evening to reassure her. I was with Vicki and Chris; she trusted them, as they knew the routine with the wheelchair, my transfer board, the whole procedure. They were a little crazed about Manilow, but otherwise, they were normal. So she begrudgingly gave her blessings, and off we went. What the hell, I tried to rationalize in the car — I had a lot of catching up to do in life.

Bundled up, with the new book in hand, we used Vicki's old beat-up station wagon, trekking to New Jersey on that chilly Sunday night in October. We arrived at the lifeless mall at precisely seven p.m. Our plan was to sit in the cozy heated car all night, then take our place in line early in the morning. Then we saw more campers arrive, fans equally as die-hard as we were, and Vicki panicked. There were several cars in the lot. We could vaguely make out the passengers, huddled in their warm coats. They had to be fans, as crazy as we were, parked in an empty lot in a closed shopping mall on a Sunday evening.

Vicki declared, for all to hear, for once in her twenty-two years, she was going to be at the head of the line. She always was beat-out for top area honors by members of the dreaded Barry's Beagle Bagels, a rival fan club in Jersey. Not this time!

Even though Vicki had a bad cold, we unpacked our gear to sleep outside: sleeping bags, food, radio, books, and whatever other provisions we could carry, and took our place beside the bookstore door. We got even more excited when we saw the giant poster of Manilow and his book in the window: "Appearing on October 12 — Barry Manilow."

Little by little, other fans braved the chill and joined the line. Next to us was a middle-aged woman, blonde and heavy set. Her husband thought she was nuts to be out there. Like the rest of us, she was determined to meet her favorite musical artist. (Her daughter would have joined her if it had been Madonna.)

The line grew, and the night turned colder. Fans from as far away as Cleveland arrived by van, as did a bunch from New England. All in all, about twenty of us spent the entire night together in line. We spent hours talking and sharing Manilow stories. That was the common bond. No sports, politics, or religion: just Manilow talk for the next sixteen hours.

It was almost like the video party I had at my house when Mari was visiting (only bigger, outdoors, and with no videos). The cassette players worked overtime, playing Manilow music all night. We swapped tapes, photos, and addresses. Some people played cards. Most were too cold to do much of anything but shiver or pace, trying to get warm. The temperature was forecasted to drop down into the high 30s, but it seemed colder than that on such a clear, harvest-moonlit night. A few wimpy fans headed back to their cars to warm up. Some sat on lawn chairs, while others sat on the sidewalk with blankets under, over, and around them. We had a little overhang above us — protection in case it rained or snowed.

Manilow fans tended to be chatty and outgoing. This group was no different. Funny how complete strangers bonded after a short time, saving each other's places in line when someone needed to get warm in the car or use the bathroom at the nearby all-night donut shop. We were in this together.

I didn't sleep at all, a combination of looking forward to the next day and not exactly feeling comfy in my chair for so many hours. Still, I wasn't complaining. I watched the stars and the growing wonder of dawn. I wished Mari could've been there. It was her dream to meet Manilow too. I had so much to tell Manilow. All the crazy stories of concerts and ticket lines over the years; the nice friends I had made through the fan club; how I loved certain songs and how they related to my life. And of course, Mari.

By daybreak there were hundreds of fans waiting in line. Radios played Barry's interview with a local radio station. If someone didn't know about the book signing before, they knew it now. Familiar faces dotted the growing crowd, fans I saw all the time at concerts. Members from Barry's Beagle Bagels finally appeared, and they tried to bully their way to the head of the line, claiming that honor should be reserved for the "official" fan club of the area. Their leader, a stocky woman in a black leather jacket (who closely resembled the then-current middle linebacker for the Eagles) was the spokesperson and chief instigator.

The ploy didn't work. Loyal fans who had waited all night now bonded and stood their ground. Everyone started booing the troublemakers like they were the Dallas Cowboys. I thought there was going to be a fight between two huge women, but thank goodness mall security arrived and started policing the line.

Around noon, two gray limos arrived. Barry and company were whisked to the rear of the store. Also on hand was an army of television, radio, and newspaper media. Reporters were asking me, Vicki, and Chris why we were there, first in line. Caught in a whirlwind of excitement, I mumbled something about loving Manilow's music and not being able to pass up the chance of a lifetime to meet him. With no sleep, I felt like a zombie, but sheer adrenaline kept me going. There would be time to sleep later.

With twelve-thirty approaching and the crowd buzzing to the point where it was tough to hear oneself think, shoppers drifted by the huge line, wondering what was going on. "Barry who?" some asked, while others gasped, "Here? You're kidding!" The line snaked as far as the eye could see. Fans gazed into the bookstore windows, shouting, "I see him! He's in there!" More squealing and screaming pierced the chaos.

The doors finally opened and Vicki, who was first in line, die-hard Vicki, after waiting so long, determined to be first, said to me, "You go first!" Surprised, I pushed inside, the entire scene surreal, as Vicki and Chris followed behind, not knowing what to expect next.

Bright lights shone ahead as we emerged from rows and rows of bookshelves. Television cameras wanted to record who this mysterious person was, the first to meet Manilow, not only there in Cherry Hill but on the entire book tour. All sorts of people in suits and dresses, publishing people with Manilow's crew, crowded into the small store. I noticed Marc, Barry's assistant, up ahead as I wheeled forward, and he gave me a wave. He had stopped by the line in the late evening the night before and shocked everyone with coffee and donuts from Barry. (These pastries was soon known as "Barry's Buns," priceless souvenirs of the camp-out.) And there, standing behind a large walnut table, wearing a beige tweed suit and tie, was Barry Manilow himself.

My first thought was, "Shouldn't you be on an album cover?" (he seemed taller in person). He looked at me, staring at first, then gestured me to wheel closer.

"Hi, Barry!" I replied, rolling to the table. Vicki was a few feet behind me, nearly fainting. Suddenly, like at school while taking a big exam, my mind went blank. Everything I planned to say, everything I practiced saying all night, went down the tubes. I stared at him like a stalker. Cameras clicked everywhere. There we were, in a stare-off.

We shook hands as Barry sat down. "What's your name?"

Luckily, I remembered. Barry was handed my book, and as he began signing the cover, I came to and knew this was my one and only chance to talk.

"'Barry, I have to tell you this real fast," I said, expecting security guards to handcuff me and drag me away at any moment.

"Sure, go ahead," he said, still signing.

"Well," I began, taking a deep breath, "I belong to the fan club and — "

"Oh, really?" he said, still signing.

"Yes, and they started a pen-pal program to match fans who love your music." I started talking faster, trying to condense the entire relationship into ten seconds. "So, I wrote in, got a pen-pal from Norway, and we met last summer."

"Great!" he replied, looking up and smiling, finally finished signing.

"Yeah, and she hopes to come back after graduation and who knows?" I stammered, coming to a dead halt as if somebody pulled the plug.

"Great!" he said again, turning to the people hovering nearby. "Did you hear that? Isn't that great? I love it when I can be involved."

"She says hi. Our dream is to see you together in concert."

"I'm sure you will," he answered, grinning.

Why don't we just have lunch together, I could tell you the whole story, we can talk music and let everyone else go home? I thought. No such luck.

"I love your music," I tacked on, something original he had probably never heard before.

"Thanks," he replied, still beaming. "Good luck!"

I turned to leave, thinking he had about enough of me. On to the next five hundred people in line, starting with the hyperventilating Vicki standing behind me. Suddenly Barry called back, "What's your pen pal's name?"

"Mari."

"Well, tell Mari I said hi," he said with a wave.

After almost running over several toes as I departed the scene, starstruck, I was ushered to the front of the store from whence I came. It happened so fast, and then it was over. Waiting all night in the freezing cold for this all-too-brief, unforgettable moment. It was so worth it! That's what I told the reporters waiting for me outside. That was my first chance to read the inscription on the book cover:

Gregg,
All Best.
Barry Manilow.

It took him that long to write that? It didn't matter that he'd spelled my name wrong.

Vicki came out next, breathless, gasping for air. She told Barry she had been outside all night, fighting a bad cold, just to meet him. "You poor thing!" he consoled. "Go home and take a Co-Tylenol and go to bed."

"I was this close to his nose!" she whined. "It was fantastic!" Her hubby just shook his head. He was used to it. After they dropped me off and I saw my much-relieved mother, I called Mari, relating the entire adventure in a few minutes. She was happy for me, flattered that Manilow asked about her, and happy I didn't forget her. How could I? She was everything to me.

Vicki said I sounded great on the radio the next morning as reporters asked us questions. I didn't bother to get up to listen to it. I always hated my voice, anyway.

————

I sent Mari flowers that May for her birthday and to wish her well on her upcoming exams. Mari's student loan finally went through. She needed to work part of the summer for expenses. We decided to meet again in August, this time for only two weeks before school cranked up again. Two weeks, although much shorter than our first vacation together, was better than nothing.

I was getting ready for my last semester at West Chester. Most of my difficult classes, like Spanish and Math, were behind me. I couldn't wait to graduate in December of 1988. There was so much to look forward to.

Mari got a job at a publishing company in Oslo. She loved it, and it was right up her alley since she was an avid reader. I missed her more than ever, and it was hard to believe it had been an entire year since we had met. This time we didn't drive all the way to New York. Mari thought it would be easier to catch the airport shuttle, which stopped at a hotel in nearby Valley Forge. That's where I met her, all smiles, looking stunning as ever in a beige outfit. We didn't shake hands as before. Instead we hugged, the warm embrace I had hungered for all winter.

It took Mari a little longer to adjust to the jet lag this time around. My late summer ragweed allergies were bad, so we did a lot of yawning and sneezing those first few days. Two weeks was too short, so we decided not to do long daytrips. She seemed satisfied with just hanging out with me, the dogs, and Mom at home. We hit the movies, our favorite Italian restaurant, played lots of Trivial Pursuit, and talked more about the future.

This was great, vacationing once a year, but we both knew it couldn't last. This was fantasy stuff. We had to share the everyday experiences that couples share, things that can make or break a relationship. We couldn't continue to live for only summer. How could we know if our feelings were real if we were always so far apart? Our situation was certainly different. Normal couples worried about money or what to have for dinner. We worried about visas and graduation and finding real jobs soon, things that were slowly creeping into our lives. If Mari decided to be with me, her life would not be easy. She would share the stares, the pain, and the hurt. She would encounter obstacles, both physical and invisible, that I met daily. How could I ask her to share all of that? But that's what she told me she wanted, to be with me when the time was right. It was either that or go back to being just pen pals again.

Often I had doubts. She was only a pen pal. This was fairy-tale stuff. It could never be forever. But when I felt that way, Mari always reassured me that everything was going to work out. I believed her.

The future was on my mind as another tearful farewell was at hand. We planned to get together after graduation and go from there.

————

It was autumn, and that meant it was time to send out resumes. Graduation was still scheduled for December. I was hoping to get lucky, as people were telling me I might have to travel or live in Philadelphia to find a good job in the social work field. Lori wasn't going to be around for transportation. I needed to take another big step on the way to independence.

Not being able to drive bugged me. There is nothing worse than depending on someone else to get around. I knew guys like Wheelchair Willie who were in a chair and successfully drove. Why not me? I had a good pair of hands. I didn't need my legs to drive.

So I contacted Vocational Rehabilitation and asked if I could be a part of their adaptive driving program. They were only too happy to help now that college was almost over. I got an evaluation with one of the best rehabilitation hospitals in the area. I looked forward to it, my confidence high after all the recent successes in my life.

On an overcast, drizzly morning, Mom and I arrived at the sprawling one-story hospital. It seemed like a cool place, ideal for those in wheelchairs recuperating from accidents or life-changing surgery. Plenty of accessible parking places, automatic doors, and ramps. A place where disability was the norm. *The outside world should take a lesson from this place*, I thought.

The purpose of the evaluation was to determine if I could drive. Then what kind of modifications would be needed? What kind of adaptable car would I need? Or would a van be more realistic, with hand-controls and a wheelchair lift like Willie's set-up?

I took a physical, then an eye exam and a coordination test. I thought I was just getting a booklet, maybe I'd take a written test, then I'd go home to study and return to take the actual test. Instead, they had me transfer into an accessible car that was equipped with hand-controls, an instructor by my side. He told me to take a spin around the parking lot. They pulled the compact gray vehicle under the carport roof in front of the building. Mom watched from inside, just as nervous as I was. Nervous wasn't the word. Scared to death! This was my first time ever behind a steering wheel. The old sink or swim theory. While we were already in the car, originally just to get used to the hand-controls, the instructor suggested we go for a little drive. It was a nice idea until I realized that I would be doing the driving.

I wasn't sure about the hand-controls. Which was the brake, and which was the gas? I froze and my mind went blank again. I couldn't remember which was which, even after the instructor told me several times. Because of my short stature, I had a hard time looking out the front windshield and over the hood. The rear-view mirror was challenging too. Even with the help of cushions to raise me higher, it was difficult to see. My first time on this side of a car. I was scared. Guys like Willie, who had driven before his accident, were familiar with the hand-controls and the rules of the road. This was all new to me. I fumbled with the ignition. I didn't even know how to start the damn car. I kept apologizing and the instructor patiently said it was okay, but he still insisted on the spin. He had controls on his passenger side of the car and could take over at any moment. "Just relax," he suggested.

The brakes screeched as we pulled away from the building. The controls were extremely sensitive to touch, which I had to get used to. Since I was left-handed, everything was backward.

The parking lot was full, which seemed odd to me. Shouldn't we practice driving in an empty lot? I thought I was doing a respectable job at first. Oh, I drove on the grass a few times, nearly taking out a garden, and I kept forgetting to stay on my side of the road, little things like that.

Then it happened. The car didn't go the way I wanted it to, as if it had a mind of its own. The instructor grabbed the wheel, swerving the car out of the way, just in time to avoid smashing into a parked car.

We came to a complete stop. He was frustrated, trying to hold in his anger. Me? I was embarrassed and frightened, shaking all over. He drove back to the main entrance, still in one piece. I was totally overwhelmed, in over my head. I let out a huge sigh of relief as I transferred back to my wheelchair. Nightmares about this experience would follow for a long time. No one was hurt and nothing was damaged, other than my confidence, which was shattered. The verdict was that maybe I could drive but I needed a lot of work. No kidding! Thirty-six lessons, to be exact. And I needed to read the driving manual.

I confided to Mom on the way home that I never wanted to drive again. "I'm not Superman," I cried with drama. "I can't do everything!"

She looked at me wide-eyed, surprised at my unusual outburst. "Greg, you don't have to do everything," she said with calm reassurance. "Why do you think you have to be Superman?"

Good point. I was ashamed to see others with challenges far more severe than mine who were able to drive, people who only used their tongue or a few fingers to steer. I admired their determination and guts to even try. I couldn't allow this one learning experience get me down. So I learned to take advantage of the local bus system and the new paratransit. After the Americans with Disabilities Act was passed, transportation was better, as someone with a disability could now ride an accessible, wheelchair-lift van.

Another step closer to independence.

Chapter 15

The Nicest Social Worker

I graduated from West Chester University with a grade point average of 3.56. Not bad. Taking my very last exam was easier than all the red tape connected with graduating: verifying my credits, the endless paperwork, ordering my cap and gown. Almost as tough getting out as it was getting in.

We did celebrate. It was an achievement to be proud of. Having started out as a volunteer at the Manor with an idea of making something out of myself, unsure, unproven, and with so many doubts, I had reason to be proud. But when the pizza got cold and the root beer stopped flowing, a calm feeling came over me on graduation night. I remembered all the classes, term papers, exams, the late nights studying, the frosty early mornings, the blazing summer school classes, the icy, steep sidewalks, and the warm friendships I made. I thought of Willie, who encouraged me to take a chance; of Mom, who always supported me and drove me back and forth to school in the early days; of Dad, who would've been so proud. I thought of the counselor at Penn who said I would always regret dropping out there. Of Mari, who gave me a reason to keep pushing forward. Of Lori, and how she hugged me after graduation, tearfully saying, "We sure came a long way together!"

"I couldn't have done it without you," I said.

Lori did her final two internships at a local mental hospital and then at a prison. She never took the easy way out. She continued to challenge herself. Now she would have a chance to make a better life for herself and for her kids. Even after she moved to Vermont, I would think of her and her amazing kindness often. She wanted to go on for her master's degree. Knowing her determination, I knew she would. She was more than transportation. She was a good friend. She guided me in times of trouble, supporting me and bringing me back to reality when I was with Silver Fox, when I started writing to Mari, whenever I needed a friend to confide in. I would always remember her fondly.

So now I could say I was on both sides of the fence in life: patient, client, and social worker. Finding a job would make it official. I promised myself that whatever I lacked in book smarts, I would more than make up for in kindness. I may not be the best social worker, but I was determined to be the nicest social worker on the planet.

––––––––––

It took a while adjusting to life after school. Nice to have weekends and evenings free. My final transcript arrived in the mail. So did my hard-earned diploma. I displayed it proudly. My textbooks went on a shelf. Another chapter of life closed.

After the holidays, it was time to find a job. The social work positions at both local nursing homes and the hospital were filled. They were jobs I wanted, jobs I knew I could do well. Now it was a matter of patience, timing, and luck.

I continued to work at the Manor part-time. I wanted to keep my foot in the door at the Manor just in case an opening occurred. Plus, I loved working with the residents. They were the ones who had planted the seed of my going from volunteer to professional. It would be hard to leave there when another job came up. The residents showed me what kindness could do. I always remembered those volunteer days — the many room visits, the reading groups, taking time to listen. Whatever I gave the residents, they gave back to me many times over. They taught me far more than any textbook could. They were the first to treat me as an equal and not look at my disability as a negative. They saw what I could do, as opposed to what I could not do. I was "differently able" in their eyes, not "disabled." I still had to laugh when a new resident looked at my chair and asked, "What room are you in?"

I was starting to see why it was recommended to stay in school and get a master's degree. "Not qualified enough" was a common phrase I encountered at interviews. Not being able to drive was biting me in the butt too. One look at my wheelchair, and I saw disappointment and surprise. Hiring someone with a disability was a positive for any company. Tax breaks, hiring an employee who may be extra motivated to prove they can work, meeting certain company requirements — all great perks. The ADA law was still in its infancy back then, so whether I could do the job or not, people could get away with rejecting me just because they "imagined" I could not do the job. I understood their concerns about transportation and reliability. Did I have the endurance to handle a full-time job? I had hoped my degree would lessen the effect of the stereotypes. Instead, I was encountering stereotypes in full force. I left so many interviews thinking that all I wanted was a chance.

Since social work jobs were pretty limited, I was forced to look temporarily for work outside of my field. I took a part-time job at the hospital, doing payroll every other week in the nursing office. At the time there was a problem with Social Security. The claim was that the peanuts I had made over the years at the Manor, mostly for school supplies and gas money, was too much and I had to repay much of the disability checks. I had returned to school to get off disability; now it seemed like I was being penalized for wanting to be independent.

I was back to being a client again, trying to straighten out the mess of red tape and bureaucracy, showing up at the Social Security office to "prove I was really disabled." I couldn't wait to find a good job and support myself. I felt like a criminal.

As equally frustrating as the stereotypes was the lack of accessibility in my job search. Always steps to battle when going to interviews. I often had to use the back door. At one place I remember using a service elevator.

I attempted to call Mari when my frustration mounted on the job hunt. She was always so reassuring and positive, and it made me feel better to hear her voice and know that everything would be all right. I tried calling her all weekend with no luck. I knew she had moved back home after law school ended. Her final exams went well, according to her last letter. Moving was a big deal. Things she had collected over the years in her small Oslo apartment, books and stuffed animals (my fault), headed the packing list.

I finally got through to Mari's mother. She didn't speak English and my Norwegian was elementary, so it was a fun conversation. All I could understand was "ikke me," which meant "not here" (or so I thought).

Mari moving to the States was still in the cards. She had things to work out in Norway — her visa, her finances, and her information from the embassy. She said she would miss her family, but she would be happier with me. Mom looked forward to her moving over. Mari would find a job here, and we would live happily ever after.

It took me a full six months before things started breaking my way and I had possibilities for a real job. Then it happened, the break I was looking for.

Woodland Center was run by the county and had an excellent reputation for being a top-notch place for its residents and employees. The ad wanted someone with a degree in social work, with nursing home experience, and extensive experience working with older adults. I checked all those boxes. The salary and benefits, especially working for the government, were excellent. The answer to my prayers! I rushed my resume out in the mail and called for an interview. My confidence grew.

Here I was, thirty-two years old, applying for a full-time job for the first time in my life. Okay, I didn't have that much "professional" experience — but how can you get the experience if no one gives you a chance?

The Director of Social Services was a pleasant lady named Dee. Like others before her, I could tell she was surprised I was in a wheelchair, but she was friendly and professional and was impressed by my college achievements. I left thinking she would give me a fair shake, despite my nerves during the interview.

A week later I got another call from Dee. The caseworker position was down to one other person and me. She didn't want me to think I was forgotten. I prayed even harder. Transportation would be solved by hooking up with the local paratransit to get back and forth to work. I was determined, motivated, and wanted to work. It would be nice to make a decent wage, to forget resumes and job interviews, with all the anxiety and stress disappearing. I could see the future more clearly now.

Another week went by before Dee called me. She gently explained that, although she admired my grit and was impressed by my life skills and college grades, she was looking for someone with more on-the-job experience. The job went to the other applicant. She promised to keep my resume on file, and if there ever was another opening, I would get the first crack at it. I thanked her for her kindness and honesty. It was back to sending out more resumes and going to more interviews. The only jobs being offered were positions where I would basically stuff envelopes all day. I continued to pray for strength.

Mari's student loan payments were coming due. Her break came before mine. She landed a job in Oslo for a big law firm. This was her dream job with such a powerhouse firm, and it was an honor to be hired, especially since she was a woman and fresh out of school. They had to be very impressed with her. I was happy for Mari. I knew we would see each other soon.

Mari ended up moving back to Oslo, where she found a bigger apartment near her new job. She would be making good money for an entry-level attorney, there was plenty of room to work her way up in the firm, and she could now afford a better place to live.

On my side of the ocean, inspiration hit. There was a professor at my community college who taught a night class once a week on government and social work. It was actually a very boring class. But Ed was a nice guy. He looked like Richard Nixon, only friendlier. He was the older, grandfather-type, and he took a liking to me. He was also a big guy in the county system, the head of Aging and Adult Services in nearby Norristown. He mentioned to me if I ever needed a favor to call him. I figured it was time to cash in my chips.

I called him and he remembered me. I told him I graduated and was looking for work — did he know of any openings? Ed couldn't promise anything, but he asked me to visit him the following Monday at his downtown office. When I showed up with Mom, I immediately had a job. I was going to work with him at Aging.

I still wasn't sure about transportation to work every day. Paratransit refused to cross Chester County (where I lived) to Montgomery County (the location of the job). I couldn't expect Mom to drive me the half an hour each day (although she said she would). The bus route stopped five blocks from the Aging office, which was in downtown Norristown (a town way bigger than Phoenixville). Would I be able to push my chair those five blocks in bad weather, trying to navigate streets and sidewalks without cut curbs? The entire idea seemed rushed and not well thought-out, but Ed said not to worry. He wanted to hire me so bad that he agreed, until I worked out another form of transportation (such as a carpool), that I could take a taxi cab back and forth to work and the county would pick up half the cost. It sounded crazy, this extremely generous offer. Ed said not to worry, so I didn't. He offered to work on paratransit, perhaps pulling a few strings in the process. Until then, relax!

The other concern was the job itself. It wasn't a social work position. It was about computers (again, computers). I wasn't sure what my responsibilities were. Something about checking numbers and coordinating schedules for county agencies such as Meals on Wheels. Good-hearted Ed gave me whatever he had open at the time. I accepted the position because I was excited to have a job — any job. It was permanent and it was full-time, and I couldn't say no to Ed after all the trouble he went through for me.

Ironically, the hospital called me later in the week offering me a temporary position for the summer. It was close to home and I liked it there, and it was social work. Unfortunately, they couldn't promise me a full-time position. Come September I would be back to searching the classifieds and sending out resumes. It was great experience and nice pay, but it wasn't for forever. What should I do?

Chapter 16

My First Real Job

I stayed with the job in Norristown. The hospital was disappointed. I hoped I had done the right thing, even though that little voice inside was calling me a jerk.

My steady cabbie was a guy named Chet. He looked like Buffalo Bill out of the Wild, Wild West — mustache, goatee, and flowing blond locks. Chet talked about his life a lot, how he had been married three times, "going on a fourth wife." Chet played country music every morning on the cab radio. He was a Randy Travis fan (so was I). Any Randy Travis song was cranked up, full blast. Only Chet always substituted the word "cab" in the title (like "Hard Rock Bottom of Your Cab" or "Digging up Cabs"). He was nuts, so we got along great.

My first supervisor was a real trip. Her name was Doris (she had this uncanny resemblance to Roseanne Barr), and it was my first professional experience with someone who didn't like me. She was always on my back about something, not in a constructive way, but a nasty way. Either I looked bored or I wasn't counting the numbers they asked me to count correctly. It was true: I didn't understand my so-called "job" or what I was there for. Neither did anyone else.

The truth was that Ed had me on the payroll until something better opened up. This position of organizing schedules in the county was the same job Doris wanted for her sniveling daughter Amanda, who also worked in the office as a receptionist. Here I was, green out of school, not having a clue, and I was awarded her coveted job.

It wasn't just me. Doris had low self-esteem issues and was grouchy to everyone — except Ed. She had him convinced she was a nice person and a wonderful supervisor. I thought of my supervisors before her at internships, and this lady couldn't hold a candle to any of them, either in ability, leadership, or personality. No one in her department had the guts to tell Ed the truth about her. She would twist it so that it was our fault.

I learned a lot about office politics and keeping my mouth shut. I was clearly intimidated. It was nice to finally have real money to help Mom with the monthly expenses, so I didn't want to make trouble. If they wanted to pay me for doing nothing, then fine. I wasn't happy, but I wasn't stupid either.

One day a group of us went out for lunch to celebrate Amanda's birthday. Doris was assigned the task of folding my wheelchair and putting it in the trunk of her car, and she complained about it. "If I hurt my back, I'll get workers' comp," she whined out loud. "They don't pay me enough to do this crap."

That year the county had their annual Christmas party at a place which was not accessible for a wheelchair. I felt embarrassed because some thoughtless person, knowing they had an employee who used a wheelchair, still picked an inaccessible location. Suggestions swirled from carrying my chair up two flights of stairs (with me in the chair), to finding another location, to asking me to ride the waiter's dummy elevator upstairs. I ended up not going at all. Later I was accused of not being a team player.

Now I regretted not taking the hospital gig. I felt trapped. After a few months, I couldn't take it anymore. I finally went to Ed and said I wasn't happy, not only with Doris, but with what I was doing (or not doing). I appreciated his kindness and the fact he had hired me despite knowing the daily taxi was costing the county a bundle. The guy gave me a break. He wanted me to experience a job and the work atmosphere until something better came along. For that I was eternally grateful.

It was a shame that paratransit wouldn't cross county lines to get me. Even with Ed's influence, they wouldn't bend the rules. Everyone who worked in the office seemed to live in or around Norristown, so sharing a carpool was out. There wasn't another kind-hearted Lori, someone willing to go out of their way to help.

Once Ed knew how unhappy I was, he arranged for an opening in the Intake and Referral Department. That meant a new supervisor named Debbie. She was a short girl with curly blond hair like Little Orphan Annie. She looked like she was barely out of school herself. Debbie was much friendlier than Doris (then again, an angry rattlesnake with an attitude would've been friendlier than Doris).

This new position was more social work. It involved doing intakes over the phone and routing people to the appropriate help they needed. It meant sending out information, referrals to organizations in the county area, or counseling people who walked in off the streets of Norristown. I loved it!

The small group of fellow caseworkers were fun to work with. Each phone call and each case were different and challenging. Some days the phone rang off the hook, and other days it barely rang at all.

Norristown was known for its share of drugs, and homeless and poverty-stricken people. The job was exciting yet dangerous too. I'll never forget the afternoon two guys had a knife fight in our lobby. The Aging offices were located on the eighth floor of the tallest building in town. Back then, security was nothing. It would have been easy for a desperate, troubled, or disgruntled client to take the elevator upstairs and gun down a caseworker. The knife fight made that clear, as these guys came into the office looking for monthly hotel vouchers. When one didn't play the game and act out the routine as they planned, the other one turned on him and tried to stab him in the back (literally). They ended up rolling on the floor, right there in the lobby, until the cops from the courthouse across the street came over.

Another time I met with a young African-American guy. He was quiet and didn't have much to say, his eyes searching the floor. He wouldn't look me in the eye as I spoke. *What's up with this?* I wondered. He was looking for county assistance, either money or a voucher, or both. I took him into the interview room, alone, which was not unusual. About fifteen minutes after he left (empty-handed), two gentlemen wearing dark suits appeared outside the office and asked to speak with the caseworker who had just helped that young guy a few moments ago (that would be me). They introduced themselves as FBI agents. The young man they were trailing was wanted for murder. They asked me what he wanted. Money, as they all want. Where did he go? He didn't tell me, and I didn't ask. All I could think about was how I was alone with this guy in the interview room.

The following week I saw in the local Norristown paper that he had been arrested and confessed to the murder.

Since the county courthouse was directly across the street, we saw well-dressed attorneys and other professionals crossing from our building to the courthouse area all the time. Walk a block away and one would find a totally different world full of hookers, homeless people, and drug addicts, many of whom made their way to our office every month. Usually around the first of the month. Everyone on the streets knew the county had money and vouchers to give away — first-come, first-served. The line formed down the hallway to the elevator, right at eight a.m. when the office opened. The free stuff was given away usually by lunch, and the rest of the month was quiet with the usual cases.

One month an older gentleman with dirty, ragged clothes shuffled into the office looking for money. Since it was almost time to close the office, there was no one left. I was the one who told him the bad news. He didn't like that answer and threatened me. I called my supervisor (by then they had hooked up a silent buzzer in the interview room to call for help). Spunky little Debbie asked him to leave the premises immediately.

When I wheeled down the hall to meet my taxi in the parking garage, the guy was waiting for me. He boarded the elevator without saying a word. I was scared. Luckily other people were on board with us, but they got off on the first floor. We still had the parking garage to reach. Again, he asked for money. I bravely told him he would have to come back the next day and I would see what I could do. As he started to move toward me, the elevator door opened. A security guard was waiting. I quickly got out and met my cab. He never did come back.

I worked for Aging and Adult Services for nearly a year. I helped a lot of people in that time and gained so much experience. I felt good knowing I could make a difference, like the time I helped an unwed teenage mother find diapers for her baby. The baby was only a few weeks old, and the mother couldn't afford diapers. Instead of just giving out money, we tried other methods to help. We learned that cash would sometimes go to drugs or alcohol instead of the intended purpose. Instead, I called numerous stores in the area. A national toy store chain agreed to donate a box of diapers. The box was slightly damaged during shipping, but the diapers inside were still good. The young mother only had to pick them up, which she agreed to do.

It was a temporary fix, and she agreed to return soon so we could plan long-term solutions, like a job to get her off welfare, assistance with school if she needed to learn a trade, or childcare so she could work. I was networking and made contacts in the area. I could relate to her plight, as I had felt like I was in a hopeless situations many times until someone gave me a break. This was real social work — right up my alley.

Every day I dealt with heartbreaking stories, and it was my job to help find solutions. Most people wanted out of abusive relationships or wanted to find shelter other than living at the Salvation Army all the time or on the streets. They just needed direction on how to start. The things we take for granted — food, shelter, money, the basic necessities — were lacking in the lives of so many. Some were unfortunate victims of bad luck, lay-offs from work, addiction, illness, or natural disasters.

It was February, and I was the next social worker in line to help a walk-in client. I wheeled into the interview room, and who wasn't sitting there but Wheelchair Willie himself, looking haggard and beat, head lowered. I rolled up to the table and touched his arm. "Willie!" I whispered.

He looked up at me with bloodshot eyes. "Hey, Smitty! What are you doing' here?"

"I work here," I replied.

His breath reeked of alcohol. Willie wore a heavy black wool jacket and faded blue jeans. He almost started crying when he saw me. I lost touch with Willie after he quit school four years earlier; I never knew the real reason, but I did suspect that his drug intake had gone way up. His girlfriend left him, he ended up in jail, and was living on the streets after he got out of prison. He was looking for money or a voucher.

Sadly, the vouchers were gone for the month. I didn't want Willie to sleep out in the cold, so I asked him if he wanted me to call the local Salvation Army to see if they had any room for the night. A hot meal and warm bed waited, if only he would agree to go. At first, he balked at going to the shelter. I began to suspect he wanted the cash for reasons other than shelter. He was kind of mad at me because I had no money to give him. I considered giving him twenty bucks out of my own pocket but thought better of it.

"Willie, I'm going to worry about you if you refuse the shelter. Please go. It's almost four, and I must leave. Come back tomorrow and we can talk. I'll try to help you some more."

"Okay, Smitty," he replied. "I'll do it for you."

As I turned to leave, he reminded me of "all the good times" we had, including the time I smoked a joint and "almost coughed up a lung" in his van. Good times for sure.

Getting back to my desk, I stopped for a moment before picking up the phone. It was sad to see my old friend like this. The same guy who encouraged me not to give up. There was room at the shelter. That was luck, seeing how it was so cold and so late in the afternoon. Ideas swirled in my mind of how to help Willie. Calling around and finding him a job; helping to find a low-income apartment until he got back on his feet; encouraging him to get back in school.

Willie didn't return the next day. It was the last time I ever saw my old friend. I kept him in my prayers that he would finally find peace.

Chapter 17
Three Wishes

One day while I was at work, a reporter called from a Philadelphia television station. His name was Mike, and he hosted a special segment on the late local news called "Three Wishes." The segment granted the requests of some very lucky viewers every week. When the "Three Wishes" segment started, I had written Mike a letter. I told Mike about how Mari and I met through the Manilow fan club, how we both loved Manilow's music, and how special she was in my life. My wish — for her — was to someday meet Barry.

Mari knew nothing about the letter. I doubted the station would find it very interesting. They had to get hundreds of similar requests every week. There were some truly inspiring stories on "Three Wishes": a mentally-challenged young man skating with his idols, the Philadelphia Flyers hockey team; a man's lifelong dream of being a disc jockey for a day; a family reuniting for the Christmas holidays.

I forgot all about the letter until nearly nine months later when Mike called me. He loved the idea and thought the entire story would be interesting to detail. He wanted it to be a bigger story than I ever imagined. Now that Barry was on tour, with an appearance at a casino in Atlantic City only ten days away, he wanted to do it now, if possible.

Now? Only ten days away?

It would all hinge on if Mari could fly over, if Mike could arrange the meeting with Manilow, and if all the other little details could be tied together in such a limited amount of time. Without really stopping to think, I agreed, planning to call Mari after work. I had no idea what I was getting into.

There was a possibility an airline would fly Mari over for no charge in exchange for the free publicity. I called Mari and related the entire crazy story. It seemed like a fairy tale. Mari was stunned. This was a chance of a lifetime. She didn't foresee problems getting a few days off work. Most of her time in the States would be over a weekend. It would only be a few days this time, not our usual lengthy vacation. She was willing to endure the flight and the jet lag. Yes! She agreed.

Everything was up in the air, like a house of cards: if one arrangement didn't work out, the entire story would collapse.

Mike kept in touch every day. Everything looked good. Mari planned to fly in for the weekend. The station planned to pick us up in a limo and whisk us to Atlantic City for dinner, the show, and the meeting. Mike would get his story. The Delaware Valley would get to share in a real-life romance. And we would get to meet Barry together. Perfect!

Then the wheels started to come off. Mari got a plane ticket (which relieved a worried Mike). But on such late notice, the best she could do was arrive the day of the show, early in the afternoon. It would be a tight schedule. The new plan was to ride the 90 miles to New York to pick up Mari, then travel south to Atlantic City (another 125 miles).

Plans still had to be finalized. Some fell through. Mike worked hard to help Mari with the plane ticket, but the airlines refused, saying that since she already bought her ticket and was flying over, they couldn't do anything. I used some of my savings to help her, since I was now working full-time and had started this idea in the first place.

Then the casino gave Mike a hard time. Even with the promised free publicity, the casino still hesitated. They didn't believe I really had a disability, sensing a scam. Mike pointed out that my disability had little to do with the wish. It was the love story angle and the connection with Manilow he was going for. In fact, he rarely did wishes where people met celebrities. He got hundreds of requests like that, even letters to meet Barry in particular. My wish was different.

Mike had never met me before, but there was no question in his mind, especially after we talked, that I was legit. If it was a scam, he would find out soon enough. I'm sure he did a little checking on his own too.

A few days later, things looked brighter, especially after I purchased tickets to the show (the casino refused to offer comp tickets). Mike finally got approval from the casino and from his station. And I got approval from Mom. Everything looked promising.

Then another last-minute snag, this time from a source I never expected in my wildest dreams to resist, made us stop in our tracks — Barry.

"Greg, wait until you hear the latest hurdle," said Mike. Manilow would not meet us (or at least that's what Manilow's people implied). Being in the business, Mike had heard stories that Manilow could be difficult. In his book, Barry even admitted that at times he "used to be a jerk." But now he was supposedly a new guy, more open and friendly to fans, the media, and the public. He was very kind to me at the bookstore signing. He did so much for charities over the years. I couldn't understand why he might be reluctant to share in this story. I tried to find any excuse I could to justify his resistance.

Mike was asked if I could transfer from my wheelchair to a regular seat. I could, but what difference did that make? It was hard to believe that the wheelchair was an issue. Or was the real reason the cameras? (There was a no-camera policy by Manilow's people). Without recording the meeting, there would be no story. Without the story, Mike would have to pull the plug on the entire event. The wheelchair had nothing to do with this story. Mike stood his ground. "You have your dignity," he said firmly. "You're staying in the damn chair." We only wanted to say hello and let Barry know how much his music meant to us. What was the big deal? I didn't want it to be a big deal. I knew Mike had to get his story. But to me and to Mari, we would've been very happy not to have all the cameras and hoopla. We simply wanted to meet the guy.

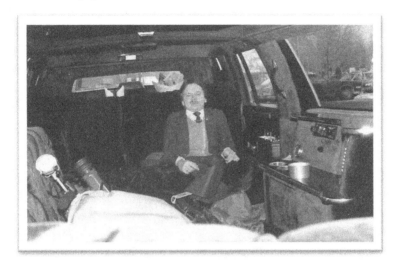

In the limo

I felt disillusioned as Mike said not to suddenly hate Manilow. We were dealing with legal hassles, long-standing policies, and insensitive publicity people who really didn't have a clue. I began to regret writing that letter. Mike felt even worse. He especially felt bad for Mari. It was too late to get a refund on her plate ticket. She was coming over, story or no story. We would have an unexpected weekend together, no matter what. We still had tickets to see the show. I dreaded calling her and explaining what happened. Now I had to prepare to rearrange plans at the last minute, such as scheduling a shuttle to pick up Mari at the airport. My faith was shaken, but I still prayed for a miracle.

Just when things looked bleak, Mike called on Wednesday, two days before the show. I expected him to officially say he was sorry, but things just didn't work out. Instead, they had reached a compromise. Manilow's team still said no to cameras backstage. But (supposedly) word got to Barry about all of this, and he either changed his mind or he never knew about the whole thing in the first place. He even remembered me from the bookstore. Whatever, it was decided the station would be allowed to film the first three songs of the show for their lead-up, but absolutely no TV cameras backstage. Although filming the meeting would've been terrific, Mike agreed to the terms. He wanted our wish to come true, especially after all the hassles. He could work around the no-camera policy.

Everything was back on!

Friday morning arrived. Dressed in a chocolate-brown suit and tie, I waited with Mom for Mike and the crew. It was ten a.m., and the day had turned sunny and cool. Butterflies soared in my stomach. Being in the limelight wasn't my cup of tea.

A huge white stretch limo pulled into our driveway. The longest freaking car I ever saw. The neighbors had to think someone had died. Emerging from the backseat was Mike himself. He looked the same as on television: medium height and weight, short brown curly hair, and an easy smile. I thanked him for everything. What a tough week on the emotions and the nerves!

Mike looked at me, shook his head, and said, "Not in a wheelchair, huh?"

Along for the ride was the cameraman, Ted, a short fellow with dark hair and a mustache, and R.J. the limo driver, an older guy with silver hair and a slight British accent. I climbed into the back seat of the huge limo, waving bye to Mom. Uncle Henry and Aunt Sue, along with Mom, planned to meet us down the shore later that night for the ride back.

As R.J. put the wheelchair in the trunk, I looked around in awe. All around me was luxury: a bar, small TV, crushed red velvet seats, and a car phone (which was a big deal back then). The front seat seemed miles away. I felt out of place, but Mike enjoyed it, taking off his shoes, loosening his tie, and lighting up a cigarette. "This isn't too bad, is it?" he said, smiling.

It was cool looking out the one-way tinted windows and watching as drivers and pedestrians squinted to see if anyone famous was inside. We stopped in Valley Forge for a few outside shots as we dropped off the cameraman to take footage of the limo cruising down the road before we doubled-back and picked him up. We were pressing for time, so we started up the Pennsylvania Turnpike on the two-hour trek to Kennedy Airport and Mari. We talked Phillies, and Mike related some show-biz gossip. Then it was time for the interview.

I tried to forget about the camera as I related how I met Mari, the connection with Manilow, and more. He asked about my broken bones and my childhood. They ended up shooting a couple of reels of film. Everything would later be edited to a mere few minutes of footage. Thankfully the worst of me would end up on the cutting room floor. I wasn't as nervous as I had imagined. Maybe the ham in me came out? If I mumbled or drew a blank, they could always start over. Mike asked if I knew any Norwegian. The first phrase that popped into my mind was "I love you": *Jeg elkser deg*.

With the interview over, Mike sat quietly, paging through a notebook, trying to put the story together. I gazed out the window as we glided from New Jersey into New York, creeping closer and closer to our destination. And I thought of Mari, who had to be close to landing in the States.

Waiting outside of customs with the camera ready to roll, I gave Mike the cue when I saw Mari. We hugged and she said, "Good to see you!" We forgot about the camera, if only for a moment. After introductions, we were on the road again, heading south to Atlantic City and the long drive ahead. Mari looked fantastic. Especially after such a long flight. She couldn't get over the whirlwind of limo, camera, and this entire crazy story coming true. The extra attention took getting used to.

Mike and the crew stopped for a quick bite to eat at a fast-food joint along the turnpike. Waiting in the limo, we had a few moments to finally be alone. We greeted each other more properly, with a kiss and a warm hug. She knew that I hated all this glitz as much as she did. If only we could sneak away into a dark corner at the show, then sneak backstage to meet Barry afterwards.

On the road again, Mike completed his short interview with Mari. His first question was why travel six thousand miles to meet Manilow? "First of all, I wanted to see Greg again," she sweetly corrected him. "And this is like an adventure. It's the chance of a lifetime."

Halfway down the turnpike, our lone camera died. Mike used the car phone to call the station back in Philadelphia. A new camera and relief cameraman would meet us at a prearranged phone booth just outside of Atlantic City. Mike worried about time, chain-smoking and constantly chewing gum. "I love the pressure," he claimed, lighting up again.

He was forming the story and upcoming evening in his mind. "Manilow music in the background as the report begins," he mumbled to himself. "Have to do some promos on the Boardwalk. When is the show? Ten-thirty? We will get some shots of you guys being seated at the theater, if we ever get another camera . . ."

We waited close to an extra hour for the news van to meet us. By now twilight was easing over South Jersey, the lights from the Atlantic City skyline twinkling across the sparkling bay. We rode into the city in style, the new cameraman, Chuck, hanging on top of the news van, filming our limo alongside the van as we made our glorious way into the seaside resort.

As soon as we arrived at the casino, we were treated like royalty. The head of the casino's entertainment and publicity department, a young blonde woman named Lola, pleasantly greeted us at the door. She apologized for any inconveniences earlier in the week. She surprised us by exchanging our tickets for seats near the front of the stage. Barry's people, including my old friend Marc, couldn't do enough for us. They said that Barry couldn't wait to meet us.

Mike was perplexed. Why weren't they this nice earlier in the week? Ah, the camera! Negative reaction would mean bad publicity. Or maybe they really did want to make amends? Whatever the reason, Mike didn't want to dampen the evening, so he went along with it, grinning through clenched teeth and mumbling, "I never had this problem with Julio Iglesias."

Mike made one last plea to have the camera go backstage to film the climatic meeting. The answer was still no. He didn't want to press his luck, so he smiled at the road manager, saying, "Can't blame me for trying, can you?" The road manager wasn't amused.

It was Friday night around eight p.m., and the casino and lobby were packed with people, many dressed to kill. Elderly ladies carried plastic cups filled with silver, heading for the clanking slot machines; casino pit bosses strolled the floors, along with winners and losers; waitresses in short skirts sprinted across the plush purple carpet, balancing trays filled with drinks. Noise everywhere, the shouts of people who had hit it big and the groans of gamblers who had lost mixing with the ringing of jackpots cutting through the hustle and bustle. Manilow fans were everywhere, their identity known by familiar T-shirts bearing Barry's likeness. The glitz and glitter were exciting as guys roared at the dice tables while squeals from Manilow fans pierced the casino racket.

After a quick dinner, we filmed the promotional spots on the deserted, chilly boardwalk. The breeze from the nearby Atlantic Ocean made us wish we had brought along winter coats. It was very quiet and calm on the boardwalk, as opposed to the chaos inside the casino. We saw a few light snowflakes flutter by as we wrapped up the filming. Mike and Mari stood behind my wheelchair as Mike announced, "Mari, Greg, I'm going inside to get a bite to eat." (Mari and I had already eaten.) "We'll tell you all about the big meeting with Barry Manilow tomorrow night. This is Three Wishes for you . . ." Reality television at its best!

Tomorrow night? Mike was planning for this report to run in two parts, he explained, the reunion with Mari, then the Atlantic City excitement. The air date wouldn't be until a month later. Could the Delaware Valley stand it?

Back then, the theater was not accessible for a wheelchair, so the usher took us through the kitchen area and backstage in order to reach our seats in the theater, avoiding the stairs to the lower level. The joint was rapidly filling up, and Mike departed to direct the action in the back, where the camera would film the first part of the show. He left us with final instructions.

"Since we can't take the camera backstage, I'm going to count on you guys to give me a detailed account of everything that goes on. Remember everything that Manilow says and look excited."

"We can't take our camera backstage, but nobody said you can't take yours," he added. "If given the chance, take as many shots as possible." Mike had a plan to somehow work our photos into the story.

We sat at a small round table on the extreme right of the stage. High rollers and fan club members filled the front rows of the sold-out theater. The first time I ever saw Manilow in concert was 1981, and I was in Row Z of the same theater, as far back as one can get. For Mari, it would be her first Manilow concert in five years since she was at the front of the Oslo ticket line. We had both come a long way.

The lights dimmed, the music played, the speakers blared, the crowd screamed, and nearly everyone stood. I tried to look around the forest of people before finally spotting Manilow kissing female fans, shaking hands, and working his way from the back of the theater to the stage. He wore a dark-blue pinstriped suit, which was in danger of being ripped off his body by overzealous female fans in the aisles. Security was everywhere. What a mob scene until he finally reached the stage!

On stage (and still in one piece), Barry sang as the crowd cheered, clapped, and sang along to hits like "It's A Miracle." Then came a string of those sweet, marshmallow ballads, songs like "Weekend in New England." During the "Can't Smile Without You" segment, he looked at Mari again — like five years earlier in Norway — but picked another girl. Mari would just have to be content with going backstage after the show.

The finale, and the highlight of the ninety-minute performance, was Barry's "Gonzo Hits" medley — over twenty of his biggest hits bunched together in one long, non-stop, twenty-minute, show-stopping treat: everything from "Tryin' To Get The Feeling" to our sentimental favorite, "Somewhere Down The Road." (Barry said to the crowd: "For those who came to the show willingly, you're going to love this medley. For those of you who were dragged here tonight, this medley is going to drive you up the damn wall!") "I Write the Songs," Manilow's signature song, wrapped up the medley. The crowd stood for what seemed like an eternity, begging for an encore. He came back with a rousing version of "Copacabana." We cheered wildly until the curtain closed and the lights came up. And that was it. We were exhausted and thrilled.

The crowd slowly filed out of the theater, a few stragglers hanging out and chatting about the show until the ushers chased them. Susan (Manilow's PR person) suddenly appeared and asked us to follow her. It was finally time to meet Manilow.

We followed Susan through a dark corridor to a gray, narrow hallway. There we waited against a concrete wall with several other people nearby. A few held copies of Barry's book while others had album covers to sign.

It was close to midnight. I looked at Mari, who by now had been up twenty-seven straight hours. She looked tired from the trip and the excitement, but she was wide awake. We were speechless, anxious for what was about to happen next.

Marc came over to greet us. As we were talking, I looked over his shoulder and there was Barry Manilow, wearing a royal-blue sweater with dark slacks. A champagne glass was in his left hand as he signed books and albums with a black marker. Barry noticed us and walked over, asking Marc to remove the red rope-railing that separated us. "Hey, hi!" He smiled. There we were — face-to-face-to-face. Our wish had come true!

Just like at the bookstore, I went blank and forgot everything I wanted to say. I asked if he remembered me from the book signing. "Sure," he said. "How could I forget?"

Mari mentioned Oslo, and Barry told her the lovely Sculpture Park in the middle of the city was a highlight of his brief visit. We chatted small talk, telling him how much we loved his music. I showed him the original letter from the fan club that I had brought along. Marc read it aloud after Barry held it up to the light, squinting without his reading glasses.

"So when is the wedding?" Manilow asked. We looked at each other and blushed — awkward! He asked if there was anything we wanted him to sign. Mari saved the day. I completely forgot about taking a picture. "We would love to take a picture with you!" she said sweetly.

"Sure," he replied, moving closer.

So with Barry on the right, smiling brightly, Mari in the middle, very ecstatic, and yours truly on the left, grinning sheepishly, Marc snapped the shot. "Let's take one more to make sure we got it," Marc suggested. A moment that would last forever. I was glad the television cameras weren't there. It was a very personal and intimate moment.

We shook hands again and said our farewell. Barry wished us good luck and a safe trip home, departing with "See you again sometime." It happened so fast, and then it was over.

When we emerged into the theater, we were met with bright lights, Mike, and a rolling camera. Our reactions? "Great!" Mari exclaimed. She felt "shaky," but it was worth it. What did Manilow say? It was hard to recall, even though it happened only moments ago. We were still in a fog.

Off-camera, Mike was happy we got two pictures. Mari was a bit hesitant about giving up her film, even though Mike promised to develop all the pictures on her roll, make copies, and return them as soon as possible. I couldn't blame her for worrying. Our proof was worth its weight in gold (at least to us).

We met my family outside the theater and said goodbye to Mike and the crew. Always thoughtful, Mari surprised him with a little crystal knick-knack she had bought in Oslo. We thanked him for everything once again. I was sorry Mike would disappear from our lives as quickly as he had appeared. He said he would be in touch soon with an exact air date of the report. As we waved, Mike looked back and yelled, "Let me know the wedding date. Maybe we can do a story!"

We got home that night around three in the morning. We were ready to crash. We had a moment to be alone and hug. Mari thought Manilow looked shorter in person. I imagined him to be taller at the bookstore. She said she held back from giving him a hug, not wanting to be the hysterical fan. But she did vow never to wash the sweater she wore again, especially where he had touched it.

———

Within the following weeks, Mike returned the pictures: there we were with Manilow. It really did happen! I sent them to Mari. I wondered what the reaction would be in Norway. Her mother wasn't very interested, referring to Barry as "some singer" in Norwegian.

Mike gave me a heads-up about the report. I was happy we met Manilow, happy for Mari, but still a bit embarrassed by the whole thing, and even more reluctant to see myself on the local news. I set my VCR, and so did family members in case I screwed up.

As the news began, they ran the promo we had filmed on the boardwalk. There I was, looking cold, as the anchorman said, ". . . and tonight on 'Three Wishes,' Mike brings you the story of a boy from Phoenixville and a girl from Norway, and their dream come true . . ." Mom sat quietly, as nervous as I was. About midway through the news, the three-minute segment began. "This is more than just two pen pals meeting," Mike said on the tape. "It's a love story." I cringed, afraid to look at the screen. Mom smiled and nodded.

There I was, wishing my wish from the backseat of the limo, a close-up shot of my mug, dissolving into Manilow singing his first song of the show. They showed everything in brief little snippets: the huge white limo, yours truly gazing out the window, even the "I love you" in Norwegian. Mike did a fine job of putting it all together. The memories came alive as I watched the Kennedy Airport segment as Manilow sang "Brooklyn Blues" in the background. There was Mari, hugging me, fresh out of customs. And there was a bit of her interview back in the limo, especially the part when she answered she had traveled so far to see me, then Barry. Finally, we were back on the boardwalk, freezing, as Mike closed with, "And we will tell you all about the meeting with Barry Manilow tomorrow night."

Same bat-time, same bat-channel.

Immediately the phone started ringing. How many people around the area watched it? Old friends came crawling out of the woodwork, my mother's friends calling as well, Mom chuckling in Slovak (she went into Slovak-mode when she didn't want anyone to know what she was saying). Fellow fans couldn't wait until the next night to see Manilow. And of course, my Manilow friends, Vicki and Chris, wanted a copy of the tape.

The second part began by recapping the previous night. We were smiling at the show while Manilow made his entrance, dancing with fans. The big moment was about to happen. For all those viewers who thought they were going to see the actual meeting they had to feel disappointed. Mike got around it by saying, "Barry wouldn't allow television cameras backstage because he considered it a 'personal moment.'" Whether Manilow felt that way didn't matter. There was no mention of the hassles. Just a positive fairy-tale-like ending, the famous photo of the three of us as Manilow's song "Looks Like We Made It" played over the fading scene.

It was well-done and magical. I didn't feel embarrassed anymore — I felt lucky and grateful for everything. Mike and Mari were very special people in my life.

After that, strangers came up to me, especially at work, saying, "Aren't you the guy who was on the news?" I heard from fan clubs from as far away as Louisiana asking me to join. The videotape was floating around the country, now part of Manilow memorabilia.

Soon it was back to "Greg who?" which I was happy about. I offered to send Mari a copy of the videotape. She said no, she would watch it the following summer when she came back.

That should've been my first clue.

Chapter 18

Breakable Heart

Mari did return in the summer, this time for only two weeks. Since she was new at work, she didn't have much time off and was lucky to get what she could. At times Mari seemed strangely distant, very unlike her. I was sure she had a lot on her mind. But she continued to say not to worry, so I didn't.

While she was in the States, we worked on her Fiancée Petition, a special visa that would allow her to work and live in the States, but only if she married an American. Applying was the first step in a long process. There were forms to complete, along with gathering birth certificates and identification photos.

For the first time, Mari saw our "Three Wishes" video. That was when she wasn't hiding her face with a pillow, peering up at times. She concluded that it was "nice."

We talked more seriously about the future in those two weeks. I was making contacts about a job for her. Children were another matter. I knew Mari wanted kids someday. We spent a lot of time in baby departments while we were shopping together at the mall. I easily imagined Mari would make a very caring mother. But I had to be honest. There was a 50% chance any child of mine would have OI. I wouldn't want anyone, let alone my kid, to have to go through what I went through.

Mari didn't have a phone in her apartment yet, so I couldn't call her as often. I knew she liked her new life as a budding attorney, living in the exciting city of Oslo and working for a well-respected law firm. That was all she talked about during her visit. Our letters continued, as did our plans. Her visa was due any day.

Then it happened. First my job. I couldn't blame the county for stopping my taxi rides. Maybe the county commissioners got on Ed's case? Anyway, I was called into my supervisors' office. It's never a good sign when they shut the door.

Ed couldn't tell me himself. I didn't blame him. He was good to me. Either I had to find another way to get to work — by bus, car, whatever (that was now my problem) — resign, or be terminated. I had a week to make the arrangements.

Not having learned how to drive killed me again. Mom offered to take me back and forth until I found another way but, as luck would have it, her car was in the garage just then. It was an old, used car on its last legs. I asked for more time until the car was repaired, but no, I had a week, period. I couldn't afford to pay the expensive cab ride each way all on my own, but that's exactly what I did for several weeks as I fought to save my first job. What was the use of working when practically all my salary was being spent on transportation alone? The bus route was not accessible. This was still the pre-Americans with Disabilities world I was living in. Paratransit was in its infancy and wouldn't cross county lines. I couldn't find anyone to carpool with. There was no angel like Lori in my life now. I was doomed.

I didn't want to quit. I didn't want to go back to life on unemployment and disability benefits. Because of transportation issues, I was forced to take a step back. Reluctantly, I resigned, giving them a two-week notice. My co-workers sympathized with my plight, but there wasn't much they could do. All they could do was wish me luck and offer encouragement that things always happen for a reason.

———

I sent Mari flowers that week, for no reason other than to say, "I love you." I didn't tell her about work. I felt something good was going to happen any day.

Usually I couldn't wait to open Mari's letters. This time I hesitated when I found the envelope on my bed after my last day of work. I changed into casual clothes first, glancing at her mail. It had taken an unusual length of time for her to write back.

The letter began as always. Well, almost. Instead of "Dearest" Greg, it began "Dear" Greg. That is where any connection to the hundreds of letters and notes in the last several years ended. I couldn't believe what I was reading. Mari was saying goodbye.

She claimed it was the hardest letter she ever wrote. She still didn't have a phone in her apartment. And Norway wasn't exactly close enough to drop by and tell me face-to-face. Our relationship would end as it began — with a letter. She loved her new job and didn't want to leave it. She was making friends and loved her new apartment in the heart of the city. She was making good money while paying off her student loans. How could she give that all up for a job she knew nothing about across the ocean?

Mari was right. I couldn't blame her family if they encouraged her to stay there. I would be concerned to see my daughter or sister move so far away. Most of all, and maybe the toughest fact to swallow, was that time and distance had made her love for me fade. There was no one new (or so she claimed). She just couldn't go through with our plans. Plain and simple. If someone new was in the picture, I don't think Mari would've told me. She knew how much that would hurt. Her letter was painful enough.

I had been great to her over the years (she wrote). That "little voice" inside told her it wasn't right after spending so little time together. Our time was like a fairy tale. It wasn't real. She "needed time to find myself." All she could offer was friendship. She wanted to remain friends. I was her best friend ever, helping her to live and love again. However, she would understand if I said no and never wrote back. She knew I would feel guilty, angry, cheated, and hurt. But as I read on, I felt nothing. Absolutely nothing.

She closed by writing, "I'm so sorry." And that was that.

I was devastated. Instead of angry or bitter, I felt foolish. I had believed her when she encouraged me "not to worry." I felt empty inside. I stared at the letter, my hands shaking. Where did I go from here? This was Mari saying goodbye, not just any girl. This girl was different. I shared so much with her — my life, my secrets, my feelings. She was my best friend. How could I ever trust anyone again? How could I ever listen to another Manilow song without crying? "When is the wedding?" everyone had asked. The wedding was never going to happen. The pressure of the visa, of leaving her new job, her family, her country, and her life had led to her decision. Welcome to the real world. A heart can break just as easily as a bone.

I wheeled into the kitchen where Mom was making dinner. She turned away from the stove and knew something was wrong. I still had the letter in my hand. "Mari," I said softly, "is saying goodbye."

Like any caring, loving mother, she didn't lecture or say, "See? I warned you." "You're kidding? Oh my God!" was her response. We were never big huggers, but she knew this time I needed a hug.

I didn't feel like eating. I couldn't sleep, and when I did, I was dreaming of Mari. One vivid recurring nightmare had me traveling to Norway, like a knight in shining armor, frantically searching the streets of Oslo in vain, always waking up in a cold sweat, my heart racing. Every few nights, I had another dream of traveling to Norway, but this time I found her. I braved the ice and cold, the long-distance flying to Oslo, and waited outside her apartment in my chair, freezing. Waited in the falling snow with fresh flowers in my hand. She would see me and run to me, hug me warmly, her heart melting, and, just like old times, we would be together again, this time for good, just like in the old black-and-white movies we loved.

"Get over it" . . . "Life goes on" . . . "You'll find someone else" . . . "It wasn't meant to be." I heard all the usual clichés. I did try to forget her. But she was everywhere. A Norwegian won the New York City Marathon. The Winter Olympics were being planned for Lillehammer, Norway. Miss Norway became Miss Universe. Norwegian language stickers were all over the house. The sweater she knitted for me hung in my closet. Life wouldn't let me forget her.

I saw her everywhere. Our favorite restaurant, the mall, the movies. Vicki and Chris did their best to cheer me up. They knew that Mari was everything to me. She was all I talked about when we went out. They loved her too.

I wasn't exactly a popular guy on the dating scene. It seemed like nothing had changed after all those years. I called a few female friends from my college days. No surprise they weren't interested. They had moved on. Until I closed one door, how could I open another? I needed time to heal.

The truth was I couldn't face the fact Mari had moved on. What good would it do to trash all her letters and gifts? The memories would remain.

Months passed without Mari in my life. Barry Manilow's music was perfect for a heartbreak. It gave me solace, and I couldn't help but smile when memories flooded my senses of the good times we shared. It was too bad we couldn't just be friends, lead our own lives on each side of the Atlantic, visit once in a while, and return to pen-pal status. Why did love have to get in the way?

I had to admit, despite the pain, I would do it all again. I got a card the following spring. An unexpected "Thinking of You" card. A fellow fan had gotten Mari a copy of our "Three Wishes" video. She thanked me again. She was offering an olive branch. My foolish pride kept me from answering. I kept busy, kept to myself, worked hard, and never forgot Mari.

Chapter 19
The Chance of a Lifetime

Things looked bleak after I left my job with Aging. I dreaded the thought of going back on unemployment or disability until I found something else. Then I caught a break.

I had worked at the Manor so long that the staff, especially Mrs. Anderson, the administrator, knew me well. I was still out of work when I attended the annual volunteer luncheon in the spring of 1990. Mrs. Anderson, a petite lady with short curly gray hair and a friendly smile, came over to me before the luncheon began and asked how I was doing. She was always kind to me. We had started working together at the Manor in 1977.

She squinted her eyes and crinkled her nose in that funny way she did when she was thinking. "Come down to the office after the luncheon," she said.

The current social worker, Bridgette, was going to have a baby. They needed someone to fill in for six months until she came back. It wouldn't be a permanent position, as they could only afford to pay one full-time social worker, but it would be great experience and a job for half a year. She trusted me like no one had before. Here she was, offering me yet another chance. She knew that whatever I lacked in work experience, I made up for in life experience.

I accepted the job on the spot. I would start immediately, orienting myself with Bridgette until she left for maternity leave on July 1.

With Peewee and Fluffy, 1990

I was thrilled, returning to where it all began. Only a block from home. No transportation issues. No more worries of sending out resumes or going to job interviews. I didn't think about what would happen six months down the road. I was just thankful that God had led me back home where I belonged.

The weeks of orientation went quickly. Bridgette was easy to work with. She had been in the field a while and knew her stuff. I learned something new every day. The job was interesting and fun. We never knew who we would meet or what kind of case we would encounter next. In that way, it was a lot like my Aging gig.

Our office was small, and we shared it with Medical Records. Much better than Bridgette's previous office, which literally used to be a supply closet. The residents were glad I was on board and filling in for Bridgette soon. Of course, they would miss her, and I suspected some families eyed me with concern. Bridgette was top-notch, and families trusted her. She was honest, reassuring, and patient with families and residents. I had my work cut out for me to win their trust as well. Bridgette did a fantastic job extolling my virtues to the families. It was up to me to prove she was right.

After July 1, I was on my own. The staff threw Bridgette a little party. She was really loved at the Manor. Everyone would miss her. I would miss her too. My caseload was a hundred and forty-four residents with a full house.

Wheeling back to our office after her farewell party, I was scared. So much responsibility fell on my shoulders, really for the first time in my life. But just like my college days, I didn't dwell on the massive caseload — I just did it.

There were meetings to attend every day, care plans and notes to write, documentation and forms to complete on a timely basis. If I didn't write it down, I didn't do it, and I soon learned documenting everything was key. There were residents to talk to and families to counsel (which was my favorite part of the job). The huge amount of paperwork was a necessity. It had to be done in a timely manner and neatly. I was conscious of falling behind and the daunting task of

Social worker

catching up. But I was on time with my notes, which impressed Mrs. Anderson and the state when they came around to do their inspections.

I especially loved the residents, and even though I was tremendously busy from eight-fifteen a.m. to four p.m., Monday through Friday, I tried to find time for them. Two things were especially important to me: first, no matter how busy I was, I tried to see each resident daily. Even if it was a quick hello and a smile, it was important to build trust and let them know someone cared and I had not forgotten them. Every single day, without fail, I touched base with all hundred and forty-four residents.

The second important item to me was continuing to feed those residents in need of assistance when I could. Even on days when I was so swamped I didn't have time to have my own lunch, feeding was important because it brought me closer to the residents. We didn't talk about their moods or family things or problems they were having. We talked about fun things or the weather or "How about those Phillies?" I never thought of feeding as demeaning or not as important as my regular duties. I pitched in and helped the nurses and aides when I could, and it was always a great experience to feed.

"Okay, Mrs. Gray, here we go," I announced as the aides brought her lunch tray bedside. After bibs were in place and secured, we went over the menu for the day: "Chicken at six o'clock, mashed potatoes at three o'clock, broccoli at nine o'clock and dessert, it looks like chocolate pudding is way up at eleven o'clock on your tray. Ready?" Nine times out of ten, she asked to start with dessert.

I was learning what it was like to be a professional. I dressed nicely every day, was on time, and often was there on Saturdays to get paperwork ready for Monday morning. The state surveyors made their annual inspection while I held down the fort. They knew I was a fill-in, but I couldn't count on them to cut me any slack. I was sure Mrs. Anderson had faith in me, but she had to worry about the inspection.

We had zero deficiencies (at least in social services). I let out a big sigh of relief during the exit interview at the end of the week. We could relax, all the department heads, all the staff. I had faith in my own abilities, but I didn't want to be the lone eye-sore on a state inspection. The staff, though always kind and helpful, were even more encouraging after they knew I was doing a decent job, decent enough to pass the rigorous state inspection. I could never be Bridgette, but I was holding my own, and the inspection verified that.

Bridgette had a boy in late August. She called me from time to time to find out how things were. I suppose she was worried too, wondering what she would come back to find. I knew Mrs. Anderson (with Bridgette's blessing) hired me because of the circumstances, but now I was proving I could handle the work.

Bridgette stopped by with the baby in the fall. She went around to see the staff and residents. They were so happy to see her and meet the baby (animals and babies were always popular with the residents). Afterward, she stopped by the office and seemed pleased, and pleasantly surprised, that things were in good shape. She met briefly with Mrs. Anderson and apparently got the same good word from her.

At the end of 1990, it was planned that Bridgette would return to work after the new year. It would soon be time to start sending out resumes again. After more than six months alone, I had become even more of a fixture at the Manor. I felt more respected by the staff and more confident in myself. I worked well with the residents and families, and soon I was hearing nice comments like, "It's a shame. Do you think they will keep you?" Even though Bridgette was well-liked, I could see that residents, families, and staff were torn.

Bridgette said she would talk to Mrs. Anderson about "needing an assistant," but she couldn't promise anything. She had asked for help before but the corporation had always said no. The workload could be handled by one, but two could share the work and have more one-on-one time with the residents. There was justification for adding an assistant to the Social Service Department, but it always came down to money with big corporations. Several families put in a good word with Mrs. Anderson. Even a few residents made it down to her office on the first floor, either by wheelchair, walker, or cane, to speak up for me.

It was the Friday between Christmas and New Year's Day. I was ready to head home to enjoy the weekend and the holiday. It was my last day at the Manor. Bridgette was expected back the following week from her maternity leave. Residents, families, and staff wished me well. Some held out hopes I would be retained, but I didn't think there was a chance. If they hadn't told me by now, it wasn't happening.

Mrs. Anderson asked to see me fifteen minutes before the end of the day. She met me in the Social Services office and thanked me for everything while Bridgette was out. "No problem," I said, expecting nothing more.

"Greg, you've done such a wonderful job that I want to offer you the position of Social Service Assistant. Bridgette needs help. Sorry it took so long to let you know, but I had to wait for the final answer from corporate. What do you think?"

I had to tell my residents the good news before I went home.

———

For the next three years, I worked with Bridgette. We rotated floors every six months so we both were familiar with the residents on every unit, splitting the Medicare floor. Our individual caseload was down to a more manageable seventy-two residents.

Bridgette and I were not only the Social Services Department, we were Admissions, too. If we had a new case, often without much notice, we were expected to drop everything else and focus on the admission. That meant getting papers signed by families or the power of attorney.

There was pressure like in any job. Keeping the beds filled, especially on the Medicare floor, was a priority and a challenge. The nursing home was a business, and an empty bed meant no money coming in. When referrals dried up, usually from the hospital across the street, we joked about needing to go out and "recruit" for residents ("If you're planning on taking a fall in the near future, I've got just the nursing home for you"). Social work in a nursing home was fast-paced and challenging. The Manor wasn't the old, stereotypical hellhole of the past, a place where old folks were mistreated, neglected, and abused. Our place was clean, odor-free, bright, and cheerful. It was a place where people came to live. More and more people needed rehab to return home. Arranging for a visiting nurse or home health aides, or ordering needed equipment, was our duty too.

Families were as different as their loved ones who came to live at the Manor. Many were experiencing grief, guilt, feelings of being overwhelmed, or extreme sadness. Family members cried at my desk, and I was there to comfort them, to show compassion and listen. Some families were angry, deflecting their anger onto staff, even onto Bridgette and myself. Some could be very demanding with staff, feeling guilty of being unable to care for their loved one. Families called for help when buying adaptive clothing, arranging for dental or eye appointments, or setting up transportation to doctor's offices or home-visits. Some merely called for guidance and support, especially new families unacquainted with nursing home life. Families helped families, and we helped put together a support group. We held regular family council meetings, too, which we organized and conducted, another source of support.

Many of our residents suffered from dementia or Alzheimer's, some more confused than others; some could recall events that happened years and years ago, as far back as when they were kids, yet not even remember their own name. It was important never to forget the families. They were the ones who knew exactly what was going on. The families struggled every day with visiting, watching loved ones decline in care and memory. And it was the families who often heard the line, "I took care of you when you were a child — why can't you take me home?" It was always so sad wanting to take your loved one home, yet knowing that going home wasn't the right thing to do.

Both residents and families needed comfort and support. We saw much depression and anxiety in our work. Some were accepting of placement; others fought it, attempting to elope, or were combative with staff. My mom was getting older, and she was going through a stage where a rash of her good friends were starting to die away. That had to be hard, watching people you knew so well slowly disappear. It was the same deal in a nursing home. Residents often became good friends with each other. A community within a community. Residents enjoyed each other's company, did activities together, and had meals together. When they heard that someone close to them had just died, the residents mourned, and the unit was unusually quiet for a few days, the staff more subdued. Who would be next?

It could grind you down after a while, the constant illness, death, and dying aspect of the job. After a period of grief, life went on. The residents knew this was inevitable, and they dealt with it in their own way. We offered compassion and a friendly, caring visit to those suffering from loneliness. I had a special place in my heart for the younger residents, those in their twenties or thirties, placed because of an accident or a debilitating disease such as Huntington's. Tough to be so young and spend the rest of your life in a place where the general population was mostly in their eighties and nineties.

One of our common duties was breaking up roommate arguments, which happened almost daily. Matching roommates was challenging, like fitting jigsaw puzzle pieces together, knowing which personalities would jive with one another. When it didn't work, someone had to move, and that was never easy. At times a resident requested a fresh start in another room or stood their ground. "Why do I have to move? Let her move!"

Generally our rule of thumb was that whoever started the ruckus needed to relocate. Common issues such as one person wanting the heat turned up high and the other wanting it cold, or one blasting the television and refusing to wear headphones . . . things like that kept us hopping. The goal was to make everyone happy, all hundred and forty-four residents. It was a new thing, sharing a room. Chances were many people had never shared a room with anyone before (other than a spouse). Spending so much time in a room made it important to share it with someone compatible and not combatable.

It was always a great day when a resident went home. I recall an elderly couple who met at our place, fell in love, married, got their own apartment, and lived very well together for the rest of their lives.

We never had to deal with anything like the COVID-19 pandemic of 2020, but we did have our share of outbreaks when I worked in nursing homes. Outbreaks always caused feelings of anger, fear, frustration, depression, loneliness, and anxiety to increase. I remember one winter when the flu ran rampant. Of course, most of our residents were elderly and compromised, so it didn't take much to put them in jeopardy. Cases of bronchitis or pneumonia were often death sentences for those poor souls. Closing our doors, quarantining all floors, and forbidding visitors for several weeks was common. It was heartbreaking when a loved one could not visit, but the residents' safety and health had to come first.

We soon learned the routine of washing our hands thoroughly for twenty seconds (while singing "Happy Birthday" twice) and other sanitary measures, lessons we continued to adhere to even after the outbreak subsided. I didn't fear getting sick as much as coming into work and making someone else sick. Wearing gloves and a mask while being close to the residents was commonplace. Reassuring the residents during lonely and sad times, while missing their families, was another regular duty during an outbreak.

The oddest outbreak I saw was when bedbugs were discovered in our building. Everything had to be cleaned, and several residents were quarantined. Bug-detecting dogs were brought in to sniff down rooms, residents, and employees until we got a handle on the bugs. Again, part of my job was to call families and inform them of the situation, keeping them informed of the progress and well-being of their loved ones. Easing fears with calm reassurance, being totally honest, and showing empathy and compassion were keys when helping residents and families during those days and weeks of crisis. Sometimes we had to move residents quickly from one room to another.

Like all facilities, our nursing home was guided by state regulations. Moving a resident was not a favorite part of my job, especially if a resident was in a private room and was happy there. When it was time to break the news to a resident and their family that a temporary transfer needed to happen, I needed all my social work skills to convince them it was for the best. The nursing home, and specifically their room, was a resident's home. Suddenly, they were asked to move out of their home, often without much warning during an outbreak situation. They had a right to feel angry. It was my job to pick up the pieces and make them feel better.

Another part of my job during an outbreak was to keep families informed, especially when visiting was restricted. We coordinated other ways to "visit," such as telephone or window visits. Communication methods such as Zoom didn't exist yet. If a resident was able to use a wheelchair, we arranged for family to gather outside of a first-floor window. It was both heartwarming and heartbreaking if an occasion such as a birthday occurred during a quarantine. Everyone loved hugs, especially on birthdays. Frustrating when a family had celebrated for so many years together and then could not. We did the best we could to make it as best we could.

I was used to the possibility of residents getting sick or dying when I worked in nursing homes. That was a tough part of the job, to say the least. But during an outbreak crisis it was dreaded, almost expected, that fatalities would happen. Leaving work every day, I never knew who I might see again in the morning or not.

There were holidays to celebrate and landmark birthdays, especially when a resident turned one hundred. Local newspapers or even a Philadelphia television station would cover the big event. There was always a party and decorations, along with a certificate from a politician, presented to the resident being honored.

Veteran's Day and Memorial Day were big, and we always made it a point to honor our vets and remember those who made the ultimate sacrifice. Our veterans reminisced about old war buddies and memories of their service. Some liked to talk about their experiences and world travel; others preferred not to talk about it at all (my father never mentioned World War II or his place in the Battle of the Bulge).

The real backbone of our facility were the nursing assistants. They did the dirty work — cleaning and showering residents, transferring and lifting folks, doing the basic, daily, mundane duties. They rarely received a thank you and were paid minimal wages, yet their dedication was unwavering. We weren't allowed to play favorites, but just like anything in life — classmates in school, siblings in a family, co-workers on the job — you always liked someone more than someone else. Many aides baked cookies for the residents they cared for; a few residents went out to the movies or home for dinner with aides. The aides laid their hearts on the line each day. It was risky, getting emotionally involved with a resident. Some vowed "never again" when they talked to me for support, but often the next resident who needed a little special TLC was taken into their heart.

One day I was making my daily rounds on the second floor when I heard a familiar voice quietly chatting with one of the residents who was waiting for her cigarette. It was none other than Wicked Joe Pickett, my childhood friend from my Hall Street days.

We had lost touch after my family moved away. Joe was no longer boxing. He was now an ordained minister of the Baptist Church. He was at the Manor to visit one of his former parishioners.

Joe quit beating people up in favor of healing souls. He made it clear that fighting was no longer in his blood — God was. Turns out Joe never really was "wicked." He used to be very "bad" in the boxing ring; in life, he was the gentlest of souls.

———————

I had no clue that Bridgette was thinking about leaving the Manor. When she told me one morning that she had given her two-week notice, I was surprised. She was taking another position closer to her home, thirty minutes away. She also wanted to spend more time with her now three-year-old son.

I grew so much in the years we worked together. I admit that I depended on her in situations I still was unsure how to handle. I thanked her for supporting me, as I knew she was on my side when the corporation approved of an assistant. I was also afraid I might not get another co-worker as understanding as Bridgette.

Mrs. Anderson looked for a new Director of Social Services. Until she found someone, after an exhaustive search and countless interviews, I was back to handling the hundred and forty-four residents alone, as I had during Bridgette's maternity leave. Three people accepted the position in six months. One turned out not to have the nursing home experience she claimed to have once she started. Another simply left after only a week once she got a taste of all the work involved. We continued to hit brick walls.

Mrs. Anderson consulted me on the resumes, and I sat in for a few of the interviews. We couldn't seem to find the right person for the job. Then Mrs. Anderson looked at me after another disappointing interview and said, "What about you, Greg? You've done the work. Why not?"

At first, I was reluctant to accept. I was perfectly happy doing what I was doing. I was okay with being the assistant. I knew the Director got the grief whenever the state stopped by and there was a problem in their department. The Director attended more meetings, and I was happy being out on the units where the action was. The main reason for my hesitation was my own self-confidence. I was still learning something new every day.

Then I thought, why not? Mrs. Anderson had the faith in me to make the offer. I might not get this chance ever again. So I accepted.

———

For the following six years, I was Director of Social Services at the facility where I started as a volunteer. Amazing! It was my dream job — and I was so grateful after all the dark days on unemployment and disability.

The actual work wasn't much different than when I was an assistant. I worked more closely with the psychiatrist and the psychologist who came into the building once a week. I worked with Mrs. Anderson more closely too. She was more demanding with her department heads than with her assistants. I was one of the top dogs now, and along with the title came added responsibility.

I would have numerous assistants over the years. Changing assistants was frustrating. After a few months of training, learning how to formulate a care plan, or completing an assessment on a resident, just when it looked like an assistant was getting the hang of it, she would quit and I had to start over again. A few cracked under the intense pressure when the inspectors were lurking.

I also had two interns, both from my old alma mater, West Chester U, who joined me for their practicums. It was great giving back to my old school by helping new, soon-to-be social workers learn the ropes. I wanted them to get excited about their duties. I wanted them to make a difference and feel good about themselves. I wasn't so far away from my own internships, and I could relate to what they were feeling.

I hated to give bad evaluations. I knew how important the internships were to graduate and get a good job in the field. Yet it was my responsibility to teach, and if they failed, I had failed as a supervisor.

There could not have been two students more opposite than my interns. The first, named Jody, was very shy and quiet. I was too when I started out. Afraid to say the wrong thing or make mistakes. I forced myself to open up more. She wasn't going to cut it being so passive, and I told her so.

My advice worked, because within weeks she was giving me advice as to how to run the department better and how I could be a more effective supervisor. I didn't need to be with her every hour of her internship, so I began to let go. We ended up with a terrific practicum. Years later I bumped into Jody at a seminar and she was doing well in the field, working for an agency that helped homeless veterans. I was so proud of her!

My second student, a young woman named Emily, was very emotional. I admired her spunk, being a single mom of two small kids, fresh out of a divorce, trying to make it in school in her early thirties. Every morning was frantic, dropping her kids at daycare, coming to her internship crying and stressed out from school and her personal life. We took the first hour of each day just to talk and let her cry. How could Emily help the residents when she was constantly in tears? She bummed me out, so I could only imagine how the residents felt. I felt bad for her, but she had to get herself together. She was still finding her way, a familiar scenario indeed, so a combination of tough love and kid gloves worked.

By the end of her nine-month run, Emily was better. I still had concerns for her in the field, but she seemed to have her life together by graduation.

I heard from Emily after graduation. She didn't find a job in the social work field, but she was working at a local daycare. Perhaps she would get back into the field someday, but for now she was happy working with children.

––––––––––

My Uncle Henry and Aunt Sue had one son: Eddie, a drifter who was on the road a lot, traveling to Las Vegas and back, making a buck wherever he could, be it selling Christmas trees over the holidays or setting up a roadside stand hawking cheap T-shirts. He was leading the lifestyle Uncle Henry would've loved to lead if he hadn't been expected to be the breadwinner and family provider. When Eddie got sick from stomach cancer and died in his early fifties, it took the heart out of my dear aunt and uncle. Imagine losing your only child, dying before you. Aunt Sue took care of her son at home until he died, helping him with a feeding tube when he no longer could eat by mouth. She had always been very sentimental, and after her son died, she cried even more often.

Uncle Henry was the stoic one, never showing his emotions. After Eddie's death, he was noticeably quieter and more restrained, like a piece of his heart had been cut away. His son was a clone of Uncle Henry, both in looks and personality. Although he never showed it in front of us, people reported seeing my uncle alone during the day visiting Eddie's grave, taking out a white handkerchief and weeping.

His card games, his fishing, and his usual routine all changed after Eddie died.

We started worrying about my uncle when he parked his car downtown one day then forgot where he had parked it. Someone called the police, and they located the car and escorted Uncle Henry home. One time, instead of pulling into the driveway of a local church grounds for a fundraiser Night at the Races, he drove into a field instead. He showed up that night in our driveway without his glasses. I asked him where they were, and he thought he had them on.

Aunt Sue knew about these episodes of forgetfulness. Most likely there were more she wasn't aware of. I know she was scared to admit he was failing. When he started to wander (even in the house) and lost his appetite, my aunt took him to the doctor, something he hated to do. Doctors were all "quacks," according to Uncle Henry.

He was admitted to the hospital and eventually to a nursing home. I never imagined my dear uncle would end up being a resident at the Manor where I was a social worker. That broke my heart, seeing my uncle waste away from Alzheimer's Disease, remembering the good times we had together over the years, reminding myself that this confusion and combativeness with staff wasn't the Uncle Henry I knew and loved. He remembered me at times when I stopped by to visit him on my breaks. He smiled with a twinkle in his eye when we talked about card games and Philly cheese steaks. He recalled those good times, yet couldn't tell me what he had done five minutes earlier.

A year later he fell and broke a hip, developed pneumonia, and died on Christmas Day.

As a final tribute, I bought a brand-new deck of cards and placed them in my uncle's coat pocket as he lay in his casket. I scribbled this inscription on the pack: "To Uncle Henry — May you find the royal flush in Heaven that you never found on Earth."

When Uncle Henry died, it was like losing my father all over again. Aunt Sue didn't last long without him. She missed his companionship, even the arguments, and she shared his fate, ending up at the Manor and dying a few years later. An entire family gone. All the years of working at the tire plant, the beautiful home in town, everything was gone. Even now, whenever I pass their old house, I can't help but think of them. There are fond memories, times that still make me smile, remembering the love and laughter they shared for so many years.

Chapter 20
Unforgettable

I met hundreds of residents and families over time. All made their mark in my mind and in my heart. Many were unforgettable in their own unique way.

There was Liz, who lived in the nursing home for over thirty years. The wife of a late army officer, she was affectionately known as "The Mayor of the Manor." She owned a Southern drawl combined with a raspy voice. Everyone said she looked like actress Shelly Winters. Everyone knew Liz. She was a fixture.

One of her daily duties was delivering the mail to her fellow residents. It kept her busy and allowed her to visit everyone. And most importantly to Liz, she knew who was getting what in the mail. "So-and-so got a postcard today from Europe." . . . "Mr. what's-his-name had a birthday package delivered." . . . "The lady with the blue hair on the second floor got a notice that she won the sweepstakes."

Liz also did the daily morning announcements. What were the activities lined up for today? What was on the menu for lunch? Important stuff to those who resided at the Manor. It didn't matter that many couldn't understand her drawl. The morning announcements with Liz were an institution. The Walter Cronkite of our facility. Trusty, reliable, and always there.

Liz had the same room near the window for years. She was at every activity or party. She often made the local newspaper when they ran a story about the nursing home. And when she died, it affected everyone very deeply, because she was the Manor.

I remember Jim, a sweet guy who suffered from pancreatic cancer. He was at the Manor several years, yet never complained and always had a smile on his face. He loved the Phillies. We talked baseball during my visits, and he told me about old players he had seen such as Jimmie Foxx and Babe Ruth. He vividly recalled the games, the stadiums, and the atmosphere. Fascinating to hear.

Sports were so cool to talk about with the residents. It was a common link between the past and present. Endless stories and endless debates about the greatest players. Like listening to a game on a transistor radio on a summer evening, it was always a part of our life, from generation to generation. I found sports to be a great equalizer when it came to forming a bond with my residents.

The modern-day player Jim most admired was an outfielder on the Phillies named Jim Eisenreich. He was a good hitter and a hustler, a gritty, determined player who never gave up, despite battling Tourette's syndrome. Jim took a liking to him. Eisenreich was an "old-school player" like Foxx and Ruth and those greats he grew up watching in person.

I decided to write to Jim Eisenreich, with a brief note about our Jim, and how it would be a nice surprise if Eisenreich could send him an autographed photo to hang in his room. The memories of my joy when baseball teams started sending me autographed items one summer when I was a kid cheered me up so much. Maybe I could return the favor? To my delight, the outfielder did send Jim a personalized color photo. Jim cherished it with pride. I sent the photo to his daughter after Jim died. She didn't need to know how he got it. Doing a little extra for my residents was always so gratifying in itself.

I fondly remembered Mrs. Steele, a former high-school English teacher. We always got along well because I was honest and fair when she had a concern. To other staff and fellow residents, she could be difficult. Mrs. Steele was feisty and opinionated, and it didn't matter if it was a nurse, a dietitian, another resident, or even her own physician; they all faced the wrath of Mrs. Steele at one time or another if something displeased her.

For instance, if she wasn't pleased with her lunch, she would immediately wheel out of her room fuming, heading for the kitchen with her issue. No one dared get in her way.

Mrs. Steele was angry about her stroke, which had left her paralyzed on her left side; angry her family forgot her, only visiting on special occasions; angry she had to be on a unit with less-functioning residents, even though she had a much-coveted private room. I could understand her anger. I would be angry too. Maybe that was why she never gave me much grief.

She admitted to me what I suspected — she was lonely. She liked her private room, but she had also isolated herself from others. She missed her cat, China Blue, who she was forced to give up after the stroke.

"I never bothered anyone," she confided. "My son never visited that much when I had the apartment. I was happy with my cat. Everyone else could go to hell."

I found two things which eased her fury: books and animals. She loved to read. Books were stacked everywhere in her room. I kept her supplied with reading material from the Activities Department, anything from paperbacks to magazines. I suggested she may want to start a reading group with some of the other residents on the third floor. Why not hook up with neighbors on the unit who also liked to read and discuss books? It would give her a purpose in life again. And that is how our weekly reading group started.

The Manor had a "community cat," a pretty orange tabby who visited the cat-lovers in the building. Bootsy could be found on any of the three floors. Bootsy somehow sensed which residents needed a friendly visit. I witnessed this special cat get on and off the elevator with visitors and staff, calmly stroll the units, stopping into certain rooms (probably for treats as well). Pet therapy was an important piece of a resident's care plan, especially for someone like Mrs. Steele, who secretly wept for her own China Blue.

Bootsy had her own little "apartment" set up in the Activity Room: water, food, cat toys, and a litter box. Everyone knew where Bootsy hung out when she wasn't visiting. Bootsy and Mrs. Steele were introduced, and they hit it off right away. Mrs. Steele saved part of her lunch for her daily afternoon visitor, especially if fish was on the menu. I often made my rounds and found Bootsy on her lap, content as Mrs. Steele gently stroked her silky fur.

One afternoon I headed up to the unit to have a heart-to-heart with Mrs. Steele. It was cool that she loved to read, but her books and magazines were presenting a problem for the nurses and aides, who could not walk in her room. Stacks and stacks of paperbacks were cluttered alongside her bed. It was also a fire hazard. The nurses noted scraps of food hidden all over the room, probably for Bootsy. The books were a potential fall risk, and the morsels of tuna fish presented a health issue, as bugs were beginning to visit Mrs. Steele.

I always hated to be the bad guy, but Mrs. Steele wasn't confused and knew the rules. Problem was, when I tried to assist her in tidying up her room, she opened her bedside cabinet, and out fell everything under the sun that she had hoarded: salt packets, plastic forks and spoons, paper cups, old newspapers, open, half-eaten boxes of cookies, cosmetics, tons of paper towels and napkins, pieces of soap, pens, pencils, paper clips, and old milk cartons.

"Oh, no! That's still good!" she shrieked as an aide helped me clean up the room. Throwing out the moldy candy took a bit of negotiating. It seems Mrs. Steele had always been a hoarder, even in her own apartment. We agreed to weekly cleaning sessions to make sure things didn't get out of hand again. The roaches would just have to go somewhere else for their snacks.

Toward the end of her life, Mrs. Steele's son started to visit more often. I know that made her happy, almost as much as visits from Bootsy. When she suffered another massive stroke, one which mercifully took her life quickly, she left us with peace in her heart.

Interestingly enough, about a week before she died, she asked the charge nurse to page me to her room. Apparently, it was an "urgent" matter she needed to see me about. When I arrived, she presented me with one of her prized classic books: *Old Possum's Book of Practical Cats* by T. S. Eliot. It was the basis for the musical *Cats*.

"I want you to have this to remember me by," she said, smiling. I accepted, although I wouldn't need a book to remember Mrs. Steele.

On the morning of Mrs. Steele's funeral, Bootsy peeked into the darkened, empty room, just in case Mrs. Steele had returned. Bootsy let out a soft meow and continued on her way, making her daily visits and spreading much-needed love and joy.

Then there was Mary Reynolds, a blind lady I visited often. Looking much younger than her sixty-eight years, her overall health had declined after macular degeneration took her vision several years before she came to us. She had a wicked sense of humor and would've made a great stand-up comic. We swapped jokes daily (a few naughty ones too), and she constantly asked me what her fellow residents and staff looked like. She was a big music and movie buff, so we chatted about the old and new stars. I teased her when she confided that she was in love with Billy Dee Williams.

"I happen to look exactly like Billy Dee Williams," I lied. I looked nothing like him at all except for the fact we were both males.

"Aw, Greg!" she laughed, her face lighting up. "You're too much. Looking so good and working here!"

Speaking of infatuation, Mary tried to fix me up one time. I had numerous crushes on different nurses and aides over the years. There happened to be a pretty aide named Rochelle working there at the time, and she happened to work on second shift. I generally saw her before I left for the day. She was assigned to Mary at night, helping her get ready for bed. Mary knew I liked Rochelle. "Rochelle said to tell you hi," she said, grinning like the Cheshire Cat. I was surprised when Rochelle told Mary she thought I was "cute," and we exchanged phone numbers. We dated a few times until I found out she not only was married but had kids. I'm glad Mrs. Anderson never found out, and Mary was a good sport to keep it quiet. It was stupid to risk my job like that, as it was forbidden for employees to date, especially with a resident playing matchmaker, but I was young and dumb back then, still getting over Mari.

I read Western novels to Mary every week. Music was also very big in her life, especially after she lost her sight. I remember bringing my portable cassette player on weekends so Mary could listen to her favorite songs for an hour or so. She loved "Don't Let The Sun Go Down On Me" by Elton John, swaying to the music. "Isn't it great?" she said softly in fascination. But her all-time favorite song was the touching "Unforgettable" duet by the late, great Nat King Cole and his daughter Natalie. We listened to that song every music session. It still gives me the chills even now when I think of Mary.

From those sessions musical ideas flowed. Mary agreed to lead a resident music appreciation weekly group. It gave her another purpose in life.

One of the few pleasures Mary still had was her cigarette break every two hours during the day. I sat with her many a time while she smoked. She lived from smoke to smoke. When the nurse was busy and her smoke was late, Mary became frustrated, almost to the point of tears. Often I used whatever influence I had to gently ask the floor nurse on duty to please give Mary and her fellow residents in the lounge area their cigarette. I knew what it was like to feel such loss of control and independence. Her smoke every two hours was more than her right — it was a matter of dignity.

A very special resident was my old schoolmate's mother. Timmy and his father visited every day for several years. They always dressed in suits and ties for their visits. And Mr. Gallagher often surprised staff with boxes of chocolates in appreciation for the care. Timmy and I would chat about our cab rides so many years ago. I helped to care for his mother until she passed away. Despite the circumstances, Timmy remained so cheerful and compassionate. What a small world it was! And our friendship continued into the future.

I would be remiss not to mention one special resident who affected me and remains in my fond memories.

I fed Teddy lunch for years. Sometimes breakfast too, if I was there early enough and the staff needed help. He was easy. The same menu every day: fried chicken and chocolate ice cream. If chicken wasn't available, then it would be macaroni and cheese or a simple baloney sandwich (hold the mustard).

We talked during lunch and in between bites. He told me about his past, his dreams of going to Florida someday, of hitting the lottery, about the Phillies, or how he won the night before at bingo. Occasionally he played a song for me on his harmonica. Christmas carols in summer, for instance. The conversations varied. He was happy to have someone — anyone — to talk to, especially someone willing to listen.

Because he was now exclusively in a wheelchair and still suffered from bad tremors, he could do very little for himself. He was able to hold his harmonica or use a remote control for his television or slowly push his wheelchair, all-important in his life, but he could not feed himself. When he tried to hold a fork, spoon, or cup he would make himself so nervous that food or drink spilled on the floor or on himself, to his anger and embarrassment. That was where I came in.

He loved watching the Phillies and Eagles on his small TV, staying up late to watch the West Coast games or listening to the ballgames on his transistor radio (which sounded familiar). A white Phillies pennant and a red Phillies cap hung on his bulletin board on the side wall, along with countless photos he had collected over the years, Polaroid snapshots of nurses, aides, and a visiting Santa Claus, plus a large, full-color cardboard Jesus. Winning the lottery was part of his master plan to move to Florida, hire a private-duty nurse to take care of him, and sit out in the sun all day, working on his tan (which he often did in the patio in the summer, much to the nurses' dismay). Hitting the lottery would just speed up the process.

"Do you want a cookie?" Teddy always offered, gesturing to the night table behind him where bags and bags of snacks sat. Good-hearted aides treated him to candy and cookies, and soon his room looked like a grocery store. The dietitian noticed he was getting a little chunky and half-seriously chastised him for eating too much junk. It got so that Teddy was giving away chocolate chip cookies to anyone passing by.

He played bingo at the nursing home, excited to win prizes like a banana. He never used bingo chips and when he did win, he let everyone know, hollering at the top of his lungs, "Bingo right here!" (his catchphrase) to the disgust of nearby residents.

Teddy was always willing to relate his fascinating history. He had been diagnosed with "mental retardation" (an outdated term now). After spending time with him and learning about his past, I seriously questioned that diagnosis and thought maybe he had been misdiagnosed all his life. He spent the first thirty-five years of his life in a local mental institution. Back in the early twentieth century when Teddy was growing up, he was shut away as an infant. It wasn't uncommon for someone deemed "different" to never be heard from again. Because of physical disabilities (cerebral palsy and a seizure disorder, which caused his limbs to be twisted and distorted, his body shaking violently), he looked and acted differently. Through no fault of his own, Teddy was "different," so his parents sent him away. Teddy could only learn from what he saw and heard. He was a product of his environment. He never received any formal education and was more or less a slave in the institution, one of the "brighter boys" who helped take care of the needier patients. When he was assimilated into the community in the seventies, he found a job at the local hospital in their laundry department. He walked to work every day, each way, for over twenty-five years. He came to us after being hit by a car while walking to a local bingo game. His fractured right hip was surgically repaired but, despite intense physical rehabilitation and plenty of determination, his broken body wouldn't cooperate.

Ted claimed to have family, but he didn't get visitors or mail. He thought he had a long-lost brother who lived somewhere in Texas, and I was given the assignment to find him. This was prior to the Internet, so tracking down his sibling "somewhere in Texas" was a tall task, to say the least. He didn't seem to mind when I reported back that my search was unsuccessful.

"I know you tried, Greg Smith," he said, smiling. "You always do."

Years later, after my Manor employment was over, I stopped in to see my special friend. He was in the same room: 211, second floor. Not much had changed, as it was with most residents. Time was frozen as Teddy "waited for God," as he put it. For old times' sake, I arrived before lunch and offered to help. With each spoonful, he smiled, his blue eyes sparkling, no words needed. We caught up on everything, from the Phillies to who left the Manor to his new roommate. Teddy knew all the gossip.

Word reached me that Teddy was dying. When I stopped in to see him, he was curled up in a fetal position in bed, side rails up, moaning as I entered the darkened room. He answered me in whispers, seeming to know I was there, peering at me through tired, glazed blue eyes, so sick. He never made it to Florida.

The snow prevented me from attending his funeral. He was buried very decently, all expenses paid by a local friend who had remained faithful to the end. In the spring I paid a visit to his final resting place, finding a small white gravestone there. The green grass was just coming in. An American flag was on the side of the marker, the same flag he had always kept taped on the side of his wheelchair. I noticed a bingo card on the flat tombstone. I added a current Phillies schedule.

Teddy had a tough life, but it was a life far more important than many. He was hard to forget. Isn't that all we could ever ask for, not to be forgotten? Residents like Ted kept me going, especially on freezing mornings when I didn't want to drag myself out of a warm bed. I knew Teddy was waiting. I couldn't let him down.

Chapter 21
Happy Birthday Mom

The nineties brought more stability to my life. My OI was under control. I was settling into work at the Manor. Mom was doing well. I continued to grow, professionally and in many other ways.

I became politically involved in my hometown. I advocated for cut curbs on every block and corner in town. It started with my very own street. I was a prisoner on my own block, unable to get off the curb independently. I wheeled to work every day, but I needed help simply crossing the street. Ridiculous! So I petitioned the borough to install cut curbs on my block. They resisted, saying there was no money for the project. I refused to take no for an answer. The recent passing of the Americans with Disabilities Act spurred me on. Under the law, physical barriers now needed to be modified. Society just needed a little nudge in doing so.

Attitudes were tough to change. I addressed Borough Council one evening asking for the curbs, not only for my use but for others in our community who might have a disability. The elderly could also take advantage of the lower curbs. The answer was still no.

Ironically, after doing some research, I found that cut curbs were originally planned for my housing development when it was built in 1977. For some reason they were never installed. I was getting grief for something that should've been there all along! A local contractor saw the story of my campaign in the paper and volunteered his services and material to fix the curbs on my block for free. Of course, the borough let him do it. I appreciated his help. Now I could be more independent. But what about the rights of others in our town who needed cut curbs? It wasn't just about cut curbs. It was about all physical barriers which hindered people with a disabilities and made it harder to get around. It was about awareness. Pretty soon cut curbs and ramps started springing up all over town. Things snowballed, and people got excited about making the town more accessible to everyone. Maybe it was the new ADA law. Or maybe folks just realized it was the right thing to do.

Fighting for cut curbs

I began to become more aware of my own surroundings. Were there enough handicapped parking spaces? It was always frustrating when the special accessible spots were taken at the store, especially when the last one was filled by a guy walking out of his vehicle. With the ADA law, new buildings had to be accessible. Old buildings would need to be modified where possible. Things were changing, in a good way, and a whole new world was opening up.

———

Mom was visiting the local pharmacy one afternoon and felt dizzy. She rested in a lounge chair until the ambulance arrived. I knew something was wrong when my brother Mark met me at home after work with the news that Mom had a heart attack.

They considered doing angioplasty, but the blockage in her heart was too severe. Several arteries were up to ninety percent clogged. Quadruple bypass surgery would be done at the University of Pennsylvania Hospital in Philadelphia. I couldn't help but remember the many times I had been transferred down to the city by ambulance. The thirty-minute drive down the Schuylkill Expressway seemed like forever. Penn was a maze of a hospital, much larger and more modern than the old Children's Hospital. I was glad Mom was at one of the finest hospitals in the world.

I held her hand the morning of the surgery. She counted her rosary beads in silence as we quietly talked. *Please, God . . . listen to her prayers.* She had been such a good person all her life. I was glad to be there for her, as she had always been there for me. I offered encouragement and hope, yet there were doubts in my mind that I would ever see her again. I was still the one who needed extra faith.

Her strong, caring heart needed repair. Her heart had been through so much in those eighty years. She was a fighter, and she made it through the bypass surgery. I was scared when I saw her afterward, even though the doctors and nurses warned us what to expect. But every day she got stronger, and every day they started to take tubes and machines away. She was walking soon after surgery. In a few weeks, she was home.

Mom's overall recovery took about six weeks. I did the best I could at home. My first time alone. I ordered out or went out to eat and found that expensive. Keeping the house going, making sure the bills were paid, the normal things adults do, were all new to me. My siblings did what they could. One ran my dress shirts to the laundromat and dry cleaners. I couldn't button the top button on my shirt (because of my deformed arms). I never could touch my own shoulders. My sister Phyllis would come over before work and helped me.

It's true what they say about not really missing someone until they are gone. I was getting a taste of life without Mom. I didn't like thinking too much about the future. She wasn't going to be around forever. Would I ever be able to take care of the house on my own? Mari wasn't going to be a part of my life, so I needed to start thinking about life without Mom.

The nights were especially lonely. I locked up, turned out the lights, and retired to my room. Louie, our new Pekinese puppy, joined me. I was glad to have company and protection. Every night I mistakenly thought I heard Mom come home from bingo like usual and poke her head in my room. If I was awake, she always stuck her head inside the door and said, "Nothing," or, "I won five bucks."

When Mom did return home, she went through a brief period of depression, something the doctors told me was normal. She was slowing down and felt sad she couldn't do all the things she used to do. Mom was a whirlwind to do what she did. She hated to be dependent on others, and I couldn't blame her. In time, she began driving again and doing most of the things she had done before the surgery, especially going to church, visiting sick friends, going to bingo, and attending just about every funeral in town.

For the family, it was more of a wake-up reminder that she wasn't going to be with us forever. That was how her surprise eightieth birthday party came to be. She had never had a party before in her life. It was time, and she deserved one. So, the family got together and started planning.

We rented the local Veterans of Foreign War hall, hired a caterer to make the food, sent out the invitations, bought the decorations, and got a DJ to spin the music. The hardest part was keeping it a secret from Mom. We thought about telling her, then realized she would never want it. Oh, maybe deep down inside she did, but Mom was humble, and I couldn't see her agreeing to a party that she knew about. No shindig for Mom. She would rather spend her birthday playing bingo. Maybe a party would really tick her off? Maybe we should reconsider? But a landmark birthday like this shouldn't go unnoticed. Mom deserved the love and recognition more than anyone, especially after her heart surgery. She was a special lady. For instance, as they were wheeling her to her bypass surgery, she was more worried about what I was going to have for lunch that afternoon. "Make sure you eat!" were her last words before she went into the operating room.

That was Mom. Always thinking of others. I think she knew how much she was loved by her family and friends, but just in case, we were going to make sure she knew.

The big party was scheduled for Sunday, April 11. We invited close family members, friends, and especially her beloved bingo buddies. Practically all of Phoenixville would be there. Only it wasn't for her funeral, as she always mused; it would be for a much happier occasion.

As April 11 neared and all the party plans had been finalized, the last item was how to get Mom to the party and keep it a surprise. She attended a regular bingo in town on Sunday afternoons if she didn't make a big dinner (usually her signature spaghetti and meatballs) for the family. What excuse could we give her to bag bingo?

My sister suggested to trump bingo with bingo by telling her there was a new bingo opening at the Veterans of Foreign Wars hall that afternoon. If she wanted to go, Phyllis would even pick her up.

Late morning of April 11, after Mom returned home from Mass, Phyllis came over to take her to afternoon "bingo." Mom knew all the bingos in the area. She was suspicious and asked if we were throwing her a party. I looked at Phyllis like, "Should we lie?"

"It is a party!" Mom said, having coffee at the kitchen table. "I knew it! You two are pretty sneaky!"

When she found out the truth, she was more annoyed than I ever imagined. She didn't like the attention and threatened to stay home, saying, "Go have the party without me."

"But it's your birthday," I pleaded. I tried to convince her that she deserved the party. Friends and family were coming from all over. The party was for them, too. It was a chance for everyone to show Mom how much they cared. "Please don't ruin the surprise. Go and have fun," I begged.

Begrudgingly, she relented, steadfast that she would have a terrible time, and this was going to be "a birthday I will never forget." That was true, but in a good way, because when she got to the hall she was surprised (or she did a good acting job) at the amount of people who had filled the VFW. When she saw the amount of work involved — from the decorations to the food to the beautiful cake — she eased up and actually smiled.

She was most impressed that her bingo buddies had taken time off to be at the party. They skipped afternoon bingo to pay tribute to Mom, a high honor (there was an evening bingo to attend, anyway). Everyone sang "Happy Birthday," the cake was cut, and all was well.

Later that night, as she sat in her favorite chair in the living room, stabbing at her vanilla birthday cake with a plastic fork, she read all her birthday cards. She had the funny habit of marking the back of each card with the dollar amount that was in the card. (When she died, I found a big cardboard box full of hundreds of cards over the years — Birthday, Christmas, Get Well. She saved every one). She admitted the party was nice. Someone videotaped the event and she would watch it now and then, especially years later when a few of the partygoers were gone. Many of her older friends died before her. Aunt Sue died a few years after the party. Mom would always have the memories of such a happy occasion.

Her ninetieth birthday party went much easier. In fact, she helped plan it: no need to keep it a surprise this time. It was held at the VFW again. New faces replaced old ones who had died, new grandchildren and daughters-in-law from ten years before.

Only a few years earlier, Mom had both of her knees replaced. Arthritis had worn her knees down to the point where she could hardly walk without pain. For Mom to complain, we knew it had to be bad. She bartered with the orthopedic surgeon that if he didn't do both knees at the same time (which, at her age and with her history of heart problems, wasn't the best course of action), she wouldn't have the procedure at all. He reluctantly gave in.

She came through the operation like a champ. Eighty-five years young and a pair of brand-new knees! Mom never had problems with her knees after that. She used a cane but still drove a car into her nineties.

So there she was at her ninetieth birthday party, holding court and her cane as she greeted the crowded receiving line of people, dressed in her favorite color: sky blue. At her eightieth, she went from table to table to see her guests. This time they came to her as she thanked everyone for coming.

"The next party is when you turn one hundred, Ann," someone encouraged her.

"I won't make it," she said, smiling. "But I do have to hang around and take care of Greg."

———

It was the first time I wore a tuxedo. I was afraid I might look like a short, squat penguin, but Mom thought I looked "snazzy" in the black-and-white tux. Mom teased me about "finding a single girl" at the wedding and how good I looked.

Mark asked me to be best man at his wedding. It meant a lot to me. I always hated weddings. I could never see myself getting married after Mari, and I thought I was destined to be alone forever.

Weddings also meant dancing. I never danced, even in my chair. I always felt out of place at weddings. But when Mark asked me, I immediately said yes, I would be honored.

Thinking of a witty, yet sincere, toast for the reception was a challenge. It was my job to make the champagne toast, and I wracked my brain about what to say for weeks prior to the event. ("To be or not to be?" "Four score and seven years ago?") The main advice I got was "Keep it short," along with "Don't try too hard to be funny." Use humor. Say something clever and original, just don't try to be funny. I got it. I always had a good sense of humor, but it wasn't wise to try a stupid joke which could potentially be embarrassing for years.

Best man

October had never been so beautiful. Refreshingly cool (after a really hot summer), sunny with sapphire-blue skies. The ceremony went off without a hitch. I didn't lose the wedding ring, which was big. My brother and his new wife, Tracey, thanked me afterward, like I had done something special. They were the special ones for asking me to be a part of their special day.

The reception site was a historic building outside of town. I didn't know there were a few flights of stairs to reach the reception room. I never did get along with a flight of stairs. I imagined closing my eyes as a couple of guys took my chair up and down the stairs. Or, I could go up on my own, on my rear end, one step at a time. One way or another, I couldn't back out. I was giving the big toast.

Luckily the bride's cousin was a college football player at Penn State. He was a huge defensive end. Three hundred pounds, six-five in height. He offered to come to my rescue. Stairs? What stairs? No problem! He merely lifted the entire wheelchair — with me in it — and carried it up the two flights (it's nice to have Superman on your side).

Red wine was at the table. I was never much of a drinker, but a glass wouldn't hurt. I toasted the newly married couple with champagne. I couldn't think of anything clever to say, so I just spoke from the heart. The booze helped me relax.

Mark, a little blitzed himself, found me and clued me in on another wedding tradition: the groom and his best man always do a vodka shot together. Straight up. It was only a small shot glass. Down the hatch it went! Moments later, the room started spinning. I could've been cited for drunk driving. Toes were nearly crushed. I felt like doing wheelies, but my hands were unable to push the chair, let alone steer.

"I think I've had enough," I informed Mom. Superman carried the chair back down the steps at the end of the night.

Mom and I quietly celebrated the year 2000. When I was a kid back in the fifties and sixties, 2000 seemed a long way away, like it was science fiction, a time we would never reach. I videotaped all the celebrations of the new millennium on TV. Uncle Henry and Aunt Sue, our annual New Year's Eve guests, were gone. I was grateful and blessed that Mom was doing so well after her health scares the last few years.

Sadly, our run of good luck and health wouldn't last too much longer.

Chapter 22
New Paths to Follow

The Manor was my dream job, but things were changing at the nursing home. Staff came and went and the quality of care, the food, even the physical environment weren't what they used to be. Mrs. Anderson tried to address all the issues; I knew she was getting a lot of heat from corporate, who did their own annual inspection ahead of the state. They didn't like what they saw. Mrs. Anderson was especially overwhelmed by the open beds. That winter we lost over forty residents to illness, discharge, or death. No matter how hard we tried, we couldn't keep the beds filled. Residents had the flu and were sent directly to the hospital. Some came back, some died, and some were taken to other facilities by their disgruntled families. Our census plummeted from one hundred and forty to just under a hundred. Open beds meant no money coming in. The hospital also went dry with referrals. Other local competing nursing homes were going through the same thing. It was a fierce fight to admit patients from the surrounding hospitals and rehab centers in our area. We started getting a bad reputation in the community. Everything seemed to snowball.

Then the state came in, and it was a bloodbath. My department wasn't affected, but it was a team effort at the Manor, and we all suffered from the consequences. The deficiencies piled up. We were given only so much time to fix everything before the inspectors returned, or else we would start being fined every day. The corporate big shots came back and asked Mrs. Anderson to step down. Demanded she step down would be the more appropriate way to put it. She wasn't even given a chance to clean up the deficiencies. They thought she was too old and couldn't do the job anymore.

It was sad. Mrs. Anderson could be tough, but she was fair and treated everyone with respect. Most of all, she cared about her residents, often leaving her office to check the units herself and talk to residents and families. It wasn't just a business to her, and that's what got her in the end, because corporate saw it only as a bottom-line business.

Her last day was heartbreaking. She sat in my office, slumped in a chair, softly saying, "Well, Greg, we have been through a lot together, haven't we?" She became administrator way back when I started as a volunteer. Twenty years earlier. I always imagined she would retire gracefully, on her own terms, with a big retirement party and tears of joy. Instead there were tears, but not happy ones.

She was so beaten. "Maybe it is time . . ." she said, her words trailing off. This nursing home was her life, her heart and soul for many years. It kept her going after her husband died. Now she was being forced to give it up.

"The last thing I'm going to do," she said, looking up at me, "is give you a raise. They have been low-balling you for a long time. You deserve it. They can't stop me from doing that."

I thanked her for everything. "You gave me a chance when others wouldn't. I won't forget you."

Several months later, I heard Mrs. Anderson was volunteering with the Red Cross. It was good she was staying active and helping others in need. That was her. That was her life.

After she left, things changed, and not for the better. The Director of Nursing was appointed by corporate to be the new administrator. She just so happened to have her administrator's license. Let's call her Nurse Ratchet.

She rarely saw eye-to-eye with me. I suspected both physical and verbal abuse by a pair of new aides against certain residents. I took my suspicions to her, as was my duty as an advocate and social worker. I was shut down even though I had heard the shouts and swearing myself. Obviously she didn't want any trouble reported on her watch. I filed reports and documented what I saw and heard and what the residents told me. It was up to Administration and Nursing to investigate.

The new administrator wanted "her people" on board as department heads. I stayed on, with heads rolling all around me. Somebody had to take the blame for the terrible state survey. Corporate was pleased, but the same aides suspected of abuse could keep their jobs.

We worked hard to clean up the deficiencies. The state came back and gave us the green light to stay in business. We started admitting people off the streets just to fill the beds. Literally. Even the homeless. Residents were being moved to other rooms and units without their consent or without their families approving, merely for financial reasons. This was against Residents' Rights, as I pointed out to the new administrator. My protests fell on deaf ears, and I was left to explain to shocked residents and families. I was running out of excuses.

Once we were clear with the state, the new leader resumed her campaign to clean house. Any allegiance to Mrs. Anderson had to go. I was called down to the office and told I "wasn't keeping up" with my work. I had no assistant, as the corporation thought better and decided to save the salary of an extra staff person. I was doing the best I could as two social workers in one, plus going nuts with admissions trying to fill the beds.

An elderly woman by the name of Mrs. Hampton was admitted directly to the third floor. Mrs. Hampton suffered from advanced Alzheimer's, among many other health concerns. At times she recognized family, but for the most part she was extremely confused, babbling and often calling out for no apparent reason. Per her social history, she was once a very refined and dignified lady, a devoted wife, mother, and churchgoer.

Her husband seemed to be a friendly guy, visiting frequently, sometimes two or three times daily, often during meals. He always insisted his wife remain in bed. The family could be demanding with staff; for example, if lunch was even a few minutes late, the husband would walk down the long hall to the nurse's station and complain. Care Plan Conferences, which generally ran fifteen to twenty minutes per case, escalated to an hour when it came to discussing Mrs. Hampton's care, allowing the family time to vent their long list of complaints.

The staff tried to remain calm and patient with the Hamptons, knowing Mr. Hampton felt guilty because he could not take care of his wife at home. He had an extremely difficult time coping with her confusion. He refused offers to attend support groups, and counseling from our behavior specialists fell on deaf ears.

I had a good relationship with Mr. Hampton as he stopped by every day to check on his wife, and I spent a considerable amount of time listening to his concerns. I only saw his son, Jackson Hampton, Esquire, at meetings, since he worked as a local attorney and only visited at night.

Every time I did encounter the son, he eyed me in a peculiar way, sizing me up with a frown before speaking. When he did address me, it was not in a friendly way. Instead his tone was patronizing, as if he were speaking to a child. During conferences, he seemed to isolate me as a source of many of the problems concerning his mother at the Manor, even concerns I had nothing to do with, including healing bedsores or making sure she was dressed in one of her favorite housecoats in bed every day.

Since our new administrator did not attend the meetings, I took the brunt of the complaints. But it was more than being a sounding board. I was used to hearing complaints from disgruntled families over the years. Something was different about this family, especially the son. I began to think I was being paranoid about this family until other staff noticed the same thing. Word began to trickle down to me from the night shift that Jackson had voiced an issue with the fact that I was the social worker caring for his mother. I had never had a problem with her, Mr. Hampton, or even the son, for that matter. Since I knew they could be demanding, I made sure I dotted my Is and crossed my Ts when it came to documentation, answering their calls and requests in a timely fashion and sending out notices of future meetings well in advance.

It seemed the son had confided to one of his favorite night shift aides that he had reservations about my abilities because of my disability. Again, the old fallacy of "being in a wheelchair must mean the wheelchair user is stupid" reared its ugly head.

His complaints were heard in the new administrator's office, either by letter or phone calls, but obviously his objections to me didn't contain solid proof or justification to fire me. First, I was the only social worker in the facility. Second, when Ms. Ratchet gave me the required "warning" for no reason at all, I denied any wrongdoing, yet understood her veiled threats. Mrs. Hampton was a private-pay resident, which meant big money was involved. With a facility already struggling to fill the beds, any threats of transferring such a resident to another facility had to be met seriously.

I wasn't sure how to handle this. I didn't have Mrs. Anderson or Bridgette around to support me. I had to do something to save my job. I decided to call Jackson Hampton and have a little chat.

I was so nervous when I dialed his work number. I had been involved in many an intricate one-to-one face-off in the past, from discussing Advance Directives to family disputes, but this was a different animal. No one had ever questioned my ability to do my job solely because I used a wheelchair to get around. It seemed so idiotic, yet here I was, waiting for the receptionist to connect me.

At first, Jackson was caught off guard by my call. He immediately asked if his mother was okay and I assured him she was fine.

"Then why are you calling me? I specifically left a note in my mother's chart that I am not to be bothered at work unless it's an extreme emergency," he said.

Oops. I didn't remember seeing such a note in her chart.

I apologized, intimidated by his voice and his stance, and I backed down, mumbling something about, "I called to see how things are going," or something really lame like that.

"I'm sorry. I am extremely busy right now," he replied. "What's the real reason you called?"

If he wanted the real reason, I'd give him the real reason.

"Mr. Hampton, do you have a problem with my ability to help care for your mother?" I asked, shocked at my own courage.

"Whatever do you mean?" he replied. The irritation in his voice was replaced by surprise.

"Does it have anything to do with my disability?"

"That's ridiculous! Why would you think that? I'm disappointed you would think of me in that way," he said, trying to make me feel defensive. It worked. Maybe I was wrong after all? I suddenly felt like a worm. Had I made the situation even worse?

"Okay," I relented. "I'm sorry. I just had to ask — "

"Wait, Mr. Smith. I'm actually glad you called," he cut me off. Glad I called? After telling me he should not be called at work? What was up? "I want you to leave a copy of my mothers' Residents' Rights with my father. I'll pick it up tonight when I visit. Can you do that for me, please?"

"Sure, Mr. Hampton. I'll make a copy and run it up to your father right away," I replied quietly.

"All right, then. I will see you at the next meeting in a few weeks." And that was that. I exhaled, hoping I was in his good graces.

I made the copy, folded it, and stuck it in an envelope before dropping it off with Mr. Hampton, who was dozing in a chair next to his wife's bed when I entered the room. He awoke to my knocking on the open door, assuring me that his son would get the paperwork. "God bless" was his usual parting line.

That brings us to why I was sitting in the new administrator's office on that overcast morning in March. The canopy of clouds outside was a sign of the impending storm inside. Was it yet another warning that I "wasn't keeping up?" If it involved the Hamptons, I expected to hear about the phone call. I did check and couldn't find a note in front of Mrs. Hampton's chart. Whatever. I had already made up my mind that I would take my lumps for that one and move on.

Instead, Nurse Ratchet walked from behind her desk, shut the door, and produced two wads of crumpled and torn white paper, along with a ripped envelope. "What is this?" she demanded.

"Paper," I replied. I didn't mean to be a smartass; I just didn't know what else to say.

She didn't find that humorous. She informed me those two crumpled pieces of paper were the same Residents' Rights I had left with Mr. Hampton the night before.

"Why on earth would you ever stuff anything, let alone a document, into an envelope like this, and give it to a family member?" she roared.

"I didn't," I replied, horrified. I took the wrinkled paper from her. Yep, it may have been the same Residents' Rights forms I had copied. But I didn't give them to the old man that way. I would never do something unprofessional like that. My mind raced, and I tried to remember exactly how I had folded the paper and sealed the envelope the day before. No, I wasn't going crazy.

"Well then, how do you explain this?" She stared at me with her icy eyes.

"I can't," I admitted.

Clearly, either Mr. Hampton opened the envelope, examined the contents, then hastily stuffed them back into the envelope, or the son had set me up. I couldn't explain the situation, only that I had this sinking feeling in my stomach. The inability to perform a basic task, such as folding two pieces of paper and neatly placing them inside an envelope before sealing the contents, fed into Jackson's discriminating and stereotypical view that I was a half-wit. For something so ridiculous, my Manor days were doomed.

Back then, the Americans with Disabilities Act was only in its infancy. Now there are laws protecting people with disabilities from unfair practices in the workplace. But that was then, and this is now. Instead of fighting, I felt defeated. How could anyone do such a thing? My faith in mankind took a direct hit, and I sank deeper in my chair.

"Greg, we can't have this," Nurse Ratchet decided, standing over me like a pet owner scolding a puppy for peeing on the floor. I was told to give my two weeks or be terminated. After ten years at the Manor as a social worker and part-time worker and volunteer, I was being forced to leave. She didn't care about all the good work I had done for so many years. She didn't care I would be unemployed. Soon I would be sending out resumes, a world I thought I had abandoned for good long ago.

Those final two weeks were rough. The residents couldn't believe I was leaving. Residents like Liz were smart enough to know I wasn't happy. But we had to make it seem like I was "retiring" — at age forty — because my health was deteriorating. "Don't tell the residents the truth, or else you may upset them," I was advised. A "retirement party" would make it official. No hard feelings?

I visited all my residents as often as I could as the clock ticked down on my life at the nursing home. I heard the new administrator was already interviewing for my position. Most of the staff were sorry to see me go. "What are we going to do without Greg?"

They did throw me a party. Many residents were there. Even Ms. Ratchet showed up to "wish me well in my retirement." There were balloons and cake and tears. After the party, I wheeled down the halls one last time. I passed room 211 where I used to feed Teddy lunch every day; the third-floor lounge area where I would read to Mary; the therapy room where I offered encouragement to the residents; the gift shop where I first started as a volunteer. So many memories.

I cleaned out my desk and wheeled home.

Little did I know, only an hour after I said farewell to my residents, Dee would be leaving Woodland Center for the day. Pulling out of the parking lot she was broad-sided by a speeding driver. She sustained multiple serious injuries. The Jaws of Life rescued her from the wreckage. Airlifted to a Philadelphia hospital, she would live but not be able to work again for close to a year.

The unexpected call from Woodland Center came first thing Monday morning. They had no idea I had worked at the Manor for ten years or that I had left. It was just luck. They needed a social worker in a bad way and still had my resume on file. They wanted to know if I was interested and, if so, would I come in for an interview as soon as possible? I met with the assistant administrator that very day. I was offered a job in their Pre-Admission Department, and I accepted.

I was happy to find a job so quickly and so close to home. I arranged paratransit as my transportation every day. Woodland Center understood if I was a little late at times: I was at the mercy of the transit system. I got to know the drivers, and it was like riding in the taxi again. I rode with senior citizens and people with disabilities. For three dollars each way, it was a way to get back and forth to and from work.

I was the first person families contacted when seeking a care facility. Normally I would do an intake interview over the phone, but sometimes we had walk-ins. A big part of my job was doing tours. Some days I did as many as five tours a day. Since it was an enormous building, a tour could take a good twenty or thirty minutes as I answered questions and described the many things our place had to offer. I had the basic speech down to a T. It was a key position, with families deciding from the tour (along with written information and brochures), if they wanted to come back for a full interview with Nursing and the Business Office with the intent to admit. If someone was being admitted, I did a social history for the social worker who would be following the case.

It was interesting because, like my first job at Aging, you just never knew who was going to be touring or doing a social history at my desk. I was making a difference again. I was always good at listening, offering encouragement, and feeling compassion for others. (Computers and paperwork? Not so much.) When families expressed sadness, guilt, or hopelessness over placing their loved one in a nursing home, I was jolly-on-the-spot to offer comfort and advice.

More often than not, I never saw the resident. Only families. I did miss the one-on-one interaction with the residents and working on the units. Now the only time I saw a resident or a unit was during a tour. But I didn't complain. It was a job, and the county, which owned the facility, treated their employees well. The Manor would always be home. But I liked the Woodland Center enough that I stayed there for the next seventeen years.

––––––––

My Manilow friend Vicki called me after 9/11. Manilow was playing at Radio City Music Hall in the heart of Manhattan on February 8, 2002. Vicki was planning on flying up from Florida and renting a stretch limo (along with three other female fans) to the concert and back home. She was ordering tickets and asked if I wanted to go.

It was always special when Barry played his hometown. This show promised to be extra special after the tragedy at the World Trade Center. I said yes right away. It had been a while since I had seen Manilow, and I got excited at the opportunity. Plus, riding to New York and back with four women wasn't a bad deal.

There was only one hitch: Mari would be there.

Vicki and Mari hit it off when the latter was in America, and they had kept in touch all those years. Mari was going to be in New York City in February on business, and she wanted to see more of the city. September 11 touched her as it did everyone. Vicki got her a ticket to the concert. The plan was to meet her at the show.

"You don't have to talk to her if you don't want to," Vicki reassured me. "But our tickets are all together. I hope you still want to go."

Why not? I hadn't done anything wrong. I had always treated Mari with love. Why should I deprive myself of a terrific time because of what happened ten years ago? Life was too short. I was over her.

It was freezing cold outside when the black limousine pulled into our driveway. I ventured out, all bundled up in winter attire: coat, sweater, gloves, you name it. Vicki was already in a good mood and may have been hitting the mini bar in the limo on the way to Phoenixville. I knew the other three girls from the fan club. Husbands and boyfriends were home this evening, babysitting or watching sports. We headed north as the purple dusk fell.

The girls talked Manilow, laughing and drinking as we motored up the New Jersey Turnpike. Our driver, a jovial guy named Tom, peppered the gang with questions about why we were going, why we liked Manilow, general small talk. He wasn't a fan, and the girls got on him. How could you not like Barry? They were determined to convert him by the end of the trip. Vicki brought along a few Manilow CDs and blasted the music to the point where Tom had no choice but listen (if he wanted a tip). I pretty much stayed quiet, looking out the window. Vicki noticed how unusually passive I was, especially around her, and she looked at me and said, "It's going to be okay."

I wondered what I would say to Mari after all this time.

9/11 really hit home as we approached New York. Usually the first thing we saw were the Twin Towers majestically looming in the distance. The skyline wasn't the same, and neither was life. It was cold and it was winter, and everything seemed so sad. Spring was so far away.

We waited to get into the Holland Tunnel. It was rush hour, and traffic was bumper to bumper. The toll-taker asked Tom, "Got anybody important in there?"

"Nah," Tom replied. "Nobody important." Nobody important? We jokingly got on him about that.

We slowly cruised past Times Square, the "crossroads of the world." It seemed smaller than it appeared every New Year's Eve on TV. We saw the lights in the sky from the area where the World Trade Center used to be. They were working there, 24/7.

Suddenly we stopped in front of one of the best hotels in Manhattan. I wondered if we had stopped because of traffic. Mari came bounding in, looking more beautiful than ever. I thought we were meeting her at the show, but Vicki felt we could pick her up on the way.

Mari sat across from me as Vicki introduced everyone. "And you know Greg, of course," she said awkwardly. Mari smiled and I smiled back with a slight wave.

She wore all black — long coat, boots, gloves — which looked stunning with her shorter blond hair. She was approaching forty now but still looked like the beautiful young girl I had first met in New York, seemingly ages ago. My heart fluttered, but I told myself I was under control.

Radio City wasn't far from there. We took pictures in front of the iconic landmark. It was windy in the center of Manhattan, skyscrapers everywhere we looked. It was too early to go into the theater, so we ducked into a small restaurant nearby to get out of the cold. We ordered sixteen-dollar salads and glasses of wine. We toasted our night and looked forward to a great show together. I caught myself often glancing at Mari.

We had fantastic seats for the show, center and halfway up the theater. The concert was predictably emotional and fun, as Manilow tried to lift every one's spirits through music. His current song, "Turn the Radio Up," was a feel-good, upbeat tune about how "everything will be all right." Near the end, former President Bill Clinton made a surprise appearance on stage and accepted a $100,000 check from Barry to the relief fund for victims' families of 9/11. Manilow had graciously donated his earnings from the show to the cause. The end to a hell of a show!

I got into the limo first as Tom folded the wheelchair into the trunk. It was strange how everyone else hung in the lobby of Radio City, all but Mari.

"May I join you?" she asked, opening the door.

"Sure. Get out of the cold. It's freezing!" I encouraged. "Another limo," I said with a slight nervous laugh. "We've got to stop meeting like this."

She sat next to me, suddenly giving me a warm hug and whispering, "I'm so sorry, Greg."

"I'm sorry too," I said. All this time, the anger, the bitterness, the hurt, the words I planned to rant if we ever met again . . . all disappeared. "It was all so stupid. It was like a fairy tale. I just didn't want it to end," I said after a quiet moment, my eyes misting. There I went again, always the sentimental one. "I should have written to you, but I didn't know what to say."

"I understand," she whispered. "And it wasn't stupid. Thank you for making it a fairy tale. It was all because of you, and I'll never forget it."

Mari thankfully broke the ensuing awkward silence by asking, "How's your Mom? And Peewee?"

"Mom is good. She had some health problems but she's good now. And we have a new dog named Louie."

"Tell everyone I said hi," she said, still looking sad.

"I will."

"I wanted to see you before . . ." Her voice trailed off. She knew I had noticed her diamond engagement ring at dinner.

"I'm happy for you," I said, my hands slightly shaking, even though it was warm inside the limo.

"Thanks." She hugged me again. "I'll always have a special place in my heart for you."

"Same here," I confided.

Just then Vicki knocked on the window. "Can we come in? It's damn cold out here and they kicked us out of the lobby!"

We dropped Mari off at her hotel, and she gave me a kiss on the cheek before she got out of the limo, disappearing into the New York City chill. That was the last time I saw her.

The ride home was quiet. We were all exhausted. Some of us were reflective. I was the first one to be dropped off at home. It was around two a.m., and I was beat.

"Did you have fun?" Vicki asked me before I left the limo.

"I did. Thanks for everything. Talk to you soon."

So what was I expecting? Mari to fall into my arms and stay for good? Not really. Maybe we just needed closure. I really was happy for her. We could both move on with life now.

Chapter 23

No Place Like Home

I was slowly coming out of my shock. I waited in the small cubicle of the Emergency Room with Mom after having just broken my femur in front of the medical facility. The ER medical staff were still debating what to do with me. I lay on the gurney, misty eyes meeting my mother's beautiful blue ones. She was trembling with fear. My right thigh pulsated, even though much of the pain had subsided thanks to the cocktail of medication they pumped into me every so often. Hard to believe our devastating fall had only been an hour earlier. It seemed like ages had passed, with so much happening in our suddenly shattered life.

They decided to admit me to the hospital. The operating room was booked, so I couldn't have surgery until the following morning. Upstairs, several nurses and orderlies lifted me into bed. From then on, they promised to use a sheet underneath me to transfer. Anytime they asked me to roll from one side or the other, to slide a bedpan underneath or change a wet sheet, it hurt. The nurses hooked me up to an IV drip filled with morphine, and I finally settled down.

Dr. Hoss stopped by in the late afternoon. He was my new orthopedic doctor after Dr. Nicholson retired. Dr. Hoss was a rare local physician who knew about my condition. He once told me I was his one and only OI patient in all his years practicing orthopedic medicine. I was a rare bird, for sure.

The doc told me what to expect from the surgery the next day. They would keep me comfortable until the fracture was fixed. I knew the routine, having been down this road many times before.

Mom stayed with me until visiting hours were over at eight p.m. "Go home and get some rest," I told her. "You need to take care of yourself, Mom. I'll be all right."

"I'll be here waiting for you," she promised, like so many times before. She kissed me on the cheek before leaving. If I knew Mom, there would be several rosaries said before the night was over.

Alone, I rested my head on the soft, cool pillow. This was my first fracture in God knew how long.

A nurse interrupted my daydreams when she briskly walked into the private room to check my vitals. "Whatever you have to do," I replied, smiling a little. A pretty nurse always made me smile.

She introduced herself as Mindy. She offered a pack of crackers and juice. "You can't have anything to eat or drink after midnight. Get it while the getting is good," she advised sweetly.

I declined the offer. I didn't have much of an appetite. I didn't even eat my dinner — baked chicken and a salad. Instead I ate the dessert: a cup of strawberry ice cream. I smiled as I wolfed down the frozen treat. *Just like one of my residents at work*, I thought. *Dessert first.*

No matter how hard I tried, I couldn't fall asleep, exhausted yet too tired to sleep. I didn't want to watch television. I missed my music. I missed my dog. I started thinking . . . and praying . . . and worrying. I hadn't had surgery since I was a kid. There would be a cast. And rehab. What about my job? Everything was on hold. I asked Mom to call my supervisor. I didn't want to get into trouble. Maybe I should go into work tomorrow after the surgery? My thinking plummeted from barely sane to irrational mode in no time at all.

My eyes blurry, I swore I saw my late father standing at the foot of the bed.

"You'll be okay, Butch," he said. "Hang in there. We'll go to a game sometime . . ." Dad disappeared into thin air like a wisp of smoke.

And just like that I eased into twilight sleep. I didn't care if I woke up or not, knowing what was coming the next day. I just wanted to sleep. Finally, no pain. My entire body felt so light, like a feather on a breeze. I didn't care anymore about . . . anything. I just didn't want to hurt. Pain, all my life. Now, let me rest . . . let me dream. Drifting into even deeper sleep, the world faded to black.

———

"I hope we can save him . . ."

Those were the first words I heard. I was in a deep fog. Nothing made sense. I heard voices calling me. "Greg, wake up!" Voices talking among themselves. "What's his pulse? It looks like he's coming out of it — "

I slowly opened my eyes and saw four nurses on either side of my bed, patting my face and hands, extra blankets covering my violently shaking body up to my neck. Why couldn't I stop shaking? "Hi," I moaned, still groggy, not clear as to what was going on.

"Hi back," one nurse replied, not smiling. I recognized her as Mindy, the night-nurse I had met earlier. "Stay awake, Greg . . . that's it. Open your eyes for me."

My eyes opened wider, the fog beginning to lift. Was it morning already?

"That's it! Stay awake! You had us worried there for a minute . . ."

There was a problem with the morphine drip. The machine either malfunctioned or I had pressed the button one too many times. I was overdosed and luckily Mindy had found me. I trembled from a cold sweat. Mindy told me to stay alert. Satisfied by my rapid consciousness, the nurses finally left the room. I was too frightened to sleep now.

All I thought about after that was going home. I hoped I didn't wake Mom when I called her later that night. She couldn't sleep, either. She was still feeling guilty about our accident. Mom said that Louie spent the night under my wheelchair in my bedroom. I didn't tell her about the bad experience with the morphine. She didn't need to worry.

The next morning I was ready for surgery. I expected to wake up in less pain, all casted up and on the road to recovery. Instead I woke up during the surgery. Yes, I literally woke up for a few moments during the surgery! I was sitting in some sort of trapeze-like chair, and I screamed. Instantly I was out again.

Dr. Hoss came to see me after I got back to my room. "Was it real? I asked.

"You felt it, didn't you?" he asked, almost in a whisper.

I nodded in reply. It wasn't a dream or a hallucination. But I had another bone to pick with Dr. Hoss (pardon the pun). I didn't know a "spike cast" meant plaster up to my chest. I wouldn't be able to sit up for eight weeks. What the hell? He knew I was upset and agreed to come back later in the afternoon to cut the cast down a bit. He did need the leg to stay in that position to heal. That was why they had me in the trapeze-like chair during surgery while he set the bone.

There was talk of sending me to a nursing home to recover. I didn't expect Mom to take care of me. She needed to take care of herself. I agreed to whatever plan the doctor, discharge planner, and Mom had in mind. How ironic would it be if I ended up being a resident at Woodland Center or even my former home, the Manor?

But Mom had other ideas. She put an end to any talk of sending me anywhere but home. She insisted she would be fine. She had taken care of me when I was laid-up all my life, and she wasn't about to stop now. Mom was Mom.

Two days later, just like when I was a kid, I was happy to finally go home. The deal was to set up a hospital bed in the living room. My bedroom was much too small for an ambulance crew and a stretcher when they would come to take me for future doctor appointments. A visiting nurse stopped by every weekday to help Mom. She gave me a sponge bath every other day. How I missed taking a hot shower!

Changing the sheets was still an ordeal. I slid down to the bottom of the bed, and the nurse and Mom hoisted me back into position. I could sit up a little since Dr. Hoss had altered the cast. Soup wasn't spilling all over myself or the bed (most of the time). I was still on huge amounts of painkillers. Percocet was the drug of choice, and it worked well several times a day. But along with the painkiller came consequences of constipation and all those other wonderful side effects. I also wore a morphine patch, which really helped. I wasn't worried about getting "hooked," not just yet, and neither was the care team, as the fractured femur was still healing.

It wasn't the most private thing, having a hospital bed in the living room, but we made do. Sometimes neighbors or friends walked in during a private moment (such as urinal duty). There was no privacy. Modesty was put on hold. The house had turned into a temporary MASH unit. I forgot all the little nuances of being laid-up. Visitors and calls were always welcome, but so was sleep, especially after a dose of painkiller.

Louie didn't know me at first. He jumped on the sofa and stared at me. "Daddy, why are you in bed . . . in the living room?" I wanted to hug the little fella. I missed the days of coming home from work, riding down on the paratransit van's hydraulic lift, and tossing an empty water bottle high in the air to Lou. He always got a kick out of that. He would let it bounce once in the driveway, scoop it up, and run for the house, leaving me behind. Every day Louie and Mom waited for me on the front porch. It was the same routine for thirteen years when they saw the van pull up: throw the plastic bottle, make the grab, then run like hell into the house. Lou would play with the bottle for a few minutes, crunching it up, then trot away in search of the next toy. God help me if ever I forgot the bottle. If looks could kill . . .

I lay there, alone at night after Mom turned in, thinking. Would I ever be myself again? I had worked so hard to get where I was. I listened to my little transistor radio like in the old days, and some nights I cried. I never let Mom see that. I had to keep my hopes high. Without hope, there is nothing.

Life had come full circle. I was recovering from a bad fracture again, just like thirty or forty years earlier. And as I listened to the soft music playing from my radio, I gave myself a mini-pep talk.

Get well soon from Richard Marx

Hey, no one had thought I would make it this far with my brittle bones, yet here I was. Not exactly where I wanted to be, in a freaking hospital bed. But I had survived tougher times than this. Hang in there and never give up hope.

Whenever I was recovering from a fracture, something would happen to lift my spirits. The same thing happened some forty years later from an unexpected well-wisher. Mom handed me a huge brown envelope from a California address. I opened it and found a glossy 8 x 10 photo from singer–songwriter Richard Marx. It was signed, "Greg, Feel better soon, Best Always, Richard." Somehow word had gotten to Richard that I had been in the hospital. It was like the old days, only without the bulletin board.

Back in 1997, I met Richard Marx for the first time. I was with a friend outside of the nearby QVC studios, where Richard was appearing to promote his new album. We weren't sure what time

With Richard Marx, 2017

he was to arrive, only that he was scheduled to appear during a segment that Sunday afternoon. I brought along a box of grape Pop Tarts, his favorite snack back then, as a surprise. We were the only two fans there, waiting for two hours in the persistent spring showers (good thing Mom didn't know).

Finally, Richard's tour bus pulled up to the studio. He got out, holding an umbrella, surprised that we were there in the rain, and asked the security guards to let us wait in the warm, dry lobby until his gig was over. He met us afterward, signed stuff, and hung out for a good ten minutes or so, chatting like we were old friends. Thus began a new bromance, one which lasts even to this day.

I always loved Richard's music. He was a talented and gifted Grammy Award-winning singer–songwriter, and even more, a great guy. Whenever our paths crossed after that April day, he was always kind and funny. Like the time I saw him at a local music store, where he was signing CDs and doing an intimate Q & A with his fans. As he was ready to take a group photo with about thirty fans, he leaned over to me in the front and whispered in my ear, "On the count of three, just as he is taking the shot, pop a wheelie!"

I met Richard many times over the years. He always had time to say hello. So, when that get-well autographed photo arrived, just when I needed it most, I was determined not to give up. I'd had plenty of fractures before. I wasn't going to let this one get me down.

———

The weeks dragged into months. X-ray and check-up appointments came and went. Before Christmas, I got the best present of all — my cast removed. It had been a solid four months since the gruesome fractured femur accident. Again, I felt like a baby chick just hatched from the shell: weak, fragile, uncertain. This time the ambulance guys took me back to my own bed. The hospital bed, thank God, was gone.

Now came my own personal rehab. The real issue was transferring on my own. I had to get over being afraid, the ever-present fear of falling. I didn't want to stay in bed any longer.

The first morning it took me close to thirty minutes to slide from my bed into my wheelchair. What was normally a three-second movement turned into a painstakingly slow and deliberate ordeal. I finally made it and let out a big sigh of relief. I was able to be independent again. Mom was a blessing, as always, but I missed my independence. Simple things like wheeling outside to get the mail. You never appreciate freedom until it's taken away.

I relearned how to transfer to the toilet (no more bedpans). I learned again how to transfer to my shower chair (no more sponge baths). It was nice to get dressed again and out of pajamas. It was nice to feel like myself again.

There was one more thing to do: get off the painkillers.

Easier said than done.

I decided I had had enough of the Percocet and its wicked side effects, so I stopped taking it. That was okay with Dr. Hoss, so we started to scale the meds down. The morphine patches were another story. The doc weaned me down from fifty percent strength to twenty-five. Still, I had nights when I went through withdrawal. Nights I couldn't sleep, watching infomercials all night. Nights I shook and broke out in cold sweats, wondering if I was going to die. Within a few days, I beat it.

By early February, five months after the accident, I was just about back to normal. I got the green light from the doctor to return to work. I was never so happy, after all those months of being inactive. I was only too glad to leave the countless crossword puzzles behind to be me again.

On my first day back, along with an office party, I had another surprise waiting for me. My supervisor was already there, bright and early, waiting for me to arrive. She said not to go across the hall to the Pre-Admissions office and instead to come into the Social Services office for a talk. An early morning "talk" was never a good thing.

I still had my job but had lost my position. I understood that I had used all my vacation time and sick days, plus extra time, when I was out. I was grateful they had saved my job. But I never expected to be reassigned to other duties. My heart sank.

I was being assigned to cover North Six, a long-term care unit in the tall North building of the sprawling complex. My caseload would be roughly seventy-five residents. Working back on the floors was what I wanted when I was hired, just like my former duties at the Manor. I missed working with residents. So why wasn't I happy?

I liked my work in Admissions. I felt like I was making a difference. I was often the first contact for families looking for placement for their loved one. They needed an understanding, compassionate person on the other end of the phone or other side of the desk when they were making that important decision. It wasn't just medical terms or dollars and cents. It was an emotional decision as well, a life-changing choice. I was good at giving folks the encouragement, support, and information they needed.

I had become the expert tour guide as well. I knew everything one could imagine on the facility, from routine numbers of total beds and what time lunch was served to more inside stuff like the results of our latest state survey. I could show a family member the entire facility, giving them information and answering any type of question they asked, and take time to listen to their concerns better than anyone in the building. I was improving at completing a comprehensive social history for the caseworker who would be following the new resident. That took a special skill as well, asking the most pertinent questions to obtain as much information as possible in order to get a true picture of the resident who was coming to the facility to live.

Alas, the powers in charge deemed that my skills were more needed elsewhere. I agreed to do whatever was asked of me. Thus, I became the social worker of North Six.

It was easy relearning how to do a care plan, write progress notes, and all the other normal social work duties I had done while at the Manor. The major differences were computers and the people. Everything, including social work, was changing over to computers. Nothing could take the place of visiting someone face-to-face, but now our notes and most forms were computerized. I never really got along with computers, going way back to my Penn days in the 1970s. It was required now, and I did the best I could with the change. I admitted it was much faster and more efficient using the machines but, call me old-school, I still missed the days of pen and paper when I could whip out a thoughtful, concise progress note and not have to worry about whether I had saved my information or not.

I soon grew familiar with my residents on North Six and their families. My same principle applied, even though it was a different nursing home: I tried to see all my residents, every day, no matter what. There was Ralph, who thought we had worked together building the nursing home long ago. "We did a hell of a job," he said, sizing up the light fixtures. There was Mrs. Pipp, ninety-seven years old and still flirting. She always liked my dimples and often commented, "If I was sixty years younger!" as she batted her eyes. She reminded me nearly once a week that she was a distant cousin of the old-time ballplayer Wally Pipp. (Pipp was best known for losing his starting first-base job to the immortal Lou Gehrig). "I never knew him. He was before my time," she said with a wink in her eye. "Now that's old!"

Meghan was only in her twenties but was with us for care after a tragic car accident. And Jake was a die-hard Eagles fan who shared stories of greats like Chuck Bednarik, Norm Van Brocklin, and Greasy Neale whenever I visited. Hundreds of resident and families. All special to me as the years went by.

————

I loved writing a column for my local newspaper called "Wheeling Around Phoenixville." I did one every other week for several years, focusing on disability issues in my community and around the country. I loved bringing inspiring stories to light, like the high-school kid in Massachusetts who only had one arm yet excelled at basketball, or rating the various Philadelphia sports venues on their accessibility to wheelchairs. It was fun stuff, and I had a devoted band of readers who followed the columns and commented on them.

In 2008, my beloved Phillies won the World Series, only their second championship in their long losing history. I thought of my father, how happy he would've been, just as I was thinking of him back in 1980 when the Phils won their first title, and later in 2017 when the Eagles won their first Super Bowl. He was a die-hard fan and I knew he was with me in spirit, celebrating at the parade. I felt he was always by my side, guiding my way and watching over me.

————

Mom started complaining about her foot. She always had problems with her feet for one reason or another — ingrown toenails, corns, bunions, you name it. Her knees were fine now, but her feet "ached" and she began using a cane. She went to a couple of foot doctors in town, just as she randomly changed chiropractors, and her right foot became infected. She quit going to the doctors, tried to treat it on her own because she didn't want anyone to "worry," and soon had trouble standing. She ended up in the hospital with gangrene of her right foot.

Mom tried her home-remedy treatments: Lourdes water, soaking her foot every night in warm water, and finally getting the right size shoes. She developed a blister, maybe from her shoes, she wasn't sure. Nothing worked. She fell in the bathroom one day while I was at work. Luckily, I had hooked her up with an emergency call system after her first fall and she was able to press the button for help. She was admitted to the hospital on the spot.

Her foot was so bad they amputated all but two toes and part of her foot. She couldn't come home just yet, so the hospital discharge planner offered a list of area nursing homes to consider. I, as power of attorney, needed to make a quick decision. Insurance wasn't going to keep her in the hospital forever. After consulting Mom, it was decided the Woodland Center would be the best place for her care needs and rehabilitation.

She was admitted downstairs to North Three, a Medicare floor. The day Mom arrived, I stopped down to see her before I went home. I didn't want to wake her. As I was leaving she opened her eyes.

"Oh, hi," she said. "Here I am." She was bummed, unlike her usual self, always positive.

"You'll be all right, Mom," I encouraged. "Work hard down in therapy and you'll be out of here in no time at all. I'll come and see you every day."

"I don't know how it got so bad," she said, starting to cry.

"Don't worry. Get stronger and you'll be coming home."

"It's a good thing you know how to take care of yourself now," she said. "I still worry about you being alone."

"I'll be fine. You don't need to worry."

"Is it time for your van?"

"Yeah, I need to go, but I'll see you tomorrow. Call me if you need anything. Ask to use the portable phone at the nurse's station."

"I will. Go home and eat. There's food in the refrigerator . . ."

"Okay, Mom," I answered.

"Say hi to Louie for me. Take care of yourself. And don't forget to water my plants."

"You eat too," I answered, wheeling to the door. "The food is pretty good here. You need to keep up your strength. See you tomorrow."

We were never ones to say "I love you" very much. I know I should've said it more. I left feeling hopeful, knowing what our therapy staff could do. Still, I had a feeling that things would never be the same again.

It was needless to tell her how I scrambled to get bank statements together for the business office and other paperwork and documentation needed to have her admitted. Mom was a bit of a hoarder, so the information wasn't exactly at my fingertips. But she knew where everything was, so if I was missing her birth certificate or another important paper, she would tell me where to find it.

Mom did very well. In fact, the very next day I found her in the therapy room sitting in a wheelchair, waiting for her turn to exercise. I stopped in to say hi on my way to North Six. She looked much better with her hair brushed, wearing her familiar clothes instead of a hospital gown. She went for rehabilitation twice a day, morning and afternoon sessions. They got her a special fitted shoe for her right foot. Soon she was walking with assistance, using a walker. Up and down the hall she went and around the busy rehab room. A few times they had to slow her down. I was so proud of her.

I spent my lunch time with her, encouraging her to eat in the dining room with the other residents. She started making friends and had a nice roommate. We brought her the small television that she had in her bedroom at home and fixed her shared windowsill with flowers. And yes, I remembered to water her plants.

For the three months she was there, she adjusted well to nursing home life. She wasn't used to having a roommate but liked the company. She enjoyed going to the weekly church services and even became one of the regular bingo players in the unit. Other than visiting her during lunch and before I left for the day, I saw her in passing. Swiftly wheeling past the clinic area, I would hear a familiar, "Hey!"

There was Mom, tiny in her wheelchair, sitting in a long line, waiting to see the eye doctor. "What are you up to?" she always asked.

"Oh, nothing, just working," I replied, and we would shoot the breeze for a moment before I continued. It was reassuring to have her there, and I'm sure it made her feel better too, knowing I was so close. My siblings visited at night when I was home with Louie, so we all had turns.

As her rehab went along and her progress continued, verified at another Care Conference, I was surprised when a few siblings "talked it over" and decided it would be "best for Mom" if she stayed at the Woodland Center long-term. She liked it there, had made friends, was on a regular routine, got her meals (healthy meals at that), didn't have to cook, and was getting therapy. What more could you ask for? They worried that she wasn't taking care of herself at home. Look how bad her foot got! She wasn't eating properly. How did I know if she really had breakfast?

All true. But it wasn't home.

"Let's leave it up to Mom," I suggested. "She's competent enough to make her own decisions." Competent, yes — but were they the best decisions? I knew she wanted to go home. She saw me now every day, and we took Louie on a leash to see her on weekends. But home was home. Her own bed. Her plants. Her independence and her rules. I knew she had gotten used to the routine and the rules at the Center. But no matter how nice it was, it wasn't her home.

The family agreed that she would choose to return home, but not because she really wanted to go home. She worried about me. She was ninety and still thought she needed to take care of me, even if it meant making a simple breakfast on weekends or looking in on me at night. She was Mom. She couldn't suddenly stop being Mom.

We did allow her to decide. "Oh, no," she said at her final Care Conference. "I want to go home. Greg needs me." (I didn't want to say I didn't "need" her, but the issue was addressed by the nurse conducting the meeting.)

"Forget about Greg, Mrs. Smith," she said. "What do you want to do?"

"I can't forget about Greg," she insisted. "And I still want to go home." There were concerned frowns all around the table when she announced that the first thing she wanted when she got home was a Philly cheese steak. I nervously smiled. That was Mom.

There really wasn't much to keep her at the Center any longer. She was using a walker. Occupational therapy taught her how to adjust to taking a shower, getting around the kitchen, and getting in and out of bed safely with her revamped foot. Her Medicare was winding down, which meant her therapy was ending. Yes, the doctor could find reasons for her to stay, such as her heart condition and her overall age, and now her foot and risk of falling. But he agreed she should be given a chance at home. He gave his blessing and plans were made.

The social worker set her up with a visiting nurse at home. Meals on Wheels was offered, as was any adaptive equipment needed. All arrangements were made for discharge. The staff was proud of her progress. Her bingo buddies at the Center would miss her. She got a new roommate who wasn't as social as her previous mate, so Mom was increasingly anxious to leave.

I had a taste of how families felt when their loved one was admitted. Going to the meetings, always alert when the phone rang at home, keeping up with the finances, and gathering all the info needed for her stay. I was on the other side of the fence as power of attorney/son. I hung in there by myself at home. I knew the routine by now of being alone. Was my family right? Did I want her home because of my own needs? Was that the real reason why she wanted to come home? The staff wished her luck as we wheeled her out to the car. I prayed we had done the right thing.

When Mom got home, she was pretty much resigned to the fact that her driving days were over. Thankfully, she admitted it. I had experience with older adults who refused to hand over the keys. A doctor then needed to get involved, and it wasn't pretty. I totally understood the reluctance. Driving was such a big part of being and feeling independent. It's a pain having to depend on others for a ride (as I knew so well). It's a red flag that the end is in sight. Mom seemed almost relieved to give it up. I guess she had had a few close calls in town even when she was well, and decided it wasn't worth risking her own health or someone else's welfare. But it was still a bummer for her.

She asked that we get rid of the car. The light-green vehicle sitting lonely in the driveway made her feel bad. When we couldn't sell it (even though the car ran surprisingly well for being twenty-five years old), we donated it to a local charity.

Mom did well at home. The visiting nurse continued her therapy. Her right foot looked great. The wound nurse at the Woodland Center did a nice job keeping it free from any more sores. Mom kept it clean, dry, and wrapped.

She was almost back to her old self, puttering around the kitchen, able to make herself toast and coffee in the morning. Family and neighbors dropped by during the day to help her out and keep an eye on her. An angel from our church named Becca (she knew Mom from church; they sat together in the last pew) came over once a week to help with cleaning and laundry. I was able to go to work feeling relieved that everything was going to work out fine.

Several months passed, and the visiting nurses stopped coming. Insurance wouldn't pay for them any longer. Despite that, Mom seemed to be doing well. We had a regular routine with our meals, keeping things nutritious but simple, like soups, salads, sandwiches, and dinners we could easily pop into the microwave.

The problems came at night. Mom rolled out of bed in her sleep two nights in a row. I couldn't get her up, so the first time, family came over to help her up; the next time, the ambulance guys helped. During the day, she seemed more unsteady on her feet. She remained sitting a lot so I wouldn't see just how shaky and wobbly she really was. It turned out her feet — both this time — were getting infected again. She tried to hide that from everyone, but soon the inevitable diagnosis arrived. Her emergency room doctor related the news of how the infection was traveling rapidly up her lower leg.

The new side-rails on her bed weren't enough. She couldn't stand for long, let alone walk. When she couldn't get out of bed one morning, I called 911. She was evaluated and admitted. Mom was destined to return to the Woodland Center, this time most likely for good.

I heard the expected "I told you so" remarks from the family. I didn't care. Mom had deserved a shot at coming home. It wasn't her fault. Just like with driving, she had to prove to herself that she couldn't do it any longer.

This time she was more depressed than ever at the nursing home. Therapy was picking her up again, but maintenance was the goal. Their recommendation was to stay for good. The worst part was that Mom wouldn't eat. We brought her favorites from home: cheese steaks, candy, donuts, anything she could have. Even her favorite Greg-gift (which I gave her every birthday or get-well visit): a box of Whitman Sampler chocolates. Godiva and Russell Stover were delicious, but Mom was old-school. She loved her Whitman Sampler where she could select her favorites from the diagram on the inside of the top cover. She always chose the caramels or chocolate nuts — I always avoided the coconut.

She was losing hope. I tried to encourage her. This time I used a tactic I had never used before — me. I knew how much she worried about me. She needed a dose of motivation so she wouldn't give up hope. Maybe I lied a little when I told her there was always hope, always a chance she might come home down the road. Without hope, there is nothing.

"I'm never coming home again," she sighed, sitting in her room in a wheelchair. She didn't want to participate in bingo anymore or go outside in the beautiful garden area. We had to encourage her to watch television and keep up with her soap operas. Staff wheeled her down to church, sometimes more than once a week. She started going to services of all denominations, not just Catholic. I was glad she attended church, but it was a red flag when she didn't care for bingo anymore. All she wanted to do was sleep. The psychologist began to visit her and prescribed an antidepressant. We made a deal, approved at Care Conference: if she started to eat and went to therapy and did her exercises, she might be able to come home for lunch on weekends. She could see Louie and get away from the other residents and the hectic, sad atmosphere of the unit she was now on, and she could spend a few quiet hours in the home she loved so much.

She agreed. I was glad family members approved. There were thoughts that once home, she might not want to go back. But Mom knew the rules. She wasn't in a prison. She needed a ray of hope to keep herself alive. Don't take away all her freedom and independence.

We had lots of family meetings back then. Sometimes the meetings ended in shouting and bitterness. It hurt because I was close to my siblings. They had always been there for me. Now it was like we were complete strangers. I could understand their feelings about Mom, her well-being, and the stress they were under. But I couldn't understand the deep-seeded resentment that came out during family discussions. "I wish you would all get along," Mom said. I had been down this road before as mediator between families, but never as one of the quarreling family members.

Without Mom at home, I soon worked out a routine on my own. Get up at five a.m., take care of Louie, get dressed, and wait for the van to take me to work. I needed a little help at home with several things Mom used to do: helping me transfer into the shower, tying my necktie for work in the morning (the Center eventually allowed me to go tie-less), and simple, everyday chores like changing light bulbs or taking out the trash. I never let Mom know I had struggles at home.

Mom's appetite improved, and she started coming out of her room to the dining room to sit with her friends. Therapy got her walking again with the walker. She still needed assistance with her bathing and dressing. With increasing independence, she was transferred across the facility to a more independent, step-down unit, a sign she was making progress. The West building was almost an apartment-like setting. There were nurses and aides on duty like elsewhere in the facility, but the residents were expected to do much more for themselves to stay in this assisted living-type atmosphere.

Mom thrived. She started attending the craft room weekly; her favorite project was stringing beads to make bracelets. She ultimately gave these cute trinkets to her granddaughters or to staff, especially the girls who took care of her every day. I often saw her in the craft room during my journeys and stopped in to say hello. She was smiling more and looked forward to coming back each week to finish a bracelet or start a new one with different colors. She was easy to spot in a long row of residents sitting at a busy table. She inevitably was the shortest lady there, barely visible in the crowd.

She returned to bingo, and occasionally I stopped in to root for her. "I only need one number," she whispered and pointed to her card. She seemed pleased when I was there to be a first-hand witness to her bingo expertise, cheering her victories and groaning at her defeats. "That woman over there," she said in a hushed tone, "won four times already today. She's lucky." So was Mom, who had a stack of silver quarters piled next to her bingo cards on the table.

"Mom, if there was a professional bingo league," I teased her, "you would be the commissioner."

We often sat together outside her room, like sitting on the front porch at home, watching the flow of traffic at the nearby nurse's station, watching who was coming and going in the hallways. Mom clued me in on her neighbors. "That one wouldn't eat her supper last night," she indicated in a low voice. "That guy over there complains too much."

A gentleman down the hall, stretched out in a lounge chair and loudly snoring, got her attention and sympathy. "Poor soul! God forgive me, I don't want to get like that. I would rather die," she said. Quality of life was so important to Mom. She felt sorrow for those around her. It did her good to come home on weekends just to get a break from all the sadness.

We began to tell each other "I love you." Every day when it was time to leave, Mom walked me to the elevator. "See you tomorrow," I said as she bent over and kissed me on the cheek. "Call me if you need anything."

"I hate that you are going home and nobody is there. Make sure you get something to eat and lock the doors at night."

"I will, don't worry," I said, looking away. If she saw me cry it would make it worse.

"Give Louie a pet for me," she said. Every day the elevator door closed, and she stood there, one hand holding onto her walker, the other hand clutching a crumpled white tissue, dabbing her tired, soft blue eyes. "I love you."

"I love you too," I replied, the door closing. I pressed the down button and slumped in my chair. Once the elevator hit the first floor, I wheeled out to meet my van, my eyes moist with tears.

Mom's visits home were something to look forward to. Usually Mark picked her up and dropped her off. He was on the fence about Mom coming home. I guess he didn't want to take sides either way. I couldn't blame him; I didn't want to be in the middle either.

Louie loved the attention and missed being spoiled by Mom. Our weekend lunches were casual and relaxing. Lunch was her choice, something she couldn't get at the Center, something like Kentucky Fried Chicken or a hoagie. Then we talked, Mom sitting in her favorite living room chair. Sometimes she wanted to take a nap in her old bed. I worried she might not be able to transfer, but she did it like a champ. She rested for an hour and Louie jumped up with her, like in the old days.

One thing Mom always did during her visits, no matter if she had an hour or four hours to visit, was slowly walk around the house and do a silent "inspection." She would straighten a curtain she felt just wasn't right or fix a bedspread. "Keep watering my plants!" she reminded me. I wondered what she thought about during her tours of the house. She was on inspection duty, the Mom of old. I'm sure the memories flooded inside her heart when she wearily gazed into each room. I stayed quiet in the living room until she returned, sat back down, and proclaimed that her home "looked nice."

"This will always be your home, Mom," I told her. "No matter what."

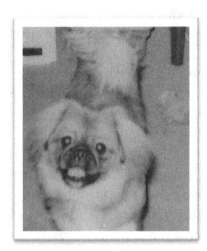

Louie

That was our life for three years. I wanted her home full-time but accepted that she needed the professional care I couldn't give. She talked of "coming home for good" but then settled back into the routine of her life. I was glad she seemed content. It would've killed me to see her hate her new home.

Things were going well. We had both adjusted to a new life.

Chapter 24
It's Okay to Let Go

Louie had not been doing well for several weeks. He wouldn't eat, very unlike Lou. I knew he had a heart condition and was thirteen years old, but I never expected to hear from the vet that he was on his way out. "Prepare yourself," she advised.

We tried pills to stimulate his appetite, and they worked for a few days; then he went back to picking. I gave him whatever he wanted, like he was in hospice care. He kept losing weight as the weeks went by. It was hard to accept the fact that Louie was nearing the end of his life.

I kept his prognosis a secret from Mom. She did know that he wasn't doing well. She wanted to see him, maybe for one last time, and we agreed on the upcoming weekend. Mark had plans on Sunday, her usual day to visit, so Saturday it was.

We had a nice visit, and Lou even ate a little with Mom feeding him by hand. We both believed he would start eating again and return to his old self. I envisioned him crunching old plastic water bottles, and Mom looked forward to more naps with Lou down the road.

We often spent time reminiscing together, be it sitting outside her room or during home visits. The memories made us smile. Mom liked to have a period of quiet time during her visits. Often it would start with "Remember the time . . ." Mom reminisced even more than usual during this visit. Perhaps she felt a bit more sentimental because of Louie.

We talked about so many memories we had shared: our old television sets that took three minutes to warm up (the kind that had tubes in the back); how a trip to the gas station included getting your windshield washed for free: saving Green Stamps in a book, redeemed for items like toasters; the weekly visits from the milk man, the bread man, the ice man, and the potato chip man; telephone numbers with word prefixes (ours was WE-3); root beer floats we used to get at the corner store in old-time Coca-Cola glasses; how we loved watching Shirley Temple movies together on Saturdays.

Every so often I helped my residents make an audio or video life summary. Think of all the memories and things like old recipes that could be saved and passed along to the next generation to cherish! If they aren't written down or recorded, they may be lost forever. Life reviews not only allow closure but validate feelings of a "job well done" in life. Mom liked the idea and wanted to do a life review.

I couldn't wait to hear about how my grandparents fled occupied Czechoslovakia for freedom in the United States; how they emigrated to the coal-mining region of Pennsylvania, looking for work; how they then migrated to Phoenixville, where my grandfather labored in the steel mill; how Mom and her siblings struggled during the Depression; how she met my father at a dance before World War II and how she became a nurse, sacrificing her career to take care of me full-time. We agreed to start working on Mom's life review on Monday.

Lou slowly walked outside with me to the driveway to say so long to Mom, our usual custom at the end of her visits. "See you on Monday," I said as she threw us a kiss out the open passenger window of Mark's car.

"See you Monday! Take care," she replied, and I watched them drive away down the street. I wheeled to the top of the ramp, following Lou into the house.

————————

A quiet weekend was winding down, and I was reading the newspaper and listening to The Beatles when my bedroom landline rang around six p.m. No one ever called that late, especially on a Sunday.

It was a nurse from the Woodland Center. They had found Mom unresponsive in the dining room. Her tablemates called for help when they saw Mom slumped over. The nurses got her into bed, took her vital signs, and called 911. They wouldn't speculate what had happened, only that they were sending her to the emergency room.

I called Mark and told him the news. I knew she would be okay. Maybe she had had an episode? Maybe with a little oxygen they would give her the green light to return to the nursing home? My brother hung up the phone, heading to the ER and promising to keep in touch with updates.

About twenty minutes went by before I heard the front screen door open. "Greg?" It was my brother Tommy.

"Hey, Tom! I'm back here. How's Mom doing?" I shouted back.

He came to the doorway, his eyes red, his voice breaking. "You better come over and say goodbye to Mom. She had a stroke."

Stunned silence passed for several seconds as I tried to process what he just said. Say goodbye? A stroke? No, not Mom. A stroke was a thing happened to others, not my mother.

I got into my wheelchair, and we walked the block to the hospital. "Don't be scared when you see her," he advised. Telling me not to be afraid made me afraid.

We found the other family members sitting in the lounge area of the emergency room. A nurse was there, kneeling and softly talking to the three. I was introduced as "brother and power of attorney," and the nurse turned her attention to me.

"Your mother has a living will. It was faxed over with her records. I looked it over. She is a Do Not Resuscitate. No machines, no feeding tube."

"Those were her wishes," I confirmed.

Everything was happening too fast. She was talking final wishes. I felt conflicted. Do whatever it takes to save her life? Or respect her wishes? How many times had I faced this conflict as a social worker? What did I advise families?

"We have to respect her wishes," the nurse stated, like she was reading my mind.

"Why don't you just ask her?" I suggested. That was when the nurse told me she was unconscious. "Can I see her?"

I wheeled alongside the stretcher in one of the cubicles and couldn't believe it. Mom was lying there, eyes closed, hooked up to all kinds of machines and tubes. I didn't say anything. I just sat there, staring at her. I didn't cry. I couldn't cry. She was just home the day before. I couldn't get over it.

The emergency room doctor explained that she had a massive cerebrovascular accident. They gave her meds to try and reverse the effects. It would take a while to see if she responded. The next twenty-four hours would be crucial. If she was going to wake up, it had to be in the next few hours. The more time passed, the more her prognosis would turn graver.

Mark pushed me home this time. We didn't say much. We held out hopes she would come out of it.

I didn't get much sleep. I said the rosary for the first time in a long time. Why was it that I seemed to pray more in troubled times? I needed to pray more often. I asked God to help Mom. If anyone deserved to wake up and get well, it was Mom. She was the one who prayed every day and had faith for all of us. Please help her now. Give her the miracle she always prayed would happen to me.

I didn't go to work the next day. Mark called me in the morning, and after taking care of Louie we went over to visit. I was hoping to find Mom in a regular room, sitting up in bed and eating breakfast, happy I had brought her another box of Whitman Sampler chocolates. Instead, Mom had been sent to their hospice unit. The nurse/caseworker asked me if I wanted to keep her there at the hospital or send her back to the Center. The floor was small, able to handle four patients at a time, with nurses close by 24/7. "Let's keep her here," I decided.

The neurologist came into Mom's room after lunch. We were all there, even my oldest brother Jim, who had driven up from Maryland. The doctor explained how devastating the stroke was. The left side of her brain was gone. No impulses, no reaction. It was unlikely she would ever wake up. If she did wake up, she would be paralyzed and not be able to speak, just for starters. She could live like this for a week, maybe more, without a feeding tube. They were giving her IVs. He doubted she was in any pain. Occasionally there would be a twitch, maybe an involuntary noise. She would get great care from the hospice nurses. Everything was comfort measures only. They would keep her clean and dry. We were welcome to stay if we liked. No restrictions. There was coffee in the lounge just down the hall from her room. Feel free to ask the nurse for anything.

Blah, blah, blah. All I really heard was the part about it being "unlikely she would ever wake up." That was so final. Mom deserved better than to just waste away and die. I knew her feelings about "not wanting to linger or be a burden to anyone." But just watching her waste away for a week? God, I struggled with that.

For three days the family waited by her bedside. We felt so helpless. I decided to go to work on Wednesday as the family took shifts being there with Mom. I knew Mom would feel guilty about having everyone there and would want me to go to work.

When the paratransit van picked me up that morning, I looked across the road to the hospital, now regretting my decision, staring at the top floor where Mom was resting. It was stupid to be at work. My mind was with Mom, and when I had a break, I called the nurses' station on the hospice unit to find out how she was doing. Everyone at Woodland expressed their sorrow that Mom was dying. They talked about her like she was already gone: "She was such a nice lady . . ."

Mom was still stable when I arrived after work. No progress, no deterioration. She was just . . . there.

My family had shared shifts since the early morning. Everyone decided to go home, take showers, grab a bite to eat, and come back in a few hours. Soon I was alone with Mom for the first time since the stroke.

I was still at a distance near the door. A nurse stopped in to check on Mom, asking if I needed anything. "You can sit alongside her," she encouraged. Mom had sat by my bedside so many times when I was sick. So many sleepless nights. She was the reason why I kept fighting. She was always by my side, no matter what. Now it was my turn to offer comfort and prayers.

Alone again, I wheeled closer to the bed. She was hooked up to machines, machines blinking and beeping and flashing numbers, machines constantly taking her vital signs, her heartbeat, brain waves, blood pressure. I looked at Mom, serenely lying there amid all this sight and sound in a peaceful coma. I reached up and held her left hand between the bed rails. Her soft, warm hand was black and blue from the IV near her wrist. I had brought a small bottle of Lourdes water, and I put a little on her hand since I couldn't reach her forehead. I said a silent Hail Mary and returned the bottle to my pocket.

The joy of her sense of humor, her kindness, and her compassion — all these loving memories flooded my senses. To think her life ended here. I whispered softly to Mom, like we were talking during one of my lunch breaks on her unit at Woodside.

"Hi, Mom. It's Greg. I'm here. I came over after work," I whispered. "Mom, in case no one explained to you, you had a stroke. That's why you can't open your eyes or talk. But I know you can hear me. I know it must be frustrating not to be able to open your eyes. You are in there, I know it. I know you can hear me. I'm not just talking to myself . . ." My voice trailed off as I tried not to cry.

"Mom, I'm doing okay at home. Louie is a little better since you saw him. There's no need to worry. We'll be all right . . ." I stopped to take a deep breath. I wasn't sure I wanted to say what came to me next.

"If you are hanging in there because of me, it's okay to let go." Those words were so hard to say because I wanted her to open her eyes and be the mother I loved for so long. I didn't want her to die.

"If anyone is going to Heaven, it's you. I don't want you to suffer. You don't deserve that. You know I love you for taking care of me all my life. You sacrificed so much for me. I'll never forget you. I'll miss you, Mom. If you need to leave this world, please let go . . . for me."

In that instant, Mom let out three quick gasps, the first noise she had made in my presence. I was startled but didn't think anything of it. Just another involuntary noise they said would happen from time to time. At that moment, the nurse returned, glancing in the room. She stopped in her tracks. "Let me check her. Her color looks different." She listened to Mom's heart, touched her pulse, and gently said, "She has passed."

"She's gone?" I asked.

"I'm so sorry," she consoled.

"She was a good mom. She had a heart of gold," I replied softly.

The nurse said to take my time with Mom while she alerted the doctor and called the coroner. "I'll be back to wash her," she said, taking away all the tubes and machines. Mom looked so peaceful without all the sights and sounds around her.

It was the way it was supposed to be. She could've died anytime, right after the stroke or even the following week. Instead she died while I was there.

The bond between a mother and a special-needs child.

God, in His infinite mercy, decided to welcome her into His arms. She wasn't going to suffer anymore.

Mom was the most caring person I ever met. So strong in her faith and her love for others. She was in Heaven with my father, reunited again.

"Mom," I whispered, "you finally made it home."

———————

The funeral director, a young guy named Charles, knew Mom well from her attendance at so many town funerals. He pointed out where Mom always sat during wakes — last row, first chair. "Everyone in Phoenixville will be at her funeral on Monday," he predicted. "She was a nice lady."

Mom looked beautiful in her sky-blue outfit. The Beatles' song "In My Life" softly played overhead as her casket was closed ("There are places I remember . . ."). I cried in church as we were leaving, following the casket down the center aisle as the solo vocalist sang, "And I shall raise him up on the last day."

Mom

There is an old tradition that on the way to the cemetery, the hearse and the entire funeral procession slowly drive by the house of the deceased. It hit me like a ton of bricks when the hearse briefly stopped in front of our house. Knowing Louie was inside, I wondered if he knew Mom was nearby for the last time. Her adult male grandsons carried her silver casket to the gravesite. I placed a red rose on her casket before they wheeled me away. So long, Mom.

The reception was what Mom wanted, a small affair ("Make sure everyone has enough to eat" were her instructions) at the local Polish club. Family, friends, and co-workers came up to me, patting me on the shoulder, whispering, "If there's anything I can ever do . . ." I nodded and thanked everyone for coming.

As the funeral director predicted, Mom had the biggest funeral in town. All her friends showed up, especially her bingo buddies. She would've been pleased.

Chapter 25
From Now On Your Name Is Bud

Life after Mom. I knew it would happen sooner or later. At first, I didn't accept her death. Why was she taken away when so many others at the nursing home lingered on? She could've lived another ten years at least. You see it all the time on the news: "Woman celebrates 102nd birthday — still going strong . . ." But it was her time. She had led a full life at ninety-three. It wasn't an easy life. Her heart broke many times. But she had her family and continued, surviving another thirty-six years after Dad died. She was ready.

There was still much to do. Paperwork to file for her insurance. Her estate documents. Making sure everything was paid. I was used to taking care of the bills by now. Mom had always been available to help if I needed advice. Now it was up to me to hold down the fort.

The family came over and took a day to clean out her room. Old clothes were to be donated or thrown away. Mom was a bit of a hoarder. We found bags of greeting cards, little packets of soap, dozens of rosaries, and religious medals she had collected over the years. Her cookbooks and beautiful crochet items like tablecloths and mittens were found in drawers. Everything went. Mom had said to the family, "Take what you want when I die," and they did.

Remaining were her beautiful religious statues in various places in the living room, some from as far away as Czechoslovakia, brought to the States by her mother. Special fellow parishioners from our parish knew she had these old statues and asked what I was going to do with them. I knew Mom would've wanted me to give her Blessed Virgin Mary to Becca, a loyal and faithful friend, someone she trusted to take care of the statue and honor it. I kept the rest.

Louie died the day after Mom's funeral. He waited until I got home from work. I held him as he passed. We buried him in the backyard with his favorite stuffed toy, Lammy, wrapped in a blanket. He was with Mom in Heaven. I felt better knowing he wasn't suffering anymore. But I still missed him. And the house was so quiet and lonely.

By now I had worked out a routine in the mornings to get ready for work. There was one morning after Mom died that I struggled mightily. Everything seemed to go wrong. First, my alarm failed to go off. I rushed to get washed, scrambling to get done before the van came to pick me up for work. I couldn't button my dress shirt no matter how hard I tried. I had to hold one end of the shirt with my teeth as I tried to button the other end with a shaky hand. The more I tried, the more the shirt slipped, and I had to start over. The button clasped the buttonhole, then slipped out. Repeatedly. It took all the energy I had to keep trying. My hands started to cramp. My breathing became labored as my frustration grew. I started to cry, yelling, "I can't do this anymore!"

I took a few moments to get myself together, taking slow, deep breaths. I did the best I could with my shirt, finally hooking the buttons together. Exhausted, I felt like calling into work and going back to bed on this rainy, cool, dreary morning. Instead I grabbed a jacket, locked the front door, wheeled outside, and met my van.

I missed Mom and Louie so much. There were times in life when we would sit and talk and Mom would ponder, "What are you going to do without me?" I tried not to think about that, brushing it off by replying, "Oh, Mom, don't talk that way. You'll always be around." Mom was going to live to see one hundred.

As time went on she allowed me to become more independent, knowing someday I would have to fend for myself. Maybe that was why, on her final visit home, instead of asking, "What are you going to do without me?" she said, "I'm glad you are doing so good without me."

Mom helped me quite a bit, like getting in and out of the shower, buttoning my dress shirts and making meals. I forced myself to learn those daunting tasks. It gave Mom peace of mind that I really would be okay after she was gone. Here I was, a grown man who needed help using such trivial things as the dishwasher. I was never expected to do anything around the house. Mom would always be there to do the laundry or wash the dishes or run the vacuum cleaner. I didn't need to learn how to take care of myself. Mom would always be around.

They say with time, the grieving gets easier. Not really. The holidays made me think of Mom even more. Thanksgiving was always a special family event in our house. Mom made the turkey and the side dishes. She was fussy and liked to entertain. I still smelled the aroma of the turkey cooking overnight, filling the house with delicious joy. Often, she stayed up late making cookies, "because it was quiet." I wheeled to the kitchen after midnight and there she was, rolling dough, wondering why I wasn't sleeping. I wondered the same about her.

The first Thanksgiving that she was in the nursing home, we joined her for dinner at midday. We ordered the trays ahead of time, and along with other families who couldn't take their loved ones home, we shared Thanksgiving the best way we could. The following year, Mom came home. We had another idea. We ordered all the food — turkey, stuffing, and all the trimmings — from a local grocery store. All we needed to do was pick up the dinner on Thanksgiving morning, heat it up, and we were ready to eat. No fuss, no muss. Mom agreed to this plan. After dinner I asked her if she was having fun.

"It was okay," she sighed, looking sad in her favorite chair.

"What's wrong? Didn't you like it?"

"It was nice. The food was good."

"Then what's wrong?"

"Well," she said, shrugging her shoulders, "I didn't do anything."

"But that was the point, Mom. You didn't have to do anything."

"I felt useless," she said, slumping back in her chair.

Lesson learned. After so many years of making the big holiday dinner, to have it all taken away, even if she did realize she couldn't do it anymore, was too great a loss for Mom to handle. So, the final year we had Mom in our lives for Thanksgiving, we compromised. She came home and we still pre-ordered the food. But this time Mom helped. She set the table and supervised in the kitchen. Like the old days, she made sure everyone had plenty to eat. She always ate last on holidays, after she knew her family was happy. That made her happy. Mom had some control again, her dignity was restored, and she said it was one of the nicest Thanksgivings ever.

Normally, I loved the holiday season. That first year without Mom, I couldn't wait until the holidays were over. Attending Midnight Mass with my parents had meant singing Christmas carols in the packed church and staying up late. Hot chocolate waited back home while we hoped to catch a glimpse of gifts under the tree before bed. Great food at the crowded Christmas table was a joy to savor, from Mom's freshly baked ethnic Slovak cookies to a mouth-watering, juicy turkey. Every year Dad drove our station wagon around town on a chilly evening before Christmas to see the colorful holiday lights. Our lights out front, usually a twinkling snowman, along with a Nativity scene, were simple yet heartfelt. Mom helped me with wrapping presents on the kitchen table while listening to Christmas music on the radio. Mom did the actual wrapping; my specialty was being the official scotch tape dispenser. Decorating the sweet-scented evergreen tree was always fun, from tossing glittering, silver strands of tinsel on the branches, to untangling strings of brightly colored lights, to lovingly placing our beautiful ceramic Nativity scene (which my brother Jimmy and his wife Marion made) under the tree. Watching Christmas movies and specials in the weeks before December 25, shopping at the small, quaint shops in town (no malls or Amazon back then), and soft snowflakes outside our candle-lit, frosty windows meant happy times. We greeted friends with "Merry Christmas" as we hung our Christmas cards around the house, along with holly, mistletoe, and wreaths.

I listened to the touching memories of "Christmas Mornings" by Richard Marx, a beautiful ballad about holidays gone by. I cried every time I heard that song, yet I still played it every Christmas. Why? I think because it brought me closer to my folks, especially my mother. The words made me feel like she was still around, baking and decorating, like the sweet, simple holidays we had shared together for so long. Would Christmas ever be the same without Mom? We vowed to try and keep old traditions alive as we started new ones. The sweetest memories never fade away, memories of innocent times, like the joy we shared at Christmas. Memories to last a lifetime. Memories to cherish when we celebrate holidays without dear, departed loved ones. Memories to get us through the daily grind of life. Memories that can never die if we keep them alive every day.

As always, music helped to heal my soul. Music always eased my pain. I listened to music after fractures when I was a kid. Now music soothed the hurt in my heart whenever I thought of Mom. I loved the Richard Marx and Alison Krauss song "Straight from My Heart." I listened to that song every night until the tears stopped flowing and I couldn't cry anymore. I was blessed to have had Mom and Louie in my life. Now it was time to move on.

———————

Soon after Louie died, friends from work encouraged me to get another dog. They saw how I was grieving Lou, going home each night to an empty house. I could hear Mom: "Louie isn't even cold yet and you're getting another dog." But they were right. I needed company. I needed protection too, since I lived alone. Having a watchdog even made Mom feel better when she was home alone. I also needed a purpose in life, something to take care of. The flowers and plants were dying, which was my fault. I just didn't care anymore. I needed life to fill the house again. The emptiness in my heart ached to be filled.

I started searching for the perfect dog. I knew I didn't want another Pekingese. Pekingese are great dogs — affectionate, smart, playful, and faithful, but another Peek would just remind me of what I had lost, and no dog could ever take the place of Louie. I didn't want a puppy. Training a puppy in my situation would be hard. Hopefully I could find a dog around two or three years old, a dog who would be around for a while, a dog already house-broken and friendly.

I tried looking locally. I went to the S.P.C.A. in West Chester. I'd never had a shelter dog before. I had this misconception that shelter dogs were tainted, maybe abused, dogs that no one else wanted. Then I thought how stupid that stereotype was. All dogs are different, just like people. Why not give a dog from there a chance? Give a homeless dog a forever home. I wanted a smaller dog, but every dog I found was either too big or too expensive. I went to shelters and pet stores (via paratransit), looked for ads in the paper, and kept my eyes open for puppies that someone from work might want to sell or give away.

Finally I went online. I had never cared for computers, but luck was on my side. I found a site in Alabama for shelter dogs. I found a cute Pekingese mix on page four under "small dogs." Only I wasn't looking for another Pekingese — that was, until I saw this little guy. A small Peek-a-Pom (half Pekingese and half Pomeranian), multicolored in different shades of brown. He looked friendly from his "smile." His name was Mr. Miyagi.

I wasn't sure if I wanted to go through all the red tape involved in adopting a rescue dog from so far away. I really wanted to meet the dog first to see if we liked each other. It would be a huge risk and a big commitment to go through the process of adopting a dog from Alabama only to find out we weren't compatible. I did a little more investigating. Mr. M. was described as "friendly, a true Southern gentleman." There was no explanation given as to why he was at the shelter. It didn't say if he was found on the streets or if he had been abused or dropped off because no one wanted him. I knew there was a big problem down South with unwanted puppies and kittens. They claimed he "didn't like to be picked up" and "didn't like his mouth touched." One note that did raise a red flag: Mr. M. didn't care for men. He preferred to be around women (I didn't blame him). That wouldn't work. I continued looking elsewhere.

I didn't find another dog I liked on their website. And I was striking out locally. Disappointed, I gave the idea a rest for a few days, almost abandoning the thought of getting another dog altogether.

I couldn't stop thinking about Mr. Miyagi. That little voice inside told me to check him out again. I scrolled down to his picture one late, sleepless night, and instantly made the decision that he was the one. I contacted Alabama and did some more research. Their shelter was legit, not a scam. Someone else was also interested in Mr. M., but after talking to a sweet lady on the phone from the shelter, she promised to hold him if I really wanted him.

I did all the paperwork online. Numerous phone calls and information were exchanged. I gave them three references, one from Louie's vet. They wanted to make sure I would be a good father. That impressed me a great deal. They didn't want to dump Mr. M. just anywhere. They cared about him.

The references were good, the check cleared, and Mr. M. was mine. He had all his shots. How did we get him to Pennsylvania? The shelter had a truck which delivered puppies once a month. They made stops in Maryland, Pennsylvania, and New Jersey. I was given a specific date and time and was told to be on time to meet Mr. M. The truck wasn't going to wait.

How would I get to Yardley, over an hour away, early on a Saturday morning? Paratransit wouldn't take me that far. Even if they did, a shelter dog wouldn't be allowed on board. This was way before support dogs were in vogue.

I hadn't seen Chet, the taxicab driver who took me to Norristown every day, in a long time, not since I had resigned my job at Aging. I looked up his number and boldly decided to give him a call. Chet was still as funny and nutty as ever. He asked about Mom and I told him she had died. He remembered Louie too. That's when I mentioned that I was in the process of getting a new dog but was perplexed about how to get to Yardley (hint, hint). Chet "booked" me for a cab ride on Saturday morning. The journey would kill two birds with one stone: catching up on old times and country music classics and picking up my new pup (plus good-hearted Chet said he would conveniently turn off his meter during the trip.) "Just buy me a six-pack on our way down and we will call it even," he suggested.

The last time I talked to Alabama, I was convinced I had done the right thing. The shelter lady informed me that Mr. M. had been up for sale quite a while. If he didn't find a forever home within the week, he was scheduled to be put down. "You really rescued this little guy," she commented. I looked forward to meeting him more than ever.

We waited in the Pet Smart parking lot on a cool September morning as other adopting parents soon filled the lot. I had a leash ready and all my identification papers. Of course, I worried. What if he didn't like me? This was a life-changing moment, and suddenly I wasn't so sure I had done the right thing after all.

Then I saw the white box-truck pull up. Exactly eight-thirty a.m., right on schedule. They started to bring dogs out in crates and on leashes. Still no Mr. M.

"Mister Miyagi, Pekingese mix . . . who is here for this cutie?" shouted a lady holding a clipboard. I waved, and they brought the pooch over to the grassy area where we were waiting.

He looked exactly like his picture. We didn't make eye contact at first as I reached for the leash. Mr. M. lifted a leg and peed on my back-left wheel. I was his. He was marking his territory. In an instant I knew we would be pals. Chet started laughing. "I like him already!"

"Nice to meet you too," I mumbled.

One of the first things we needed to do was get him groomed. He didn't look or smell too good from his thousand-mile trip. The only stops were to occasionally pee. Back in Phoenixville, my groomer took him in, and groomed and bathed the little guy before he reached his new home. He sure was house-broken, and they didn't kid about how smart he was, for when we got inside, he immediately ran to the back door and asked to go out. I was just as relieved as Mr. M. was, hoping the house-broken part was true.

The only thing I didn't like about Mr. M was his name. I couldn't say it very well. I had never seen the Karate Kid movies, and I wanted something simple. The Alabama lady said they named him that when he arrived at the shelter, so he wasn't used to it yet. I looked at him when he came back inside and said, "From now on your name is . . . Bud." Not original, but easy.

Bud was great from the get-go. I figured he had probably been on the streets at one point, because he kept trying to dump over the trash basket in the kitchen, looking for scraps of food. At night I would hear him prowling the other rooms and the crash of a trash can. Once he started getting regular meals, he stopped the trash-picking stunts.

I hated to leave him home during the day, but I had to work. I bought him some new stuffed toys and gave him a few of Louie's old toys. I used these to my advantage in the mornings. Bud still had a little "rabbit" in him, and I had to be careful he wouldn't bolt out the door and head for Alabama. Until he got used to his forever home, I needed to back out in the morning, which wasn't easy to do with the wheelchair. I tossed a toy deep into the living room for him to chase as I shut the door.

He never made a mess while I was gone, not even an accident. All my misconceptions about rescue dogs faded away. Now when I came home from work, I had someone with unconditional love to greet me. I had a purpose again. I may have saved his life, but he also saved mine. I was glad I had taken the risk and found Bud.

In February we had a terrible ice storm which knocked out my power for five days. No heat, no electricity. The power went out on a Sunday afternoon while it was still light outside. It usually came right back on. It didn't this time. My landline eventually died. It grew dark early, and I searched for flashlights. I didn't trust candles. I got an extra blanket for overnight and hoped the power would return by morning.

I imagined there would be no work the next day because of the storm. The only contact I had with the outside world was my transistor radio. They were working to restore power, but it might not be back "for a few days." Ice piled up outside the front door. My family still wasn't in touch much. Plus, I figured they were battling the ice storm as well, with no power. It was me and Bud, alone.

I didn't keep too much food in the refrigerator and freezer, so no worries about things spoiling. But not having food wasn't a good thing either. I did have fresh bread, peanut butter, crackers, and other essentials on hand. Plus, Bud's dog food.

Our days were spent waiting. We couldn't go anywhere. No one was coming to check on us. I had no phone or Internet. No television. I felt like Daniel Boone in the wilderness. It's one thing to lose power in the summer from a thunderstorm. At least you can open the windows and leave if you had to. The aftermath of the ice storm was still evident just outside my door. Bud squeezed himself out the backdoor to pee and then hurried back in. The highs during that week were in the teens. The nights grew even colder. One night I had three blankets on, plus layers of clothes, yet I still trembled. What scared me more was Bud. He slept at the foot of my bed but was shivering so violently I could feel him shaking. I wasn't going to let him die. I got one of the blankets, wrapped him up, and held him against me all night. We both survived.

By Friday, the ice had cleared enough that the paratransit van arrived to pick me up for work. I was dressed and ready to go, thinking they would come, washing and dressing in the dark. I couldn't use my electric razor and didn't own a regular razor, so I went to work looking macho. I didn't want to leave Bud, but I wanted to find out how close we were to power. If I stayed home, would someone come and find me? I couldn't be sure. I gathered all the blankets for Bud to keep warm and left.

The radio said power was slowly coming back all around me. The local high school had been an evacuation place for people without power to go for heat and food. I found out from the van driver that not all of town was out of power. In fact, the part of town where most of my siblings lived was fine. When I got to work, they had just gotten their power back. The elevators were finally working. It had caused chaos at the nursing home, but everyone was trained for such events. I heard a rumor that Phoenixville was back online. When I passed one of our physicians in the hall, he asked how I was doing. I told him the temperature in the house was down to forty-three degrees. He strongly suggested I take Bud and get out of there if the power wasn't back on. "You could die in your sleep from hypothermia," he warned.

The van driver couldn't go fast enough to get me home. He had heard the same news — the town had power. I worried about Bud. When I opened the door, I was met with heat. I was never so happy in my life, especially when Bud greeted me and didn't try to escape.

He found his forever home. I found a lifelong friend. And we really did save each other in more ways than one. Upon a routine dental exam, my vet shared the news: Bud had seven broken teeth. Two were infected and five others were jagged and rough. Plus, he had suffered from a fractured jaw sometime in his past. Bud had his share of fractures too. Apparently, whoever abandoned him at the shelter had also abused the little guy.

The vet extracted his broken teeth. I was so glad he was no longer in pain. That night, after his surgery, I held him in my arms as I had when we faced the ice storm together when he was a puppy, tears in my eyes. I wasn't ashamed that I was so old yet crying for my dog.

We went through so much together over the years. Maybe Bud wasn't the "perfect" dog I was looking for. But we ended up being a good match for each other. Perfectly imperfect. I never knew the bond we shared until that day. Broken bodies — unbreakable spirits.

Chapter 26

Is There Someone Special Out There?

I went back to West Chester University around this time in my life. My friend Rick was a professor there and taught social work classes. I had met him back in my Manor days when he came in weekly to help us do individual and group counseling. I always admired his kindness and gentle approach. He wanted me to visit because he was retiring from teaching after the spring semester. He was heading to Florida with his wife to live the much-deserved good life.

I touched base with Rick one pretty April day, and he asked me to visit one of his social work classes. We worked out a good date and time, and I rode the paratransit van down Route 202.

This was my first time back at West Chester U since 1988. The campus sure had changed, and the memories flooded back as soon as we parked. Students hustled everywhere, many wearing backpacks, still many more checking their cell phones. The crowded chaos had not changed (although we didn't have cell phones back in 1988). It looked like twenty-five years ago: students sitting on the floor in the halls, studying, listening to music on headphones, talking, and texting. I kind of wished I could return to those carefree days when Lori and I were at WCU. So much had happened since then.

Rick was his usual cheerful self as he greeted me. He had an infectious smile, a thick gray mustache, and wire-rimmed glasses.

As always, he was dressed impeccably. Didn't look like he had aged a day since the last time I saw him. He was a former champion body builder who ended up getting his doctorate in social work. I could see why the residents loved him so much back in the good old days. He knew that, no matter what, things would be all right. He made you feel that way just by spending time with him. Always positive. Rick paid me the ultimate compliment when he introduced me as "a social worker's social worker." I wasn't sure that was true, but coming from a truly great social worker like Rick, it was a real honor.

For the next hour I sat in a circle with twenty young students and answered questions. Most were female and most were seniors, a group due to graduate soon and enter the challenging world of social work. I thought about how cool it would've been to have a seasoned, experienced social worker come talk to us back then. Maybe I wouldn't have made so many mistakes, but I suppose everyone needs to learn the ropes on their own to appreciate the successes.

We talked social work, but I also fielded questions about OI and what it was like to get around in a wheelchair. To me, the key points to remember about social work were simple: 1) Always keep a sense of humor; 2) Listening is more important than giving advice; 3) Never forget about feelings; 4) Have empathy for others.

"You'll find your niche in the field. Don't give up and don't allow yourself to get burned out. Be honest, be real, and be nice to others," was my advice.

I mentioned that I had a bit of a challenge getting into the building because of the rocky gravel parking lot leading to the sidewalk and into the building. A few students agreed and suggested they contact someone on campus to make the campus more accessible to wheelchairs. Awareness is the first step to change. It was like old times.

I had a great time with the students that afternoon. "You guys are the future," I said before leaving. "Make everyone proud."

Becca helped me weekly with the cleaning and shopping. Local Rotary Club members cut my grass in the spring and summer. People heard about my needs and were nice enough to offer their assistance. Well-meaning friends advised me to sell the house and move into a handicapped-accessible apartment. I wouldn't have to worry about the grass or shoveling snow in the winter. It was a great idea, but now I had Bud. Plus, home is home. If I could pay my taxes, I wanted to stay in my parents' home for as long as I could.

Most of my family started dropping by as time went by. I began going to family cookouts and special events. Forgive and forget. Our folks would've wanted it that way.

It was New Year's Day, 2015. I had just gotten back from one of those family functions. I fed Bud and relaxed in my room, preparing for work the next day. Always a downer to go back after the holidays. I had the Sci-Fi Channel on TV, slightly paying attention to the Twilight Zone marathon they were heavily into. A commercial came on about a "senior dating site," one I had never heard of before. It caught my eye and, for reasons I can't explain, I memorized the website address.

I had tried the Internet dating scene before, even when Mom was alive. I was always honest about my disability and put a legitimate, up-to-date picture (that really was me) on my profile. I was too naive to know that lying was a big part of those dating sites.

I didn't get very many replies (more like none). Why should I put myself through such heartache? Those sites were like bars: very superficial. If you were attractive, you had a shot. Who wanted to go out with a little (but cute) guy who used a wheelchair? Nobody — or so I thought.

But once again that little voice inside told me to check it out. I never had much luck with computers. But I had found Bud. And I was tired of being alone and feeling lonely. I was still afraid of rejection and having my heart broken for the umpteenth time in my life. The new year might change my luck. After spending another holiday season without someone special in my life, I made the brave (or stupid?) decision to try again. Loneliness trumped fear.

The site was geared to older adults. Anyone over fifty could apply. Same usual fees and rules, which no one really abided by. I checked out some of the local female profiles for free. If interested and you wanted to contact her, you had to sign up. That was the catch.

I'd had it with long-distance relationships. I wanted to find a nice woman nearby, someone I could see occasionally, not just once a year. Someone with a car . . . oh yes, that driving issue was rearing its ugly head again. Another strike against me. What woman would want to drive on a date, handle a wheelchair, and use her own car each time?

The girls at work were nice and would politely say no or say they had a boyfriend or whatever the excuse. I didn't push it because I had to see them every day. There was added emphasis on the topic of sexual harassment at work, so I had to know when to not cross the line, even if it was something as innocent as going to a movie. Not worth losing my job over. Better to keep work and personal life separate. Many fish in the sea, as they say — but which harbor were they in?

Bookstores and grocery stores were good places to meet. I could start going with Becca once a week to the grocery store, but that might be a little awkward, trying to pick up a female shopper in the produce department while another woman was pushing my cart full of frozen dinners. Church was another possibility. I'm sure Mom wouldn't have approved of that tactic, even though she always said, "I wish you would find a nice girl." I could hear her say, "You go to church to pray, not to fool around."

My age was working against me, too. Here I was, pushing sixty. Most women my age were grandmothers by now. I had nothing in common with a twenty-something female. Make that thirty-something or even forty-something female. God, did I feel old!

So this senior dating thing didn't sound too bad. At least I would be in the ballpark age-wise. The REO Speedwagon song "Blazin' Your Own Trail Again" was playing in my mind as I completed a profile and added a picture (me in a suit and tie at work, from after I had won "County Employee of the Year" my first year at the Center). I rarely wore a suit in real life, only to funerals and weddings, neither of which I attended very often. I was always a jeans and sweatshirt guy, preferably Phillies or Eagles gear. I hoped whoever answered me liked sports, too.

Actually, I didn't add many "requirements" to my profile. Beggars can't be choosers. Just someone nice. And local. And not attached. Preferably no kids. I loved children and always thought I would've made a cool father, but I was way beyond that. Still, what were the odds of finding someone like that?

Having common interests was important. Being a good communicator. And, of course, someone with a good personality, who liked to laugh, had a good sense of humor and a caring, kind heart. Oh, and she must like dogs. Bud made sure I put that part in. Me? I was honest, a hopeless romantic, with a good sense of humor, a fan of sports, music, and movies. I left out the "I don't drive" part for now. Why push it? I posted the profile and waited.

I checked my inbox each day for the next week. Many ladies viewed my information. Like sharks circling fresh bait. No one responded. I wasn't surprised. My confidence sank. Then, out of the blue, someone did respond! It was a girl about fifteen minutes away. She claimed she was forty-six, had two kids who lived with their father, and lived in a three-story apartment. Didn't she read my profile? Maybe not, as I was quickly learning that photos count the most. Many people on those dating sites didn't really care if you took the time to write a sensitive, intelligent narrative. They only looked at the photos.

She must've thought I was cute, because she did answer my profile. She wanted me to meet her the next Sunday afternoon. She would cook chicken for dinner. She included her phone number in the reply. This was going way too fast for me. I did call her to see if she was for real. She wasn't playing games. She was very direct in what she wanted. Extremely direct. But she wasn't my cup of tea, so I politely declined. Before she hung up, she parted ways by saying, "Your loss."

This online dating thing wasn't going to be easy.

One week left in January. Still no luck. The "new" profiles of local senior females were recycled every week. Pretty soon there was no one new to contact. I decided if I didn't find anyone by the end of the month, it wasn't meant to be. Maybe I was destined to be by myself? I was happy now but knew I could be happier. I was lonely. However, I wasn't going to pay for an extra month, or three months, or even a six-month membership and waste my money on rejection.

When all seemed lost and my membership was down to the final three days of January, there was Holly.

Holly joined the senior dating site a few days before I planned to sign off for good. We could've easily missed each other. I found her new profile one morning before work. She was everything I hoped for. She lived only twenty minutes away. She was a widow with adult stepchildren. Short and pretty with a friendly smile, she had Farrah Fawcett long, curly blonde hair. She looked younger than her age, which was a little older than me. She worked as an IT specialist for a major communications company, plus she had her real estate license. Animals were one of her passions, and she owned three beautiful retired horses on her small farm. She loved to cook, quilt, and enjoyed movies and music. Who could ask for more?

I wrote her the nicest introductory email I could muster at a drowsy six o'clock in the morning. I probably should've waited until I was a bit more coherent, but Holly was someone I wanted to know better. Knowing the guys on these dating sites, it wouldn't be long until her mailbox was full. I let my profile do the talking. First letters are always so hard to write. I didn't know what would separate me from others, but I hoped for a reply.

The first thing I did when I got home that late January afternoon, even before feeding Bud (who wasn't too happy about that), was check my email on the site. Sure enough, there was a response from Holly. I wanted to read it, yet prepared myself for the usual, "You sound like a nice guy, but . . ."

It turned out Holly really liked my profile and first email. She thought I was funny and cute. Most importantly to me, she didn't seem fazed by my disability. So we exchanged emails for the rest of the week. Then I started a conversation via instant message one evening. Before you know it, I offered my phone number. My excuse was that it was easier to talk than type, which really was true. My typing sucked. I also wanted to hear if this special lady sounded true. Remember what happened to me earlier in the month with the first reply I got to my profile? Funny, I had thought then how "fast" she was to include her phone number and ask me over to her place for chicken without really knowing me — and here I was, doing the same thing!

We planned to talk on Saturday night at seven o'clock. Our emails all week were fun and light-hearted, nothing too serious. We both looked forward to the next email and the next, one building on the other. We had a lot in common. Even though Holly wasn't a sports fan, she was willing to learn. I really wasn't a country music fan, but I was willing to listen. We compromised and grew closer.

Funnily enough, Holly had once lived in Phoenixville. She used the gas station around the corner from me. Our paths may have crossed many times before, or maybe we narrowly missed each other. Thirty-five years earlier, we lived within a mile of each other and never knew it.

When Holly called at exactly seven o'clock, I was delighted by her cheerful voice. She was just like her emails — fun, bubbly, and smart. I was dazzled. So much so that our planned short chat

turned into a five-hour marathon. We talked about our pasts —
her husband had died not too long before. Because she was lonely
and one of her sisters was vacationing in Mexico, she decided to
take a chance as well. She had two sisters, and even though Holly
was the oldest, they were very protective of her. Neither knew
she was on the senior dating site.

As I expected, Holly's inbox was crammed with mail. Every
day she got more and more replies. Most of the guys wanted to
meet her right away, understandably so. One demanded a "full-
length body shot" before he would continue to correspond. Some
were nice, some were rude and crude, some were goofy, and
some were boring. Some were too far away, as she was looking
locally, too. Some were way too young for her (under fifty), and
some were from women. She found my original email and profile
refreshingly "normal." Me, normal?

I told her about Bud and my life. I was honest and answered
anything about my disability she wanted to know. I made sure I
thanked her for giving me a chance. Of course, I had not met her
yet to see if it really mattered. I had been down that road too
many times before where someone said, "It's no problem," then
we met and it was, "See you later."

The five hours flew by. We agreed to talk again the following
night at the pre-determined time of seven once again. I hung up
and couldn't wait.

I forgot that the next day was Super Bowl Sunday. New England
vs. Seattle. I watched the Super Bowl every year. I was the kind of
intense sports guy that couldn't do two things at once, like watch the
game and talk on the phone at the same time. Not if I really wanted
to get into the game. But there was absolutely no thought of sending
her a "let's reschedule" email. I wanted to talk to her more.

Talk we did, another great conversation until eleven o'clock,
when we reluctantly said our goodbyes because of work the
following morning. Somehow the subject of the Super Bowl came
up, and she figured out I missed the big game for our chat. I scored
huge brownie points right there.

Holly gave me her number, and I started calling her during my lunch break. She worked at home, so it was easy. She began leaving messages on my voicemail at my work desk, plus every night at seven we talked for several hours. It was heaven to find someone who really seemed to care.

I decided to sign off the dating site. I wasn't going to pay for February. I was so lucky to have found someone special. Holly stayed on the site because she was only a week into her membership. She was still getting tons of mail but, other than responding to an eighty-eight-year-old guy looking for "friendship," she decided she had found someone special too.

We didn't talk about meeting yet. The following weekend, Holly drove right by my house on her way to King of Prussia. She was going to surprise me with a quick visit but chickened out. I'm not sure what I was doing that Saturday afternoon. Probably not much, as usual on my weekends. "That's fine," I told her. "When the time is right, we will meet. Right now, let's just take our time and get to know each other."

That was a lie. I wanted to meet her badly but didn't want to sound like the rest of the lonely vultures contacting her. I tried to play it cool but wasn't very good at it. I know she wanted to see if I was "real" or not. We agreed to meet the following Saturday, which happened to be Valentine's Day. What a perfect day to meet that someone special! My parents were married on Valentine's Day. Was it a sign?

After a seemingly endless week of waiting, Saturday — Valentine's Day — finally arrived. I was nervous about meeting Holly in person for the first time but also had a good feeling. After all the emails and phone chats we'd had the last few weeks, I knew she was a sweet person. I didn't expect her to instantly fall in love with me. Frankly, I wasn't sure what to expect. Continuing our friendship would be a good start.

I was prepared. Like my usual romantic self, I spent the last week gathering Valentine gifts. I didn't want to come on too strong, so I kept the gifts fun: a sweet Valentine's card, letting her know how I felt (yet not too psycho); candy (the gift shop at work was one-stop shopping); a stuffed teddy bear; and a DVD copy of the movie *Marty* starring Ernest Borgnine, the film we planned to watch together after our pizza.

I loved that movie. It was made in 1955, the year before I was born. Black and white, a very simple story of a lonely butcher from the Bronx looking for love. Borgnine won an Oscar for his performance. I could relate to the story, especially when Marty laments to his mother, "Ma, I'm nothing but a fat, ugly man, a fat, ugly man!" It had laughs in it too along with the drama and lamenting, so I hoped it was a good film to watch on a first date.

It was cold outside, but it didn't snow as we feared it might. Holly knocked on my front door, and the barking Bud greeted her first. She looked like a doll, all bundled up in her white winter jacket, bunches of blond curls flowing down her back. She was very friendly, and there was no indication of disappointment or surprise. She was just the sweet Holly I was growing to know.

She wore a red blouse and jeans for the occasion. She smelled great too. I was swooning but tried hard not to let it show. Bud eyed her suspiciously but didn't growl. A good sign. He liked every woman he saw, anyway.

I thanked her for agreeing to meet me at my house. It was not a good idea. Better to meet in a public place the first time. I offered to wheel out to the driveway to prove I was who I was, but she declined the offer. She understood my situation and took a chance to meet me at home. Still, she did the wise thing and gave her youngest sister (the one not in Mexico) her number and my address, promising to call when she arrived and saw that everything was on the up-and-up.

The pizza arrived and we ate in the kitchen while Bud begged for scraps. The talk was light-hearted, pretty much the same as it had been on the phone. I invited her into my bedroom to watch the movie, only because I didn't have a DVD player in the living room hooked up to our ancient TV (the kind that had tubes in the back). Was she thinking, "Wait a minute! First, he wants to meet at his house, then he invites me into his bedroom on the first date. What the hell?"

I gave Holly my Valentine gift bag full of goodies. She knew I couldn't gift wrap (a major flaw in my character), so the candy, the bear, the DVD, and the card were all stuffed in the decorative bag. She was impressed. We watched the movie, barely touching each other, as we sat on my bed. She seemed to like "Marty" but hardly said a word. I knew the wheels were turning.

Two hours flew by and it was time to go. We both thought meeting for only a few hours would be a good start. Before Holly left my room, she had something to tell me. Was I the irresistible, hopelessly romantic guy she always dreamed of and was ready to spend the rest of her life with?

She politely said that everything was nice, she thanked me for all the Valentine presents (she sweetly brought me stuff too, homemade brownies, which she knew I loved) but she didn't think it would work out. It had nothing to do with my disability. It was her. She just wasn't ready for this dating world yet. Yes, she applied to a dating site, but . . . maybe it was too soon after all.

I looked into her blue eyes and said, "I understand," which was another lie. I really didn't understand. At least she was honest. She didn't run away as others had or break my heart on the phone or in a letter.

Bud had grown fond of Holly, especially after she offered him a piece of pizza crust (the way to Bud's heart was always through his stomach, like me and brownies), so he followed her out to the living room. She gave me a hug, said she was sorry, smiled, and waved. I followed her outside to the front porch, without a jacket, my heart broken. I waved back when Holly got into her black SUV and pulled away. I watched her taillights flicker in the dusk, sure I would never see her again. She was so nice too. I felt she was "the one." Mom would've liked her. No more heartache. *I'm done with love*, I thought.

I opened the front door to wheel inside, and out shot Bud like a brown bat out of hell! He obviously was looking for Holly and more pizza. "Bud! Get back here!" I yelled. I watched him scamper up the street (wrong direction, Bud — Holly went down the street). I was in a panic. How to get him back in? It was getting dark, there were no neighbors outside, the February chill was growing colder, and I was up shit creek without a paddle.

I didn't know what else to do, so I wheeled back inside (leaving the front door open in case Bud decided to do me a favor and scamper back inside). I sped down the hall to my landline and called Holly on her cell. She wasn't far, and I hoped she would pick up.

"Greg?" she answered. "What's wrong?"

"Bud got out. He may be headed back to Alabama. Can you please come back and help me?"

"Sure. I'm just around the corner. Be there in a second."

I waited on the porch for Holly. Bud was a distant speck up the street as he checked out every bush and mailbox post he could find. She pulled in the driveway, quickly got out of the car, and asked, "Where did he go?" I pointed up the street, and she ran after him, yelling, "Here, Bud! Pizza!"

The pooch saw Holly, saw she didn't have pizza, ran by her, and raced back into the house. "Thanks," I sighed. "I don't know what I would've done without you."

"No problem," she laughed. "Get in the house! It's freezing out here!"

I closed the door behind me and watched her pull away again. I would miss talking to her every night at seven o'clock. I turned around and there was Bud, crying for more pizza.

I was down in the dumps all night. I vowed to never touch my computer again. Damn computers!

Sunday was typically slow. I tried to keep busy. Football season was over, another bummer. Seven o 'clock came and went. I watched TV for a while, shut it off, and went to bed. I stayed awake for hours. I always liked to listen to the radio or music while falling asleep. Maybe it was just my imagination, but I swear all it did was play sad songs that night. The last straw was the beautiful "All Alone Am I" by Alison Krauss. I love that song and I love Alison Krauss, but that put me over the edge. I turned on the light and sat up in bed.

It was nine o'clock and I said to myself, "This may really be stupid," as I picked up the phone and dialed Holly. It was strange calling her at night instead of the other way around.

"Hi," I began when she answered. "I'm sorry. I don't mean to bug you. I'm not a stalker. I just miss you. I know you said it won't work, but there is no reason why we can't be friends . . ." I didn't want to come off as being desperate or lonely or needy. But I was. Bud's great escape may have hurt any slim chances I had to keep Holly in my life. How could I have a girlfriend when I couldn't even manage my own dog? I was a fool to make this call.

Guess what? Holly missed me too. She had spent her Sunday thinking and brooding. She missed our nightly phone date. She didn't want to try and find someone new on the dating site. Having the courage to make the call earned me more brownie points.

She said she was "still thinking." Nothing was set in stone, and she needed time. I wanted to call her during my lunch break at work the next day but hesitated. I would give her the space she needed.

My old landline rang at exactly seven on Monday night. Friends would be a good way to start. We started seeing each other every weekend. Then it was weekends and Wednesdays. Then almost every day. It was the closest I had ever come to having a "normal" relationship. Holly drove over around noon, stayed for a few hours, went back to take care of her horses, then came back for the evening before heading back to her farm around midnight. Almost every Saturday.

I continued to call her every night when we weren't together. I also called during lunch at work. First thing in the morning, as I opened our office, when the red light was lit on my desk phone, I knew Holly had left me a message overnight. It was so nice knowing someone cared.

We spent most of our time at my house, but if we wanted a real relationship long-term, we had to go out sometime. To dinner, movies, shopping, or to her place. There was a hitch, however, one I failed to mention: I couldn't get in her SUV. I was used to sliding into the front seat of a regular four-door car using my transfer board. Wheelchair Willie had a van, but not as high as Holly's. Getting into her high SUV would be like climbing Mount Everest. But I wasn't going to let that be a deal-breaker. As tough as it might be, I was never more determined than to get in that damn SUV.

Our first date away from home was going to be a special one: my childhood buddy Bobby Rydell was singing at a local restaurant/ballroom, and we had tickets. It would be my first time seeing Bobby in over thirty years. I had sent Bobby a get-well card after his liver and kidney transplants not long before. I was glad he was doing better.

Holly was all dressed up, wearing a white blouse and black slacks. She looked gorgeous. Now came the mountain climbing. With it parked in my driveway, I lined up my wheelchair to the SUV. The transfer board was at an uphill angle. I tried again and again to slide uphill, using all my upper body strength. I had a flashback of the fractured femur fall.

After a few tries, almost getting into the front seat and sliding back to my wheelchair, I mustered one final push and made it. Exhausted, but happy. Practice makes perfect, and soon it got easier to get in and out of her SUV. Getting out was much better, almost like sliding down a chute at a water park, tumbling into my chair.

I loved Holly for her patience. She didn't need that hassle. But she didn't seem to mind and handled the wheelchair like a pro. I still blamed myself for not learning how to drive so long ago. I knew that I needed to stop beating myself up about it after all those years.

Holly loved that SUV. She saw what a challenge it was for me every time we went out. She didn't have to do it, but she surprised me by trading in the SUV for a white, conventional vehicle. That was a big move for her, even though she claimed she "didn't need the SUV any longer."

What were the odds that I would find someone so sweet, who lived local, and who cared?

Back to Bobby Rydell. We had a nice dinner, Italian was our favorite, and Rydell sang for about an hour. He did all of his hits, the same songs I remembered from *American Bandstand* on television, the same songs we sang together as I sat on his lap in his dressing room at the Atlantic City Steel Pier when I was only four and a half years old, and the same songs I used to sing for the nuns on Sunday afternoons. I brought along scrapbooks and pictures of our meeting back in 1961, hoping to reunite after so many years, but Bobby was sick. He made the performance, the trouper he was, but he got out of a sick bed to do it, he told the crowd. He sang great, still with a clear voice for someone his age, but he left immediately after the show.

So we started going places together. Holly needed to catch up, too. She had traveled quite a bit when her late husband was healthy. In fact, they explored Yellowstone National Park and much of the West, a favorite spot for Holly. Then Bob got sick, and they didn't travel as much during his battle with cancer. Our excursions were mostly daytrips. It was spring and the weekends were ours to have fun in as new worlds opened to me: shopping at the mall, strolling the boardwalk at the Jersey Shore, or checking out the beautiful flowers at Longwood Gardens. We saw a lot of movies together. She liked Westerns, Star Wars, and romantic chick-flicks; I liked sports films, documentaries, and movies about dogs. We compromised, and I would catch myself trying not to fall asleep during her Hallmark movies. My snoring always gave it away.

She loved country music, and my musical tastes broadened as we went to local country festivals and I savored the new delights of great artists such as Keith Urban and Willie Nelson. I taught her baseball. We went to a Phillies game together, and she knew the names of all the players. We watched football on TV at home. Holly wasn't as keen on football, although she tolerated my Eagles games the following fall.

At Longwood

I was her personal social worker whenever she needed one. She was my personal IT specialist whenever I needed one (which was all the time). We were good for each other.

The first time I visited her horse farm was magical. She had three older horses, each nearing thirty years old. They grazed in her pasture all day. She had a few barn cats, her Schnauzer dog Zip, and various wild animals who lived on the property. It was close to the small town of Pottstown yet was isolated, with a lovely flowing stream running just outside her door and all sorts of trees growing on her several acres of land. And of course, flowers everywhere.

She made her house more accessible for me. It was nice spending time at her beautiful farmhouse, and she made me dinner there quite often. Inside her farmhouse, I glanced at all the memories she had gathered from her previous life. The many photos of her husband and their travels together; pictures of her relatives, both old and new; her carefully arranged and well-cared-for knick-knacks and cute artifacts she had collected over the years. I smiled because they reminded me of things Mom would've done.

This is a special lady, I told myself. She had had a different life too; one she would never forget and always cherish in her heart. I didn't want her to forget. I only wanted to share her heart and her life, not be a replacement. Holly changed my world so much, bringing life back to my existence. After Mom died, the house looked dreary and gloomy. Everything outside seemed brown, dry, and dead. I had a few trees cut down out front, trees that were too close to the house and presented a threat during bad weather. The last thing I needed was a tall tree crashing on the roof during a violent thunderstorm. Cutting down dangerous trees was fine, but it left the yard looking barren. Holly suggested flowers to dress up the house and front lawn. I started getting into gardening. Soon there were flower boxes and baskets hanging from the front porch railings. We planted small evergreen trees and added nice touches, such as bird feeders and bird baths. Inside we started adding green plants and white, lacy curtains. Life and color were returning to Dianna Drive.

I finally purchased a cell phone. I was always old-school about electronics and technology, mostly due to my fear of all the new gadgets on the market. Holly encouraged me to toss the landline and go with a cell. Admittedly, it was much easier to use. I didn't want a phone that could do a thousand different things. I wanted a phone that was easy to use. Texting was yet another new world. I didn't start to turn geeky yet, but I came close.

There were so many special times now with Holly. Like dancing in the kitchen when we asked Alexa to play Hank Williams's "Hey, Good Lookin'" as she made breakfast. Remember how I said I hated weddings because I couldn't dance? Holly taught me that I could still "dance" in my chair. In fact, we took wheelchair dance lessons together. She surprised me with unexpected gifts.

An Easter basket in the spring, a surprise birthday party in November. Christmas was fun again with decorations and real Christmas trees; and since we found each other on the twenty-seventh, we shared little anniversary remembrances on the twenty-seventh of every month.

It was the relationship I had always dreamed of and never had. Here I was, approaching sixty. I was sure Mom would've loved Holly. I was even more convinced that Mom, up there in Heaven, somehow had a hand in helping me find her. We visited her gravesite together on Mom's birthday, April 11. I brought flowers for Mom and made sure Dad's American flag was still at his grave. Uncle Henry and Aunt Sue were buried in the next row. So many memories of a time gone by. Holly whispered, "I wish I could've met them."

After knowing Holly several months, I met her two sisters and their husbands at a local restaurant. They were very nice, and we soon grew to be family. I earned their stamp of approval, which was important to me. I think it helped when I brought them all gift bags of goodies, which I knew they would love. More brownie points!

Bud loved Holly, which was important to me too, and we took him to nearby Valley Forge Park when we could. We shared picnics and simple times together. I missed her so much when she went to places like Sedona, Arizona, with her family, or to an all-sister getaway to Cape May, New Jersey. We kept in touch via the new wonder of texting. It made me appreciate her even more when she came home.

Holly learned more about disability awareness. She shared the stares and was astounded at the inaccessible places we ran into and the limited parking spots at different locations. In many ways, she became an even bigger advocate of disability rights than I was. I tended to accept the things I couldn't change after so many years; Holly viewed my life with a fresh set of eyes. She was determined to change the injustices she encountered with me. She was not only my friend, my love, and my companion, she was my champion.

I could see us spending forever together.

Chapter 27

Survivors

Holly was gardening at her farm when she crouched down and felt a severe stabbing pain in her head. Bewildered, she called me, even though the pain had subsided.

"Call the doctor," I said. "Right now!"

She did, and they ordered tests, both blood tests and a CAT scan. They found a brain tumor, about the size of a walnut, at the top of her skull. She had never had any indication of problems before. In fact, other than bum knees and a bad back, Holly was healthy. She ate right, exercised, and kept active.

"You'll be okay," I said, hugging her later that night. God and Mom didn't help me find her only to take her away.

Holly went to a local neurologist, who advised her to wait. "Let's keep an eye on it for a few months," he advised. Not satisfied with that answer, she got an appointment with one of the leading neurosurgeons in the world at the University of Pennsylvania. His name was Dr. Bram.

I had not been on the Penn campus since my days studying computer programming back in the seventies. The new children's hospital was located next to the sprawling, shiny glass Penn medical buildings, one of the best groups of hospitals in the world.

Soft hands, I thought to myself. Shaking hands with a brain surgeon was like shaking hands with a world-class musician or a famous painter. Holly liked Dr. Bram from the start, and so did I. A soft-spoken gentleman in his sixties with a friendly smile, he oozed confidence. I sat alongside Holly in his office as the neurosurgeon asked her numerous questions and discussed the results of the scans that were forwarded to him. The good news was, he didn't think the tumor was malignant. He knew his tumors after so many years and thousands of operations. His calm manner rubbed off on Holly. He was positive she would ultimately be fine. A long road was ahead.

He recommended the tumor be removed. No waiting. It was still small enough to reach before it started tangling itself around arteries and veins. It was too close to the main artery in the brain to fool around with. Get it now while the getting was good. Holly could wait and think about it. But the longer she waited, the more likely the tumor would start to affect her senses. Loss of vision, more painful headaches, possible weakness on one side of her body, the list went on and on.

It wasn't much of a choice. Holly agreed to the surgery. Dr. Bram got out his laptop and scheduled it right then and there. She was booked for the morning of Monday, July 18th, less than two weeks away.

We left Bram's office still shaken. One day she was fine, the next day a brain tumor? It didn't seem real. Dr. Bram was very reassuring, however, and he explained all the details of the impending surgery. She would still have her lovely blond curls; they would make an incision where it could hardly be noticed. The operation would take seven or eight hours, depending on how things went. She would be in the hospital for a few days, then recover at home for about eight weeks. No driving during that time.

Those were just the basics. A lot to take in and digest. I went home and prayed. Even though Bram sounded very positive, I was still the ultimate worrier.

Holly rarely cried in front of me. She did get misty-eyed at the movies when we watched a good love story or a tear-jerker about dogs. I can only remember her crying once before the surgery, when she saw me crying. I tried not to think about life without her now.

Holly was always learning, always interested in information, always proactive, and the brain tumor issue was no different. She looked up everything she could find on the Internet about her type of tumor and everything about the upcoming surgery. Me, I would rather not know and deal with it when it happened, but Holly wanted to be prepared, for better or for worse.

We left my house for Philadelphia on the morning of July 18th. It was still dark, but there was a hint of the coming dawn on the horizon. Holly's two sisters and their husbands traveled with us. More of Holly's family would meet us in the waiting room at Penn. We had to be there early for prep, as surgery was scheduled for seven o'clock sharp.

We stayed with Holly for as long as we could. I held her hand through the side-rails of the stretcher. She was already hooked up to IVs and machines. Both Dr. Bram, his assistant, and the rest of the team popped by. Just like that, she was gone, and the long wait began.

I waited with Holly's family, who by now were like my own family. I was glad they liked me, even after they found out how we originally met. I had a history of disapproving families. We read newspapers and books, worked on a laptop, napped, and mostly watched the clock while sitting in the waiting room. I tried to believe my own words: "You'll be okay . . ."

Almost seven hours later, we briefly met with Dr. Bram, who brought us the good news that the surgery went well. They removed the tumor, and the prognosis was good. Most importantly, it was not cancerous.

Soon we met Holly in the ICU. She was wide awake and alert, far more alert than any of us expected, her head wrapped with bandages. We were amazed how well she looked and sounded, considering that she just went through major brain surgery. She mentioned something about "needing to take the car down the expressway." A little off, there. I wore a midnight-green #20 Brian Dawkins Eagles jersey. Somehow my jersey was included in the conversation when Holly laid her head back on her pillow and sighed, "God, I hate football!"

Her family thought she might still be loopy until I interjected, "No, she's right. She really does hate football!" That made me feel better, knowing she was the same Holly.

"I'll call you tonight at seven," Holly said when we were ready to go.

"No, you won't!" I scolded. "You just had brain surgery. You need to rest. I'll talk to you tomorrow if you're up to it. We'll be down to see you."

Damned if my new cell phone didn't ring exactly at seven. We briefly talked. "I told you I would call," she said wearily. How could I be mad? I wasn't — I was grateful.

Holly's brave recovery continued through the summer. She wasn't allowed to drive for several months, so her family made sure we saw each other. Bud missed her, so he was also included with any meeting. The visiting nurse checked in with her. By all accounts, she was doing remarkably well for what she had been through. Her follow-up appointment with the neurosurgeon was after Labor Day, and all her scans and tests showed no more signs of a tumor.

I was so glad she was getting better with each passing day. I didn't tell her I wasn't feeling well. It wasn't my legs this time.

———

Everything seemed to hit me at once. First another kidney stone, despite the fact I was drinking gallons of water every day. Second, my acid reflux was getting worse. A non-stop, persistent cough was the tell-tale sign. I started to get indigestion in the 1990s, including from my favorite cuisine, Italian. Maybe it was age, but I couldn't take spicy foods any longer. I adjusted my diet and got on medication. Then I had a routine colonoscopy and endoscopy, and they found Barrett's disease of my esophagus. A precursor to cancer. During the testing, they also concluded I had a leaky valve in my heart. So that was why I had been so tired lately and short of breath! Between stress at work and worrying about Holly, I was tired at the end of each day.

They thought the heart issue might be a byproduct of my OI. So was the escalating scoliosis in my back. The trunk of my upper body was slowly turning to the left. I felt like a Philly soft pretzel. Someday would I be able to look behind myself like in *The Exorcist*? Everything went back to my OI, including my toes often turning purple (poor circulation). OI haunted me, even in my later years.

I was breaking down. Like an old car in need of repairs, we all age and sometimes need a tune-up. But my problems seemed too sudden and too acute, more than just the normal aging process. No one really knew what to expect from someone my age with OI. It was uncharted territory. I didn't suffer full-blown fractures any longer, but now the OI reminded me of its presence in chronic ways. I was getting more and more stress fractures. They hurt for a few weeks, then went away. I was getting them everywhere — my legs, back, ribs. Arthritis was my constant companion in all my joints and bones. Whenever they did X-rays or bone scans, it was difficult to read the new cracks from the old, with all the lines zigzagging here and there. I was coming full circle from my childhood.

I began to assemble more and more doctors, all younger than me. I now had a cardiologist, an endocrinologist, a pain management physician, and a medical genetics doctor (along with my usual family doctor, orthopedic guy, and urologist). My calendar was full of doctor appointments every month.

One of the first was the medical genetics doctor. Her name was Dr. Kallish, and she was excellent. A short, cute blond with curly hair and a nice smile, I found her looking on the Internet at Penn. I typed in Osteogenesis Imperfecta, and there she was. She happened to be one of the leading authorities on OI. Hardly anyone in the suburbs was familiar with the condition, so I was happy to find someone near home who understood what was happening to me.

I started seeing her every six months, and she gave me information on OI that even I didn't know. Turns out I was one of the oldest people around with such a severity of brittle bones. I was glad to still be kicking, especially after she reminded me the life expectancy of someone with OI was twenty-five years. I had more than doubled the average life span. She helped make life easier by suggesting different equipment and treatments. Lighter wheelchairs to make pushing easier; a shower chair with a roll-in shower so I didn't need to transfer as often, hopefully avoiding slips and potential falls; special cushions to make sitting in the wheelchair all day more tolerable; and new medication to help ease the pain.

I continued to visit a pain management physician on a regular basis. Now my pain was mostly from stress fractures and arthritis. It was a constant trial-and-error process of what medication worked to relieve pain. I never did like to take the hard stuff, like Percocet, because of the side effects (especially constipation). Medication would normally be something to "take the edge off" the pain, not something that would knock me out or make me woozy all day. I was glad there were pain management doctors. Pain was starting to be taken more seriously compared to when I was a child. OI was tough enough to deal with. No reason to be brave and try to "tough it out" like when I was a child. After a lifetime of so much hurt, there was no reason to hurt.

My doctors listened more. OI was still a rare animal in the scheme of things. The survivors were the only ones who knew how bad the pain could be.

My deteriorating physical condition started affecting me at work. I knew it but didn't want to admit it. I was determined not to allow my body to call the shots when it came to my life. But in the end, my body won. The docs were closely monitoring the heart issue, and I was on new medication for the Barrett's disease. No matter what I did regarding cushions or wheelchairs or pain meds, I had a tough time with the persistent pain. Not enough pain meds meant I suffered all the time from the ravages of wear and tear on my old bones. Too many meds meant I couldn't function at work. There was no happy medium.

I had found Holly and the future was worth living. I had another reason to keep going. Carefully weighing all those considerations, I took the early retirement package the facility offered all employees at the beginning of the year. I did so with a heavy heart and a bittersweet feeling in my soul. I would miss my work and my residents.

Once I got into social work, I imagined myself doing it forever. I had to be real and admit I couldn't do it anymore. I was proud, after close to thirty years, that I never did burn out. My candle was extinguished with one final puff. No one warned me it would be so hard to leave behind.

Social work in a nursing home was changing. In the past, the emphasis was the resident. Getting to know the residents you cared for was of the utmost importance. How could you do a proper assessment, care plan, or write a comprehensive progress note if you had no clue about your residents? When I left, it was required to spend much more time chained to a desk, doing computer work. Computers were never my forte. People were. Numbers and machines were gradually taking the place of people. Many of my younger co-workers were much more technical and computer savvy than I was. They could zip through an assessment in no time. Me? I was still old-school. I struggled, which made time at my desk seem even longer and more agonizing. Back in the good old days, I visited a resident for twenty minutes, then whipped out a note in the chart. With pen and paper. Now it seemed the computer ruled and the resident came second, and the time requirements were reversed. And it was all because of machines. Progress notes, care plans, assessments — everything was now being documented on computers. It made the job faster and more efficient, but that didn't always mean things were better. When I went home that afternoon, not checking in on all fifty of my residents (as was my daily custom), I knew things had changed. The simple ways of my early social work career were fading, with new, faster-paced, more impersonal ways of doing the job being thrust upon me.

After making the decision to retire, I missed feeling wanted and needed. I didn't have a plan, and I soon got bored at home. Waiting for the mail to arrive was the highlight of my day. My body wouldn't let me do what I wanted anymore, but my spirit was still willing to try. While the rest of the world continued, I felt guilty about no longer being a part of that world. Why? Why, even after all I accomplished, despite my challenges in life, did I still have this intense burning in my soul to keep going? A feeling that my role in this world was never good enough?

They teach you how to become a social worker, but no one ever teaches you how to stop.

I dreamed of work almost every night. I tried staying away but couldn't, and found myself visiting my residents on weekends. Now I needed them more than they needed me. Gradually, I tapered off and began to let go. Thank God Holly filled the emptiness in my heart. She reminded me that retirement doesn't have to signal the end of an active life. It can simply be the start of another chapter of life. Sharing life with Holly, now more than ever, saved me from days of sleeping until noon, or endless hours of mindless late-night television, or simply doing nothing. That wasn't me.

Wheelchair Willie, Lori, even Dad might say, "Give yourself credit, Greg. Job well done! Now get your butt in gear and move on to the next great adventure."

———

Around Christmas, the Penn doctors recommended that Holly have proton beam radiation. Her tumor was the kind likely to come back, so they advised a round of thirty-three treatments, every weekday for a month. One of the side effects was losing her beautiful hair.

The proton beam treatments at Penn began in March. Holly's radiation schedule varied during the thirty-three treatments. The unpredictable spring weather cooperated, as did the Schuylkill

Expressway as we made the daily forty-five-minute commutes to the city. We met so many wonderful people there — staff, patients, and families. Young, old, black, and white; all races and nationalities. Tumors didn't discriminate. All brave folks. *This goes on every day*, I told myself. *It never ends.*

On Holly's first day of treatment, as we anxiously waited in the lounge area, we heard the loud clanging of a bell. It sounded like a school bell, a series of two or three clangs echoing from the other side of the lounge. We investigated and found that a bell had been set up near the elevators, and each time a survivor completed their entire treatment, they rang the bell in joyful celebration. Pretty cool stuff.

Holly drove to Philadelphia and back daily. I was with her most days. Parking attendants and receptionists became familiar, friendly faces. We met local patients and patients who temporarily moved to Philly until their treatment was over. Some were getting both radiation and chemotherapy. Things could always be worse. I felt especially bad for the children. Many had lost their hair; many looked tired and worn-down; many wore big smiles, knowing that with each treatment they were getting closer and closer to completion. Hope was a key word I heard often at Penn. I was touched by the bravery I witnessed from those courageous kids. In a small way, I could relate.

Holly didn't get sick from the radiation but, as the doctors predicted, she grew more fatigued. Some days she had her treatments in the mornings and some days in the afternoon. Everyone, from her radiologist to the nurses, was so reassuring and positive, carefully explaining every detail. The most support she needed through the entire ordeal was when she started losing her hair. I'm sure she worried how that would affect me. The answer was not at all. She was beautiful, no matter what. Inside and out — even more so now as her inner beauty glowed brighter than ever. We hugged and cried together.

We traveled around the area to find an appropriate wig. They warned that her hair may not fully grow back for close to a year.

The wig was close to what her hair looked like before treatment. She also wore hats, caps, and bandanas. Holly was far from vain, but I understood how this deeply affected her.

Day after day, time after time, the regimen continued. Finally, the treatments came down to one last dose. The last day was also the only time we were caught in a traffic jam on the expressway. God was on our side and we were lucky to avoid accidents, closed exit ramps, snow, spring thunderstorms, and road projects that presented obstacles.

After the final treatment, Holly, the ultimate warrior, proudly stepped up to the bell. She triumphantly rang the bell and smiled as cameras flashed around her. In that instant, Holly officially went from patient to survivor.

———

Even though I wasn't a social worker at a nursing home any longer, I still tried to keep busy doing what I knew how to do best.

I developed a seminar on visiting loved ones in a nursing home setting. I spoke to a small gathering at the local library. Sometimes visiting a nursing home can be an unpleasant experience. My talk was about how to get the most out of visits. Almost every day my residents used to say, "I wish more people would come and see me." I did an oral presentation and showed the outstanding short film *Peege*. It was a real tearjerker. Between the brochure I developed and the presentation itself, I hoped to make future visits a little easier for both families and residents. I loved to read, and there was always another sports biography, classic novel, or trivia book waiting for me to get lost in it. Reading helped me write. I needed another purpose in life after I retired, and finishing this book was that purpose.

Another new project I started after retiring was writing a blog. I always liked writing, going back to my "Wheeling Around Phoenixville" columns in the local paper. My column gave me the discipline to write. I decided to write a similar blog, focusing on disability news, issues, and awareness. If I heard about someone in the news who was achieving something extraordinary (like the Tony-Award–winning actress on Broadway who happened to use a wheelchair), I wanted to make readers aware. New television shows like "Speechless" (which featured a wheelchair user as a main character) were welcome additions. Stories about people with disabilities who do extraordinary things in life — like climbing Mount Everest or skydiving — were highlighted in my blog, proving that anyone can do anything if they try hard enough.

Some of my finest articles were about the actor, author, and activist Michael J. Fox. He was always an inspiration to me. He made me strive to do great things in life. Since I saw him in the first *Back to the Future* movie, I was always impressed with his humor, honesty, and wit. But it wasn't until after Parkinson's disease entered his life did I know what a special guy he was. I was a fan not only of his talents, but of his immense dignity and extraordinary courage. *Unbreakable*, the film starring Bruce Willis and Samuel L. Jackson, touched my life on a personal level. Refreshingly, the villain in the film had Osteogenesis Imperfecta, proving that not every person with a disability is a hero. *Unbreakable* was the first film I ever saw that dealt with OI. I read how the director and writer of the movie, M. Night Shyamalan, was always fascinated by the bone disorder (he wrote a Mr. Glass into a pair of movies — *Unbreakable* and *Glass*). I was blown away to see the condition depicted on the silver screen. Any sort of awareness is great. I left the theater happy to be the real Mr. Glass.

Holly sold her farm after her beautiful horses died. She ended up moving to Phoenixville, buying a cute house only blocks away from me. When her beloved dog, Zip, also died, I convinced her to fill that emptiness in her heart by getting a puppy (sound familiar?). She found the perfect dog — a white Morkie named Katie. She was a ball of energy and had a lot of fun keeping Bud on his toes. And like most good things in our lives, we found this tiny, furry, fluffball of love where else but on the Internet?

Katie and Bud

Bud was still commander of his domain, both in the house and in the backyard. In the past he would try to bolt out the front door, looking for greener pastures. Then one day a friend was over to cut the grass. Unfortunately, he left the side gate open. I was relaxing on the deck, thinking Bud was patrolling the backyard, making his morning rounds. I soon heard this distant barking. It seemed to come from the front of the house. Was that Bud? Couldn't be. I looked out at the backyard — no sign of Bud. I finally put two and two together . . . it was Bud! How did he get out of the fenced-in yard?

I think I must've broken my own personal wheelchair sprinting record, racing from the deck, into the house, and through the kitchen, all the while yelling, "Hold on, Bud! Don't leave!"

When I got to the screen door, there he was, standing on the welcome mat, wagging his tail and grinning. He barked one more time. I interpreted it as, "It's about time; let me in!" His Alabama-bound days ended. He was happy in his forever home.

———

Mom's garden was full of life again. Along with planting flowers, we built a beautiful pond and rock garden. Birds flocked from everywhere to take a bath in the pond. Mom would have loved the St. Francis statue that welcomed the birds. I think she would be proud of her garden again.

Like everyone else in the world, we were affected by the deadly 2020 COVID-19 pandemic. Pennsylvania had a stay-at-home order, which was fine by me. With my history of bronchitis and my limited lung capacity, along with my age, it all added up to yours truly being a prime compromised candidate for the virus.

Throughout the crisis, I kept nursing home residents and staff in my prayers. The COVID-19 crisis had an especially horrible effect on nursing homes everywhere. Along with the physical suffering so many endured came the daily anxiety and fear of the unknown, as well as the loneliness of isolation. I prayed for the health care workers, who risked their own well-being to care for the elderly and compromised, and for the families and friends who could not visit, facing an uncertain fate of their special loved ones. Even if I didn't know each personally, I knew their stories well and could relate to their plight in so many ways.

Pond and flower garden

————————

I was sitting with Holly in an office at Penn, waiting for the endocrinologist to see me. This was my second time seeing her, after being introduced back in the spring. I had seen so many new doctors in the last few years. This was just another usual visit. Yet I couldn't control my nerves. Why was I so stressed to see Dr. Mona? I did all she asked to prepare for this appointment: new bloodwork to satisfy the many different tests she wished to check; another urine collection (always fun); and completed all paperwork that was due. My bloodwork in the spring was good. I increased my water intake and was concentrating on raising my calcium, too. I added weekly salmon to my diet (great for increasing Vitamin D, which she also requested); I started drinking more milk (preferably chocolate); I liked most dairy products, especially ice cream (probably too much, but ice cream was a pleasure in life I just couldn't ignore). I began taking Vitamin D supplements, which I liked. Chewable gummy bears were always good. Why didn't medicine disguised as gummy bears exist when I was a kid?

Dr. Mona was treating me to strengthen my brittle bones and to prevent more kidney stones. She asked me to start taking a 500 mg horse pill every morning to increase my citric acid level. When Dr. Rose was my urologist, he suggested the same thing by spiking my water intake with a squirt of lemon juice to give it an extra zing of taste. I had trouble swallowing pills. I had to crush everything, even going back to my childhood days. Otherwise, count on major gagging. I was always embarrassed by that: here I was, sixty-two years old, soon to be sixty-three, spitting out pills like our dogs Bud and Katie, even tiny baby aspirins that should be no problem. Now I had a legitimate alibi since I was diagnosed with Barrett's disease of the esophagus. Dr. Rock, my gastroenterologist, recommended that I either crush all my pills or substitute liquids or capsules.

The last time I saw Dr. Mona, she recommended I think about having an infusion done once a year to make my bones stronger. This new procedure had not been approved by the FDA for people with OI, so I had some concerns that I wanted to discuss with her. I had another worry too. She mentioned having a bone scan done down the road. I probably had one done somewhere in my past, but I honestly couldn't remember. One procedure and one test seemed to jumble with another test and another procedure. I just couldn't keep track anymore.

So my plate was overflowing as we waited, and waited, and waited. Things like infusions were some of the new treatments and techniques used for OI patients in 2019. The surgery I had long ago, designed to keep the weak lower leg bones from curving and breaking so easily, still existed. Fresh fractures were still casted, but the modern-day casts were funkier and more decorative than ever before. Now I was beyond any kind of surgery, even for the progressive scoliosis in my back. My upper torso continued to slowly rotate to the left, the trunk of my body distorted and deformed. I was evaluated by a spine doctor; nothing could be done. Just as well. I had gone through my share of surgery. Quality of life was the priority now. Whatever it took to live a long, pain free, and unbreakable future. For yours truly, those new treatments — like the proposed infusion — were my options to make life more bearable.

I was beginning to sustain more fractures with each passing season. Only now, they didn't happen with such fury, so devastatingly fast, the crunching of my bones and that all-too-familiar knifing pain. Now they snuck up on me disguised as stress fractures. They often happened in the spring and fall when the weather changed or during a rainy time of the year. I could literally feel it in my bones. A stress fracture feels like arthritis, only the pain is more centralized in one spot. They occur often in the thigh and femur area from additional stress while sitting or transferring. Those went away in time. The docs didn't treat them with casting, especially when the cracks were in my ribs or my back. Treatment was generally heating pads, pain meds, or pain patches (although patches were expensive and often not covered by insurance).

It was a matter of waiting it out with sleepless nights and painful mobility, pain that wore on my body. Clean fractures heal in six to eight weeks; stress fractures linger.

If any of those new procedures helped, why not try? Participating in certain experimental treatment may not only benefit me but OI patients in the future. If I could help lessen fractures for those after me, why not?

As we continued to wait, my eyes scanned the small room. It was painted in ugly army green and gray, surprising since the outer edifice and lobby area of the medical building was so cheerful. The usual medical equipment hung on the wall or sat on the cabinet: purple latex gloves, different instruments like blood pressure cuffs, jars of gauze, and tongue depressors. A computer was on, hooked up to a small desk. Pretty standard stuff.

Holly nudged me, pointing to a yellow blob near the sink. "Remember that?" she asked.

How could I forget? I couldn't believe when Dr. Mona revealed what it was, to satisfy our curiosity: a five-pound piece of fat. It looked like the famous Blob in the 1950s horror classic of the same name, which oozed around my hometown of Phoenixville, destroying our historic Colonial Theater.

Just then Dr. Mona whisked into the room. "So, how's it going?" she asked as we shook hands. I had forgotten how pretty she was — tall and thin, dark eyes and long dark hair pulled back. She brought my recent blood work up on the computer screen and seemed pleased. Same with my urine output (I passed that exam, drinking extra water on collection night to make sure I met the quota). She continued to scan the screen, reviewing my electronic records as she asked, "So, tell me what happened regarding the pills?"

"Oh, I couldn't take those. I would have to crush them, and you said no crushing allowed."

"That's right, no crushing allowed. So why didn't you take them?"

"Well, Dr. Rock said I needed to crush all my pills since she found out I have Barrett's. I have this little pocket in my upper esophagus that sometimes catches food and pills." (I left out the part about how I was a real wuss and couldn't swallow pills of any kind.)

"They were big," she acknowledged. "That's okay." (I felt vindicated and my manly pride was still intact.) "So how's your calcium intake going?"

"Great," I said, perking up. "I'm eating salmon every week."

"Hon, she said 'calcium,'" Holly gently interjected.

"Oh, of course. Well, eggs, milk with cereal twice a week. Chocolate milk. Lots of ice cream."

"Have you had any more fractures since I saw you last?" she asked.

"No. Just the usual aches and pains from seasonal arthritis. Why?"

"Well, your recent blood work shows your phosphorous levels are high. They were high last time, and even higher now. We may have missed a recent fracture."

Was that the reason why my legs hurt so much last spring, and even now, into fall? Had I been going along with fractures and didn't even know it? Maybe I couldn't tell the difference anymore between arthritis and stress fractures.

Dr. Mona asked how my breathing was. I knew this concerned all my doctors. Since I had limited lung capacity due to my short stature, OI, and scoliosis, they worried about conditions such as pneumonia, bronchitis, and different kinds of pulmonary infections potentially being fatal.

"It depends," I said. "Sometimes good, sometimes not."

She suggested buying a breathing device that would keep my lungs clear. She also recommended singing, which apparently was good for the lungs. I had a flashback to my days as a child, singing Bobby Rydell songs for the nuns on Sunday afternoons. She warned that because of the progressing scoliosis, my breathing might be affected as my body changed. I was afraid of that, as I knew how sometimes it really was harder to breathe on days my back ached more.

"So I think now we can move on with scheduling the infusion I talked to you about last time. You have concerns?" she said.

"I do," I admitted. "Can you please review the whole thing again?"

She rolled closer on her stool and looked me straight in the eyes. She once again explained how it was used for people with osteoporosis, certain cancers, and arthritis. It was not FDA-approved for treating OI, but it had been tried on OI patients with success. In fact, 50% of the cases reported less fractures during a long period of time after treatment. It was given by IV once a year, a thirty-minute dose of Reclast (zoledronic acid). Some side effects were flu-like symptoms, jaw swelling or pain, and in even rarer cases, stress fractures in the femur area of the legs.

After she explained everything about the infusion treatment, she asked if there were any more concerns. I hesitated. This was important, so I needed to be open about my fears. As I became quiet, Holly, my angel, spoke for me.

"Greg is afraid to be lifted onto a table," she said softly.

"Why are you afraid, Greg?" Dr. Mona asked in a low voice.

"Oh, I've had some bad experiences with being lifted," I replied, my voice cracking. Who was doing the lifting determined how gently it was done — or not. No matter how much I tried to explain before the lift, often lifters grabbed at the wrong area of my legs. Usually it was one person behind me, under my arms, and another person in front, holding onto my legs. I'm still a very light weight, maybe a hundred pounds, so all it takes is 1-2-3 and up we go. But during the lifting anything can happen, from cracks to full-blown fractures, as I close my eyes tightly, my heart pounding, trying to relax, fearing the next fracture. *Try not to think about it. Try not to think about it*, I would repeat to myself during a lift.

My eyes starting misting with tears. I bit my lip, trying not to cry. I looked at Dr. Mona and whispered, "Too many fractures."

"I know," she said. I could see her think as she stared at me.

"Can it be done in my chair?" I asked, hoping she would say yes, fearful she would say no.

"Of course," she replied. I sighed in relief. "Actually, it's better if you stay in the chair. We often do the intravenous infusion in the chair. No problem."

So it was decided to go ahead with the infusion. Since she knew how fearful I was about being lifted, she asked me to only consider the bone scan for now. "It may not be needed if your phosphorous levels are back down. Don't worry about it, okay? We will work around things." She smiled, and I felt so much better. I scheduled to see her again in a year.

It was time to go. So many exciting things were on the calendar soon. A concert, a fall apple festival, an Eagles football game, and my birthday.

"Let's go home," Holly said as we gathered the paperwork.

Fly, Eagles, Fly!

"Good idea," I agreed. "You know, between the flu shot earlier this week and today, I'm going to need some extra TLC," I said, smiling as we headed home.

———

Two weeks after my visit with Dr. Mona, I did have the infusion.

I had the infusion at Penn in Valley Forge, in the same department where people go for chemotherapy treatment. Holly and I sat in the lobby with cancer patients and cancer survivors. It was just like when Holly was undergoing her radiation treatments a few years earlier. Mostly older and middle-aged folks, with a sprinkling of younger people there too, some wearing hats and some not, all waiting their turn. It was a quiet waiting room. Some people read their own paperbacks and some nervously paged over magazines. The Home & Garden Channel on TV was background noise; nobody was really watching it.

Two people stepped up after their daily treatment and proudly rang the bell near the front of the room, signifying the end of their chemo treatments. The entire room applauded as pictures were taken by family and friends. It was kind of cool how strangers reacted to these brave folks. Everyone was linked together as someday their chance to ring the bell would come.

The receptionist called out numbers and names, directing patients to the rooms in the back where their nurse and treatment awaited. Most had been there before, smiling at the receptionist when their name was called.

"Gregory, number twelve!" got our attention, and we headed back.

We passed faces we had seen in the lobby, now hooked up to IVs, lying or sitting on soft gray recliners, receiving their treatment. Some had been there for hours, while others were just beginning or ending. I was lucky. This infusion was a once-a-year thing, taking no longer than thirty minutes. A young nurse named Brianna hooked me up to the IV as we talked Eagles. Funny how an Eagles sweatshirt can also link total strangers. "Did you watch that game last Sunday?"

Slowly the liquid dripped into my veins, this experimental juice that supposedly would make my bones stronger. Wouldn't old Dr. Nicholson love this? Treatment for OI had come such a long way.

This wasn't a cure. Far from it. A cure would have to come from the terrific researchers and scientists out there who are working hard to eliminate OI from our lives. This infusion was simply a way of putting a techno Band-Aid on the problem. If we could lessen even one fracture in a life, it was worth it.

I wasn't thinking of being this noble fellow, helping future children with brittle bones, as I stared at my bedroom ceiling. I felt more like a guinea pig, feeling stupid for allowing Dr. Mona to talk me into this treatment as I lay there in pain. I could almost feel my bones absorbing the fluid, the wetness seeping into my old, thirsty, dry bones.

Just transferring into bed was a challenge. I suffered many broken bones in my life, but this felt different, like everything was cracking, snapping, and crumbling, my joints and muscles aching loudly in pain.

Initially, it went well, with no side effects. However, the next morning I could hardly get out of bed. It felt like all my bones were broken. Bones I had never broken before now hurt. Bones in my face, bones in my neck, and bones in my fingers. My back and rib cage area were especially sore. The only relief I had was to lie flat on my back and not move an inch.

"Damn," I mumbled to myself. "This sucks!" I knew Dr. Mona only wanted to make my life better, and I would calm down tomorrow and come to that realization. For now, the only thoughts drifting in my mind were things like, *It's easy for her to say, "Get this done." or "Let's try this." I'm the only one who knows how much it hurts.*

I slept for the next eleven hours without moving, wondering if life would ever get back to "normal." Normal for me was pushing my wheelchair pain free. Normal for me was using my upper-body strength to transfer my body into bed or into the car from my wheelchair. Normal for me was pushing around the block for exercise, an activity I adopted after retirement, something to keep me strong and give me a good cardiovascular workout. Normal for me would not be normal for most people.

Usually my dreams were about my past. Never about walking. On this night, I had such an incredibly vivid dream of the future: A small ceramic Christmas tree sat on a windowsill, its colorful lights twinkling in the dark. I was alone in the dark room, lying in a hospital bed, covered to my neck with two warm blankets. Where was I? In a nursing home? Hospital? At home? The years with Holly were some of the best years of my life. We went places and did things together. Where was Holly now?

I had come full cycle in my life; my bones still broke by merely sneezing, coughing, or turning over, like when I was a child. There was another gruesome feature to the end of my life: my soft bones were so fragile now, they disintegrated to powder upon touch. No wonder the bed was lined with feathery-soft pads and cushions. The slightest movement might cause an explosion of bone. Was this my fate in the future? Few OI survivors live to old age. Few really know what does happen to someone with brittle bones when the natural aging process makes the bones even more brittle. Would my bones (or whatever was left of them) still be encased in plaster casts like before, or would my caregivers just let the fractures happen? Shoot him up with painkillers and keep him comfortable in bed? When does it end? How does it end? I was alone and afraid, trembling under the blankets.

"No!" I woke up screaming. Lifting my head off the sweat-stained pillow, I recognized my bedroom. I squinted my eyes as early dawn sunbeams lined the lacy white curtains. "It seemed so real," I whispered.

My body was feeling better. The soreness had shifted to my shoulders and arms. Ironically, my legs, which took the brunt of the hundreds of fractures for over sixty years, felt great. I began to feel like myself again. Getting another infusion treatment would be a bridge I would cross in another year. I was happy to be "normal" once more.

I vowed not to dwell so much on past regrets or wonder about future events. We are only assured of today. Make the most of now.

————

The black cemetery gates were open, as Father Bernie had promised. We pulled in and slowly drove the length of the driveway. We parked near the center large cross. Yesterday was Good Friday. Today, April 11 — my mother's one hundredth birthday.

One of her favorite Easter flowers was purple hyacinths. Holly set the plant in front of my parents' gray tombstone. No one else was in the cemetery. The weather was chilly for April, the breeze not helping matters. The trees were beginning to bud tiny spring green leaves. A sign of life and hope all around us, even in a graveyard. So peaceful here. A stark contrast to the chaotic world outside the black, wrought iron gates during the horrible COVID-19 pandemic. No problems with social distancing here.

I spoke too soon; Mark approached us from the driveway. "Here for the birthday party?" he joked. "Did you bring the beer?" We both agreed that Mom's hundredth birthday party would've been spectacular. Even here, at her final resting place, Mom was still bringing us together.

We exchanged small talk. How was everyone coping during this crisis? If you need anything, just call, etc. My eyes wandered to Aunt Sue and Uncle Henry, buried a few feet behind the Smith grave marker. It was hard to believe that Uncle Henry would've been 108 years old; Aunt Sue 102. When ages hit triple digits, it's as if people lived in an entirely different time and place. How swiftly time goes by.

One hundred today. Mom was born on Easter Sunday. I reminded my little brother of her logic: "If you are born on a holy day, you are going to Heaven." If anyone was in Heaven, it was Mom.

My dearly departed loved ones. They were only sleeping here; they would always be alive in my memories. Gazing at the tombstones, although each died years before, their final resting place still moved me. The gravestones of so many familiar names, Slovak and Polish families, many neighbors and friends that lived in town, folks my parents knew, worked with, laughed with and cried with, they were resting in our parish cemetery. Fleeting memories of those souls who had touched my life, now before me in eternal peace, flashed before my eyes like old photographs, before fading away.

Soon it was time to leave. One final silent prayer and one last farewell to my folks. The American flag beside Dad's grave waved from the breeze. We said so long to Mark, wishing him a happy Easter while keeping our six-foot distance. *Easter will sure be different this year with the raging pandemic,* I thought. *Hopefully we will see him this summer for a cookout when life returns to normal.*

————

I read that Bobby Rydell was doing a book tour for the book he wrote, *Teen Idol on the Rocks,* and he was coming to a bookstore in Broomall, Pennsylvania. I asked Holly if she wanted to go, so off we went.

Meeting Bobby Rydell, 1961

There was a small line inside the front of the store when we arrived. There were three people ahead of me, all holding copies of Bobby's book, Rydell vinyl records, or photos of the singer. I had my own book and an extra item.

A younger lady came into the store at the back of the line. She hesitated while checking out the line, mumbling, "Who is the guy? Do I know this guy?"

I looked at her and shook my head. He's only a rock 'n' roll icon. Damn millennial.

When it was my turn to approach the table, I got my first good look at my childhood idol, the first time I was face-to-face with Bobby Rydell in over fifty-five years. I sat there, just staring at the guy who was so damn nice to me, the source of so much joy when I was a child. Where did the time go?

"Hi," he said, reaching across the small table to shake hands. "How are you? What's your name?"

"Hi, Bobby. I'm Greg."

"Nice to meet you, Greg," he replied, taking my book and opening the front cover to sign. "Is that with one G or two?"

"One," I said. "And we've met before."

"Really?" he said, looking up from the book. I produced the black and white photo of Bobby and me in his dressing room in Atlantic City in 1961. We were both grinning from ear-to-ear. There I was

Meeting Bobby Rydell, 2016

sitting on his lap, wearing that same stupid butterscotch checked jacket and bow tie. "I was only four back then," I said. A chill went up my spine. Such a special moment.

He stared at the picture, mesmerized for a moment. "How old are you now, Greg?"

"I just turned sixty last week."

"My God, Greg!" he gasped.

"You wrote me this letter after we met."

Bobby quickly scanned the handwritten letter that I kept in a clear plastic sleeve. The letter read how nice it was to meet, how sharp I looked in that jacket, and how Bobby had recently met his own idol. *Perhaps you heard of him*, the letter read. *Frank Sinatra.*

"That's my writing, all right," Bobby whispered to himself.

The people behind me seemed fascinated by the reunion but also wanted their moment to have their book signed, so Bobby quickly finished signing my copy and posed for a new photo with me, taken by Holly. He handed the book back, saying, "Nice to see you again, Greg."

Back in the car, I read his inscription:

To Greg,
My lifelong friend.
Best Wishes Always,
Bobby Rydell.

I closed the book and smiled.

Chapter 28
Always Look Up

Everyone loves a good love story. My story is no different.

The flowers in front of the house and around the pond were lush and vibrant with color. Scents of jasmine, carnations, and roses sweetly filled the perfect morning in late July. Every summer morning, I could be found watering our garden with great care. Thunderstorms were sparse during the summer of 2020. The baskets and boxes of flowers on the front porch loved the cool shower from the garden hose.

Watering our flowers gave me a chance to daydream, usually about the day ahead. My nephew Adam was getting married later in the afternoon. I knew Holly was also looking forward to the wedding. She loved my family, as I loved hers. And she loved weddings. She is hopelessly romantic — another reason why I love her.

With car keys in hand, she kissed me on the porch before heading out for a bit. "We're going to have fun today!" she said, smiling. I was never too crazy about weddings. They always reminded me of something I secretly missed, something I never thought would happen to me in my life — finding someone special, someone who was my best friend and my soulmate all in one. Someone I wanted to spend forever with.

The last few months had been so sad. My brother Tommy had suffered a sudden, fatal heart attack in May. My first sibling to die. Then his wife Sue was diagnosed with cancer only a few weeks after his death. She passed away in the same hospice unit where

Mom died. The COVID-19 virus raged all spring. We were fortunate to be well. We needed some happiness in our lives soon.

"You really love weddings, don't you?" I responded.

"I do," she replied, smiling and giving me an extra smooch.

"Do you want to?" I asked softly.

"Want to what?"

"Want to get married?"

Holly looked at me, wide-eyed. "Are you kidding?"

"No. I'm not kidding. Would you marry me?"

I surprised even myself with the question. I had been thinking about asking her for a long time but I just didn't know how. I was always pretty awkward about that kind of stuff, yet here I was, asking the one special woman in my life to marry me, while holding a garden hose.

And she said yes!

After all my life of hearing "No," after all my life of hearing, "You're a nice guy but . . ." it floored me when Holly said, "Yes, of course I will. I love you so much!"

Holly was my best friend. After five years of dating, at times living under the same roof together, through the good times and bad we shared, it was time. I was lucky to find her. Brushes with sickness and death only solidified our love. There was no one like her, ever.

It was fun telling family and friends the good news. Many were surprised, some screaming, some crying. We wanted a small ceremony with a nice reception. But because of the pandemic, gatherings of more than twenty people at a time were not allowed. We would have a larger party the following spring if the virus disappeared. We had so much to celebrate.

Me? Getting married? Weddings were for other people, not me. I was in a wheelchair. What chance would I ever have of getting married? It was still hard to believe, even three hours from saying "I do."

I was alone for about an hour, just me and Bud. I had to admit, I looked pretty sharp in my light-gray suit, white shirt, and burgundy tie. Burgundy was the main color of the wedding. Burgundy, white, and yellow mums adorned the back-deck where the ceremony would take place. I even had one of those elegant hankies a guy stuffs into the pocket of his suit jacket, also in burgundy.

Everyone, including Holly and her sisters, left until just before the ceremony. They were getting dressed a few blocks away and didn't want me to see the dresses they were wearing. Some sort of superstition, custom, or ritual. The bride assured me that it wasn't a burgundy gown. Oh, she'd had her eye on one a month ago while shopping for a special dress. In fact, she called me from the shop saying, "Is it okay if I don't wear burgundy? I think I found something else."

"Sure. Wear whatever you want. You'll look great in any color," I reassured her. That was true. I was marrying a really pretty girl.

But no matter how much she apologized for not wearing burgundy as we had agreed upon, I had a sneaking suspicion she was going to wear burgundy. She wanted to surprise me. So we teased each other about the color she ultimately picked for our special day. It was autumn, so I tried to weasel it out of her: burnt orange? A shade of red? Gold? Maybe forest green? "No hints" was her determined answer.

That was the kind of relationship we had had for over five years. Breezy and fun. Not once did we argue or fight. Was something wrong with us? In this day and age, we actually got along!

Bud looked very dapper in the white wedding scarf I bought him for the occasion. "Best Dog," it read in bold black letters. He sat with me in my bedroom. Soon the house would be full of guests. Well, as many guests as we were allowed to invite during the pandemic. Bud eventually fell asleep in his "apartment," his favorite place to chill. It used to be my bedroom closet until Bud took it over.

It had been just me and Bud for a long time. Two bachelors on our own. No more slumming it alone anymore. We were happier now since the two lovely ladies, Holly and Katie, entered our world. It was so damn lonely before.

Holly and Katie

Earlier in the morning, Holly's brother-in-law Chuck asked me, "Are you nervous?" Actually no, I wasn't nervous at all. I was looking forward to married life. I couldn't recall the exact quote, but it went something like, "If you keep looking back, you miss seeing what is right in front of you." For many years, I didn't see the future. My future was foggy. Things became brighter after I met Holly. Now I had a future.

I heard someone at the front door. Was it the caterer already? I wheeled to the living room and let the florist in. Boxes of corsages filled the living room.

I loved Mom's smiling picture above her favorite chair. That was how I remembered her best, seven years after she died — always smiling. I would miss her a little extra on this special day.

———

October 10 — Holly looked beautiful, as always. And yes, she wore burgundy (I was right!). And in the warmth of the early afternoon, with trees of red, gold, and orange foliage all around us, we said our vows and became one forever.

The Reverend Joe Pickett, my childhood friend, officiated. Holly and her sisters decorated the living room and the deck with flowers. Katie wore a doggie dress and looked like a little princess, while Bud guarded the catered food in the kitchen.

Our wedding song was the beautiful "The Best of Me" by my friend, Richard Marx. We danced. Everyone cried.

Hours later, after everyone had left, I rolled out to the deck as the sun set. I was alone, breathing in the cool air. It was a perfect day. I thought of how far I had come — from a childhood full of pain, to my rewarding life helping others, to losing my parents too soon, to all the ups and downs and twists and turns my life had taken. A life I was lucky and blessed to have lived; a life, despite the pain, full of happiness and love as well; a life I would do all again without hesitation. A life leading to this special day, when I vowed forever with my love, my soulmate and my best friend.

In my misty daydreams I swore I heard the distant echo of Mom calling my name from the backyard below. I scanned the yard, hoping against hope she had gotten a heavenly day pass. Mom always said, "When you die, you can't ever come back. If you're in Hell, the Devil won't let you out, and if you're in Heaven, you're so happy you don't want to leave."

The yard was shrouded in shadows. Crickets chirped peacefully. No Mom. I felt a warm hand on my right shoulder. Holly joined me on the deck as I peered into the growing twilight. "It's okay to let go," she said. She was right. It was okay to let go of my grieving, to let go of the pain, to let go of my past. There was a brand-new life ahead. Break the chains of the past and embrace the bright dawn of the future.

I looked back and touched the soft hand on my shoulder; only it wasn't Holly who stood there, offering comfort. It was Mom. She smiled, just like in her photo, then she was gone.

Epilogue

I found my Dad's Purple Heart (circa 1944) hidden away in an ancient steel box in the house. I knew he had a Purple Heart but rarely saw it. I thought it may have gone with my father when he died, but no. I debated whether to wear it or not. Dad earned it, not me. Holly encouraged me to wear it for him. Now I wear it with honor and pride. Dad is next to my heart every day.

I also found musty photos of Mom, both when she was young and later in life. I stare at the pictures as they stare back at me, as if we are communicating to each other: I miss you.

We renovated the house this year, and as we cleaned out a closet in Mom's old room, we unexpectedly found my parents' wedding photo. This surprise would've been wonderful enough to find; however, in the same box and on the very bottom, was my mother's wedding gown. It was like finding a precious artifact, a priceless

Philadelphia

Baltimore

treasure, a family relic that was meant to finally see the light of day. The dress was slightly yellowed with age, yet nonetheless perfect. My heart melted when I touched the soft fabric. I can only imagine what this gown meant to my mother. She kept it for seventy-one years until she died. Memories of a happy time in her life, as if the cherished dress had come alive out of the photo, reminding me never to forget her. As if I ever could.

Retirement gave us a chance to travel a bit more, so we have taken a road trip every summer following the Phillies. We invaded Camden Yards in Baltimore and PNC Park in Pittsburgh. It was odd being the enemy for a change, but both places treated us well. At Oriole Park we met up with my brother Jim, and in the land of the Pirates, we took good-natured ribbing from Bucco fans. Holly and I wore our red Phillies gear proudly. It didn't hurt that the Phils won in Baltimore and in Pittsburgh as we rooted them on.

Pittsburgh

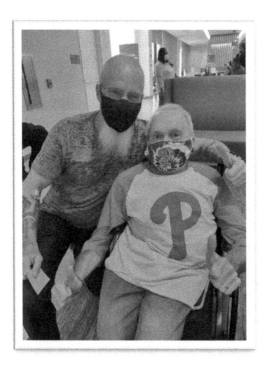

Reuniting with the great Pat Croce, 2021

I missed baseball during the pandemic. Old, reliable baseball. Sixty years on, I still listen to ballgames on my transistor radio. Baseball survived the pandemic, and so did we. I will never take life for granted ever again.

What I am most fearful of now is a big crowd. Not that I have agoraphobia; I fear people bumping into my legs. But I can't stay away from ballgames and concerts; life wouldn't be the same without them.

During the pandemic, I was sitting in a hospital waiting room, ready for routine blood work, when I noticed a guy sitting near me. We made eye contact; he wore a mask, as I did, which was still required. We started talking, and lo and behold it was Pat Croce. We had first met 22 years before at a 76'ers game. I asked if he remembered me and he answered, "Sure I do. Who else gives me Lourdes water?"

That was pure luck, being at the right place at the right time. Or maybe it was another blessing from God in my life.

I was never one to just sit around and do nothing. My desire to help others still burned inside of me. So when a local non-profit organization called Orion Communities asked me to join its Board of Directors, I jumped at the chance. Orion was doing my kind of social work, offering hope to individuals and families experiencing hardship due to poverty, disability, or illness, offering shelter, food, clothing, and transportation, all with compassion.

I'm proud that my hometown of Phoenixville recently added an all-access playground to our park. Kids in wheelchairs can swing and play like able-bodied children. Every time we pass the park and I hear the children laughing, I remember the happy times of my childhood so long ago. The pain, the rejection, and the sorrow has disappeared. I am now at peace. It took me a lifetime to clearly see the wonderful world around me. Now, if I ever get depressed, all I have to do is look at my legs. I used to think of my legs as symbols of pain. Now I see them as signs of hope and strength, my battle scars of life. They remind me to always look up.

Cheers!